BLACK ELECTORAL POLITICS

National Political Science Review

Volume 2

NATIONAL POLITICAL SCIENCE REVIEW

BLACK ELECTORAL POLITICS

National Political Science Review

Volume 2

Lucius J. Barker, Editor

Transaction Publishers
New Brunswick (U.S.A.) and London (U.K.)

ISSN: 0896-629-X
ISBN: 0-88738-821-3 (paper)
Printed in the United States of America

Contents

Editor's Note 1

SPECIAL ANNIVERSARY SECTION

NCOBPS: Twenty Years Later
Mack H. Jones 3

NCOBPS: Observations on the State of the Organization
Dianne M. Pinderhughes 13

FEATURE ARTICLES

Racial Belief Systems, Religious Guidance, and
    African-American Political Participation
    *Michael C. Dawson, Ronald E. Brown, and Richard
    L. Allen* 22

White/Black Perceptions of the Electability of
    Black Political Candidates
    Linda F. Williams 45

Electoral Politics, Affirmative Action, and the
    Supreme Court: The Case of *Richmond v. Croson*
    W. Avon Drake and Robert D. Holsworth 65

Political Responses to Underemployment among
    African Americans
    Cedric Herring and Gloria Jones-Johnson 92

The Politics of Desegregation in Higher Education: Analysis of *Adams*
    States Progress
    Joseph "Pete" Silver, Sr., and Rodney W. Dennis 110

SYMPOSIUM: Big-City Black Mayors: Have They Made a Difference?

Introduction
    Michael B. Preston (Symposium Editor) 129

Big-City Black Mayors: An Overview
    Michael B. Preston 131

Black Mayoral Leadership in Atlanta: A Comment
    Mack H. Jones 138

Mayor of the Colony: Effective Mayoral Leadership as a
    Matter of Public Perception
    Georgia A. Persons and Lenneal J. Henderson 145

Black Political and Mayoral Leadership in Birmingham
and New Orleans
Huey Perry 154

The Political Legacy of Harold Washington: 1983–1987
Robert T. Starks and Michael B. Preston 161

Black Political Power in the City of Angels: An
Analysis of Mayor Tom Bradley's Electoral Success
Byran Jackson 169

The Politics of Detroit: A Look Ahead
Wilbur C. Rich 176

Mayor W. Wilson Goode of Philadelphia: The Technocrat
Bruce Ransom 183

Black Mayoral Leadership: A Twenty-Year Perspective
William E. Nelson, Jr. 188

BOOK FORUM

Review Essays: Black Politics

The Pioneering Books on Black Politics and the
Political Science Community, 1903–1965
*Hanes Walton, Jr., Leslie B. McLemore, and
C. Vernon Gray* 196

Independent Leveraging and Local Community Development
Mary Coleman 219

Bibliographic Essays: Race, Class, and Urban Politics

Race, Ethnicity, and the Politics of Resources
Charles V. Hamilton 223

Separate and Unequal Societies in Urban Politics
Susan Welch 228

Social Science, Public Policy, and Persistent Poverty
among Urban Blacks: A Review of Current Thought
Roland Anglin 234

Urban Politics
Zelma A. Mosley 244

Race, Class, and Politics: A Conceptual Critique of
William J. Wilson's Model of American Racial History
Eric Moskowitz 249

Book Reviews

On Account of Sex: The Politics of Women's Issues 1945–1968
reviewed by Sarah Slavin 264

Slavery and Its Consequences: The Constitution, Equality, and Race
  reviewed by Rickey Hill 267

Coleman Young and Detroit Politics: From Social Activists to
Power Broker
  reviewed by Hanes Walton, Jr. 268

Strategies for Mobilizing Black Voters: Four Case Studies
  reviewed by Marilyn K. Dantico 269

Political Power in the Postindustrial City: An Introduction
to Urban Politics
  reviewed by Michael O. Adams 271

Urban Reform and Its Consequences: A Study in Representation
  reviewed by Raphael J. Sonenshein 273

Book Notes

The 1984 National Black Election Study Sourcebook 275

Urban Minority Administrators: Politics, Policy, and Style 275

When the Marching Stopped: The Politics of Civil Rights
Regulatory Agencies 275

Editor's Note

This second volume of the National Political Science Review (NPSR) is dedicated to the Twentieth Anniversary of the founding of the National Conference of Black Political Scientists (NCOBPS). Founded in 1969, the anniversary was celebrated at the annual meeting of the organization held in Baton Rouge, Louisiana, in March 1989, and is commemorated in this volume by a special introductory section that includes formal addresses delivered on the occasion by the organization's first president (Mack H. Jones) and by its then-current president (Dianne M. Pinderhughes.)

The major focus of this second volume of the NPSR, however, is on attempts by African Americans to use electoral politics to achieve their political objectives. This allows us an opportunity to assess the symbolic and substantive dimensions of the "from protests to politics" drive begun by black leaders in the late 1960s and continuing today. In the some twenty years of this resort to politics, blacks have made important gains in electoral politics. At bottom, however, the importance of these gains can be best assessed when subjected to more rigorous theoretical and empirical analysis by scholars who come from a variety of backgrounds and who utilize a variety of approaches and methods.

One of the overall reasons for establishing the NPSR was that research findings reported on and reviewed in its volumes could bring to the academic marketplace additional perspectives and insights that might not otherwise be forthcoming on important topics of scholarly research. This would seem to hold special importance in dealing with topics such as black electoral politics, where perception, sensitivity, and ingenuity of data collection and use can prove as important to the validity of the research as does the use of rigorous and systematic methods and approaches. Hopefully, both can be found in the articles in this volume.

Just as in volume 1, this volume includes major feature articles, a special symposium, and a Book Review section. The general theme, "Black Electoral Politics: Participation, Performance, and Promise," is well reflected in each of these sections. The feature articles, for example, are the contributions "Racial Belief Systems, Religious Guidance, and African-American Political Participation;" "White/Black Perceptions of the Electability of Black Political Candidates;" "Electoral Politics, Affirmative Action, and the Supreme Court: The Case of *Richmond v. Croson;*"

"Political Responses to Underemployment among African Americans;" and "The Politics of Higher Education: Analysis of Adams' States Progress." These articles should add greatly to our understanding of American politics, of which black electoral politics constitutes an essential part.

A major feature of the issue is a special symposium on "Big-City Black Mayors: Have They Made a Difference?" The symposium includes introductory and concluding essays that place the topic in conceptual and historical context. The core of the symposium consists of brief but succinct case studies of the promise, problems, and performance of selected big-city black mayors: Harold Washington of Chicago, Tom Bradley of Los Angeles, Andrew Young of Atlanta, Marion Barry of Washington, D.C., W. Wilson Goode of Philadelphia, and Coleman Young of Detroit. Another contribution analyzes "Black Politics and Mayoral Leadership in Birmingham and New Orleans."

This volume of the NPSR once again includes the Book Forum, one of the most expansive and informative book review sections that can be found in any scholarly journal. The section consists of two review essays, one of which focuses on "The Pioneering Books on Black Politics," and five bibliographic essays on race, class, and urban politics. The section concludes with a number of regular book reviews and several short book notes.

We continue to be grateful to the many persons who continue to contribute to the NPSR: to our editorial staff and assistants, especially to my graduate assistant Kevin Lyles of Washington University, who has kept the administrative work of the NPSR office going while I was on leave at Harvard during the 1988–89 academic year.

Our greatest appreciation, of course, goes to the authors whose contributions appear in this volume as well as to those whose submissions enlarged the range of choices from which selections could be made. And we continue to express gratitude to the many reviewers who invariably heeded our request to give rather detailed appraisals of various manuscripts and a number of whom somehow managed to do so in reasonable time frames.

We sincerely appreciate the many comments that have come our way regarding the initial volume of the NPSR, and continue to solicit your contributions and suggestions as we attempt to make the NPSR a major forum for the communication of scholarly research.

NCOBPS: Twenty Years Later

Mack H. Jones

Prairie View A. & M. University

During the height of the most recent peak in the struggle for black liberation in the United States, the civil rights movement (CRM) of the 1960s and 1970s, the clarion call to organize was one of the most profound and most promising developments of that era. The call to organize was profound because it rendered superfluous the simplistic debate about integrationism versus separatism as a strategy for black progress by affirming that self-directed and self-defining organizations of those with common purposes and objectives are absolutely necessary, though not sufficient, conditions for progress. It was promising because if the call were brought to fruition, it would create a black community characterized by interrelated and overlapping sets of organizations that could serve as a fulcrum from within which a common ideology might surface. Should such an ideology develop, it would be grounded in the experiences of black rank and file who would constitute the membership of the diverse but interconnected organizations.

By that I mean to suggest that the call to organize presumed that individuals would join sets of organizations that reflected their economic, social, cultural, and political stations in life. Membership in these overlapping organizations would bring together black people from all walks of life, and through their self-interested behavior, as opposed to moral preachments about the virtues of unity, they might arrive at a common definition of reality and vision of the desired future.

The NCOBPS was one of the organizations that grew out of this awareness of the need to organize and the virtue of organizing. Those who were involved in the preparatory conference called in 1969 at Southern University were assembled to discuss professional problems of black political scientists within the discipline in general and within the American Political Science Association (APSA) in particular. As we de-

Prepared for delivery to the Twentieth Anniversary Banquet, Annual Meeting of the National Conference of Black Political Scientists, Baton Rouge, Louisiana, 17 March 1989.

liberated, our focus and concerns quickly broadened. Rather than situating ourselves within the ongoing process and limiting our concerns to achieving equity within that process, we began to challenge the process itself. We also began to realize that it was necessary for us to define ourselves and our mission unencumbered by the assumptions of the existing order. What political science should be and what black political scientists should be doing were for us to decide, with APSA and the discipline being merely one more feature of the total environment in which we were obliged to function. Our grounding in our experiences would provide the basis for our answers to these two fundamental questions.

The substance of our work, the nature and content of the political science knowledge that we generated and passed on, would grow out of our own experiences and serve our own needs. We would no longer receive and pass on to our students and colleagues parochial knowledge generated by mainstream political scientists to serve the needs of American society as they saw them. We came to recognize that mainstream American political science was nothing more than a self-serving, Eurocentric, parochial view of political life thinly disguised in the ill-fitting garb of science and universalism. The ultimate objective of mainstream political science, as we understood it, was to justify and sustain the existing configuration of power in the United States and the world. The long-term interest of black people, on the other hand, would be served by ending the Euroamerican domination of the world.

Similarly, our professional activities and community service would not be limited to efforts to scale the walls of APSA. Rather, they would be bound by our description of the black predicament and our sense of our responsibility to the black community.

This meant that we, the founding members of NCOBPS, committed ourselves to developing a new, a different political science, a black political science, and we committed ourselves to developing an organization that would be a part of that interrelated network of self-defining and self-directed black organizations involved in the struggle for black liberation.

This commitment was demonstrated by the conscious decision not to organize as a caucus of the American Political Science Association but as a separate corporate entity that met at a different time and place and had no formal connection to APSA. It was also manifested in our decision not to seek tax-exempt status, because this would diminish our efforts to be politically assertive. Our first efforts to produce a journal also reflected this commitment. The *Journal on Political Repression*, as it was entitled, was designed to produce serious scholarly works, both theoretical and empirical, that would clarify the nature of the relationship between the systemic requisites of American political economy and the continuing inequality and repression of black Americans.

Our desire to be an activist political organization was also dramatized by our efforts to form regional liaison committees, including the Washington Liaison office, that were designed to involve the membership in the political life and struggles of the black nation, both nationally and within the various regions. This commitment was also reflected in the symbolic trappings of the organization. Our motto, "Seeking the Key to African Unity," indicated our understanding of the inseparable link between the plight of African Americans scattered throughout the diaspora. The naming of the awards bestowed by the organization also dramatized our desire to link our efforts to the ongoing struggle for black liberation. Our community service award was named for Mrs. Fannie Lou Hamer, the heroine of the freedom struggle in Mississippi. The outstanding student award was given in honor of Sammy Younge, the Tuskegee student who was martyred in the antisegregation struggle of the 1960s. Our faculty award was dedicated to the memory of Professor Rodney Higgins, who was instrumental in training a generation of black political scientists at Southern University.

To be sure, there were differences among us on several important questions. There were those who believed that to be relevant was to be engaged in some fashion with our white mentors, either protesting what they were doing or clamoring to join them. The idea of a separate black organization unmoved by the dynamics of APSA struck them as a retreat into irrelevance and acceptance of second-class status. There were also those who were hostile to the idea of a black political science. For them, mainstream American political science was not the parochial product serving identifiable and hostile interests that some of us believed it to be, but a scientifically generated and universally valid and therefore useful enterprise. There were also those who felt that to publish in a journal on political repression compromised their career interest.

Within the ranks of those who accepted the idea of a black political science growing out of the black predicament and driven by the anticipation and control needs of the black community there remained differences on major conceptual issues. Some of the most memorable entries in my own files are exchanges with colleagues such as Ron Walters, Matthew Holden, Alex Willingham, Leslie McLemore, and others on such conceptual issues.

One argument for a black political science was made by me in the first presidential address to this organization twenty years ago. My argument proceeded from two related sets of assumptions: one dealt with the responsibility of the political scientist to the larger community, and the other focused on the instrumental character of knowledge.

Hans Morgenthau's highly insightful and equally neglected theory on the purpose of political science informed my argument regarding the parochial character of American political science. Morgenthau argued that the ultimate responsibility of the political scientist is to tell the truth about power in a society, how it is organized, accumulated, distributed, and exercised. But, he says, one of the cornerstones of every society is the desire to disguise the exercise of power and to have the basic assumptions that justify the existing configuration of societal power accepted as part of the natural order of things rather than being subjected to systematic examination. To question them, according to Morgenthau, "is tantamount to questioning the worth of society itself, its justice, its rationality, its very right to exist" (Morgenthau, 1966:69). If we accept this premise, as I am inclined to do, we are forced to conclude that a relevant or a useful political science is necessarily subversive. Those of us who committed ourselves to the development of a black political science not only accept the role of being subversive to the existing and accepted configuration of power in the broader society, but we must also take a similar posture toward the configuration of power within the black community as well. Our responsibility to the community is not simply to lead the cheers and run errands for black leaders but to serve as a source for enlightened understanding of the black predicament. This means critically examining the politics internal to the black community and assessing its relevance for the ultimate objectives of the struggle.

Those of us who share the instrumental interpretation of knowledge start from the assumption that social science knowledge is a tool created by human beings for human purposes. We believe that social science knowledge is generated by a people to serve their anticipation and control needs. That is to say, that mankind seeks knowledge in order to be able to anticipate impediments that compromise our ability to realize societal objectives. Using the knowledge generated, strategies are developed to either control these impediments or to adapt to them if control is beyond our reach.

Anticipation and control needs are socially determined. They arise when the society's definition and description of its current predicament are juxtaposed with the societal vision of the desired future. Problems are framed by our views of the discrepancy between what is and what ought to be. The most important factor in determining both the definition and description of the current predicament and our vision of the desired future is the societal worldview. The latter is a social product, but it is conditioned disproportionately by the interests and outlook and by the values and ethic of the dominant forces in society. The rise of social science disciplines and the paradigms and frames of reference employed therein grow out of and serve the interest of dominant societal forces. Thus, the problems that set in motion the generation of social science knowledge are problems as perceived by identifiable interest, and the product of that process, which is to say the substance of that scholarship, is necessarily conditioned by and serves those same interests.

Thus, all social science is parochial and unique to the people whose problems it addresses. The idea of a universally valid and useful social science is nothing more than a testimonial to the power of those dominant forces that are able to force or persuade others to accept their definition of reality and their prescription for the future.

As DuBois said in a slightly different context, "It is a matter of beginnings and integrations of one group which sweep instinctive knowledge and inheritances and current reactions into a universal world of science, sociology and art" (DuBois, 1970:181).

To meet the challenge imposed on ourselves by these views required that we disabuse ourselves of the fundamental assumptions upon which all of our prior training had been based because, as Lerone Bennett had said, we were disposed to view the world whitely (Bennett, 1970). The call for a black political science did not mean black scholars studying about black folk and white scholars studying about everything else. Rather, it meant black scholars starting with our own beginning and from that beginning, from that vantage point, from that particularity, moving to understand everything else.

During the early years of our existence as an organization, some of us struggled to develop new conceptual apparatuses through which a new, black political science would be developed. The doctoral program at Atlanta University had that as the centerpiece of its founding mission. Other political scientists here and there also joined in this effort. Valuable contributions were made, which dramatized the limited utility of mainstream American political science, but the new black political science did not arise.

To say that the effort to do so was stillborn may be an overstatement. But it certainly has yet to get beyond its most rudimentary stage. The forces of the status quo responded to the black-studies movement in general and the call for a black political science in particular by charging that they represented undue parochialism and a retreat into the warm womb of noncompetitive segregation.

In a similar vein, the hope that we would produce a radical subversive political science that exposed the deceitful power machinations both in the broader society in general and in the black nation went unfulfilled. Ironically, but perhaps understandably, if our work was at all subversive, it was more subversive toward the leadership structure within the black community than it was toward the power structure within the broader society. And more often than not, the critique of black leadership was atheoretical and burdened by the self-hate syndrome that has historically plagued black self-criticism. The problems of black leadership and organizational failings were not put in a systemic context so that we could understand how the decadent and predatory character of black politics was conditioned by the dynamics of the overall oppressive system. As a result, the criticisms of black leadership reinforced the impression that the problems of black folk were merely those of ineptitude, graft, and a lack of sophistication.

Thus, we are forced to conclude that we have made little headway in realizing the major goals for which we were established. What is more unsettling is the fact we no longer seem to be committed to them. Within NCOBPS there is no debate around these issues. Black political science and political scientists have been mainstreamed. There are no voices calling for alternative interpretations of reality. We are, I think, becoming indistinguishable from our white counterparts. What started out as a challenge to the mainstream has become a part of it. Black political scientists, like other privileged elements of the black community, are becoming functionally integrated into the polity, while the presumed rewards of such participation continue to elude us and the conditions of our working class continue to deteriorate. These contradictions cannot be understood from the vantage point afforded by mainstream scholarship.

This move toward the mainstream must be aborted, because much remains to be done. The responsibilities we identified twenty years ago still beckon us. Let me move to a close by offering a few scattered comments about the particular tasks that lie ahead.

To begin, I believe now, as I believed twenty years ago, that there is a need for us to develop a liberating scholarship, a scholarship reflective of what C. Wright Mills has called the sociological imagination (Mills, 1959). That is, a scholarship that allows us to understand how the troubles of individuals are linked to societal problems; a scholarship that allows us to understand the interplay between man and society, biography and history; a scholarship that helps us understand the relationship between capital accumulation and social deprivation and depravity, between the affluence of Euroamerica and the poverty of Africa and African Americans.

As a necessary precondition for such scholarship we must develop conceptual devices that allow us to capture and build into our research and analyses both racial and economic factors and both material and psychological dimensions of politics. Our frameworks must allow us to capture the essence of the U.S. political economy and culture and the place of blacks in them, as LeRoi Jones once said, in exactly the same terms that America has set for us, not as we wish it to be, not as it is for the privileged few, but exactly as it is for us as a people (Jones, L., 1966).

So much for problems of conceptualization. Let me turn to another matter of concern—our responsibility to be involved in liberating political practice and our concomitant responsibility to interpret our actions and those of our compatriots. False modesty aside, we are the ones who are paid and given the time to study and think about politics. We have a responsibility to produce coherent, insightful interpretations of our practice as a people, interpretations that serve as bridges from one movement to the next, from one generation to the next. We also have a responsibility to bring our insights to bear upon contemporary international developments.

Presently the political state of black America cries out for analysis and interpretation. When NCOBPS was founded twenty years ago, we were in the latter stages of a decade of intense activism. That period of mass protest and violence was succeeded by one in which emphasis was placed on formal politics. The slogans from protest to politics, green power instead of black power, aptly characterized this period. Black elected officials, particularly big-city mayors, congresspersons, and the heads of a handful of civil rights organizations, became the acknowledged and unchallenged black leaders.

At the local level, black organizations are beholden to these leaders for their survival. Consequently, there is little if any authentic black opposition to the system. What passes for black opposition are individuals and organizations fully integrated as functional parts of the very social order that calls forth their need to exist as adversarial structures.

Of course, this functional integration of the leadership element of the oppressed community into the repressive apparatus of the state is nothing new. Nevertheless, it remains a serious problem and deserves our most critical thinking and analysis.

Let me indicate why I think this is so important at this stage of our struggle. On the surface, it appears to me that the gains realized by blacks as a result of the struggles of the recent past have been and continue to be distributed in a fashion that not only accentuates class differences in the black community, but that also gives the black middle class objective reasons to support policies and programs detrimental to the interests of black rank and file. Time does not permit a comprehensive development of this argument this evening. Suffice it here to say that this argument rests on what I take to be three commonly recognized facts.

First, middle- and upper-income black professionals are found disproportionately in the public-sector bureaucracy. Second, increasingly, as the labor market provides fewer and fewer opportunities for black rank and file, the well-being of the black community is dependent upon government-sponsored intervention strategies such as transfer payments, subsidy programs, and set-asides. Third, as blacks become more concentrated in the service sector of the economy, their well-being is contingent upon maintaining the irrational and wasteful consumerism upon which the service sector rests.

These factors lead the black leadership class to support uncritically the dominant economic philosophy, which assumes that any and all production is good and which equates economic growth with development. To the extent that the deteriorating conditions of working-class black communities are the product of unplanned economic growth and the production-for-production's-sake ethos, black leaders and their followers unwittingly work to reinforce their own oppression. They never raise, or perhaps even glimpse, the really important question, namely, to what extent do these patterns of production actually serve to reinforce the structural conditions that give rise to the "black problem."

Similarly, black leadership is disposed to embrace the reformist, intervention strategies of the liberal wing of the American ruling class without attempting to determine whether they weaken or reinforce the structural conditions that create and sustain the unequal conditions of blacks in American life. Under these circumstances both black leadership and the followers who defer to them become hostage to the irrational economic and political order that creates and sustains their unhappy plight.

In a similar vein, recent developments in world politics, the role of the United States in it, and the significance of these developments for understanding the black predicament deserve our attention. The Reagan-Thatcher policies have raised the economic exploitation and political repression of Third World peoples to unprecedented levels. They have reinforced the inequitable international division of labor that results in the systematic transfer of wealth from the impoverished lands of the Third World to the affluent countries of the West. The ultimate outcome of these policies manifests itself in what is euphemistically called "the Third-World debt problem." Through the International Monetary Fund and other international institutions, the United States and its allies force Third World governments to adopt public policies that further impoverish their peoples in order to pay these debts.

This economic strategy of the West is supported by the companion military strategy called "low intensity conflict" (LIC), which declares the United States is in a constant state of war with the peoples of the Third World (Klare and Kornbluh, 1988). The United States and Great Britain have their rapid deployment forces and France has its *force d'intervention* to maintain order among the exploited.

The United States has led an ideological/propaganda offensive to camouflage its real objectives and win the support of the American people. The increasing impoverishment of the Third World, according to this ideology, is said to be its flirtation with socialism, and the solution is said to be privatization. In the final analysis, privatization can only mean selling the national patrimony to international cartels, with the local bourgeoisie serving as bagmen.

In the midst of all of this, the United States has concocted a "human rights" standard to judge other governments, while at the same time it trains and supports those who direct death squads to terrorize their own people. The human rights campaign is buttressed by the Reagan-Thatcher claim that the West is morally superior to other countries. To assume that Western policymakers, like those of other major powers, may have anything other than benign altruistic intentions toward the Third World is to assume that other regimes are the moral equivalent of the West, and this, to the Reagan-Thatcher axis, is heresy. This claim of moral superiority pales in credulity when we are reminded that it comes from a civilization that gave the world centuries of slavery, American and South African–style apartheid, and World Wars I and II; that developed and used on human targets atomic weapons and agent orange; and that is now working feverishly to develop ethnic weapons (Larson, 1970).

These developments certainly deserve more than our silence.

Unfortunately, black political scientists have been more inclined to be cheerleaders for, than constructive critics of, our leaders and these developments. It is our responsibility to put all of this in a coherent theoretical context and help to ascertain the implications of these realities for developing strategies for liberation.

Recently, a smattering of black social scientists have begun to raise questions about the role of contemporary black leadership and about the efficacy of certain intervention strategies. Most of these efforts have been grounded in the backward-looking neoconservative philosophy and, hence, have little prescriptive utility for those concerned with black advancement. Some of the others have been presented in an atheoretical context, and as a consequence, they have been received as merely liberal critiques. And as such, they can easily be construed or misconstrued as a continuation of the thesis that the unhappy state of the black community is simply the result of the ineptitude of our leaders and our backwardness as a group.

Neither set of critics makes a useful contribution to our efforts to understand our plight and fashion strategies for our advancement. We must move to a higher calling. And this brings me to the final issue I want to raise this evening, and that is the need for us as individuals and as an organization to become involved in efforts to develop an authentic movement *against* the system, which would complement the current inauthentic black opposition within the system. This opposition to the system would enhance the prospects for changes in the system.

There can be little doubt that the oppressed condition of blacks as a group is systemic and, therefore, can be changed only through fundamental changes in the system itself. The same can be said regarding the plight of the oppressed of the Third World. This change will occur only when enough people believe that it is both necessary and inevitable.

This generation of black academicians must take the initiative in demystifying the nature of the U.S. economic and political order. Through our scholarship, we must show how it functions to maintain poverty and decadence at home and repression and underdevelopment abroad. We must disabuse ourselves of the notion that its problems are merely the unintended consequences of human progress or simply manifestations of human nature. We must show that the system we have now is the flawed creation of flawed men; that it was created by one variety of men to serve one variety of interests, and that that variety of men and the system they have created are not even suggestive of the limits of human possibilities. We must be brave visionaries. As Martin Luther King said, we must form the core of the colony of dissenters. We must affirm our belief that mankind can produce a fair and just society, and we must commit ourselves to its construction.

References

Bennett, Lerone, Jr., 1970. *The Challenge of Blackness.* Atlanta: Institute of the Black World.

Du Bois, W. E. B. 1970. "The Negro College." In Meyer Weinberg, *W. E. B. A Reader.* New York: Harper and Row.

Jones, LeRoi. 1966. *Home.* New York: William Morrow.

Jones, Mack H. 1977. "The Responsibility of Black Political Scientists to the Black Community." In Shelby Lewis Smith, ed., *Black Political Scientists and Black Survival.* Balamp.

——— . "Mainstream Political Science and the Black Experience: Issues of Epistemology and Utility." Unpublished manuscript.

Klare, M., and P. Kornbluh. 1988. *Low Intensity Warfare.* Pantheon Books.

Larson, Carl. 1970. "Ethnic Weapons." *Military Review* (November).

McLemore, Leslie, and Vernon Gray. 1969. "The Participation of Blacks in the 65th Annual Meeting of APSA: Some Random Impressionistic Comments." Unpublished manuscript. See also personal letter Mack Jones to McLemore and Gray, October 10, 1969 and Willingham to Brothers (McLemore and Gray, 1969).

Mills, C. Wright. 1959. *The Sociological Imagination*. New York: Oxford University Press.

Morgenthau, Hans. 1966. "The Purpose of Political Science." In James Charlesworth, *A Design for Political Science: Scope, Objectives, and Methods*. The American Academy of Political Science.

Willingham, Alex, with Mack Jones. 1969. "A Preliminary Statement to Black Political Scientists." Unpublished manuscript.

NCOBPS: Observations on The State of the Organization

Dianne M. Pinderhughes

University of Illinois (Urbana-Champaign)

On this twentieth anniversary of the founding of the National Con-ference of Black Political Scientists (NCOBPS), I want to offer some observations on the state of the organization. I will talk first about the role of black political scientists in the discipline of political science and within the organization. Second, I will discuss some of the major strengths and weaknesses of NCOBPS. Finally, I will offer some obser-vations about the structure of the organization and make some recom-mendations about reforming it.

The Role of Black Political Scientists within the Discipline

The 1960s marked the era when not only in the streets but in academe a relatively large cohort of black scholars entered a variety of disciplines. Those who had entered before came in smaller numbers and entered the profession by focusing, at least in the initial stages of their careers, on the operations of American political institutions. By the mid to late 1960s, however, larger numbers of blacks sought graduate training, and they entered with an explicit interest in the politics of race and in the impact of American politics on the status of blacks. They were not easily accommodated, and black academic organizations like NCOBPS, the As-sociation of Black Sociologists, the Association of Black Psychologists, and others were formed in the late 1960s, both in light of these rejections and during an era of high ideological intensity and interest in alternative group-based approaches. Immediate products of, or significantly influ-enced by, the civil rights movement–black power–black nationalism, black scholars reshaped the existing disciplines and added to the repre-

Presidential address at the Business Meeting of the National Conference of Black Political Scientists on its twentieth anniversary, 17 March 1989.

sentative structure of the disciplines. Integration into the profession was not the only, or a sufficient, goal of this cohort.

In more recent years, black politics have moved away from the ideological intensity of earlier years toward a somewhat greater concentration on electoral politics and political integration, including efforts by blacks to claim the presidency. There are, of course, not at present any black senators or governors, although there are increasing numbers of black legislators (only Utah, Vermont, Idaho, Hawaii, Maine, New Mexico, North Dakota, and South Dakota have none). There are still constant developments of black community organizations and other types of black nationalist groups; I would not dare to suggest that the integrationist wing is dominant.

Black political scientists in the discipline today also press for accurate, complex representation of politics in the black community. Our own organizational structure provides us with the opportunity to concentrate on the many and varied ways in which the politics of race affects the world; and many, although by no means all, of black political scientists participate in the national or regional associations of political scientists as well as in NCOBPS. And important numbers of blacks who are political scientists do not participate in NCOBPS at all.

The role of NCOBPS over the years has expanded significantly. The organization is important in the following areas (although this list does not intend to be at all comprehensive).

First, the annual meetings of the conference include panel presentations, written papers, and oral communications, as well as the times between panels, which I think all of us value so much. It is on these occasions over the last twenty years during which we have developed a rather distinctive and always highly critical set of perspectives on the study of racial politics. I think the most difficult and simultaneously the most valued criticism we receive in the profession on these topics, broadly identified as black politics, is centered in and around NCOBPS.

Second, the results of this creative process are apparent in the outpouring of publications by NCOBPS "members," and I use that in the broadest sense of the word, in recent years. The appendix contains a representative list of members' volumes, with apologies to all of you whom I have forgotten or about whom I do not yet know. There are obviously many other important works, among them Mathew Holden's and Milton Morris's books.

Third, and most recently, the first volume of the conference's own publication, the *National Political Science Review* (NPSR), has just been published and will continue to need your interest and support.

Fourth, the broad-ranging activities, with the *Roster* and with *Focus*, among others, of Eddie Williams, Milton Morris, Linda Williams, and other staff members of the Joint Center for Political Studies are very important. Sheila Harmon's recent pioneering work in satellite teleconferencing, Elsie Scott's leadership as executive director of the National Organization of Black Law Enforcement Executives, Vernon Gray's leadership as commissioner in Columbia, Maryland, and Leslie McLemore's activities as congressional candidate in Mississippi deserve special recognition. Ron Walters founded the National Congress of Black Faculty; Curtina Moreland, Mitchell Rice, and Oliver Jones have been leaders in the Conference of Minority Public Administrators.

Our members are leaders in and of educational, academic, professional, and policy-making institutions throughout the nation. In twenty years, I think this is a great deal to point to.

Major Philosophical Forces within NCOBPS

The NCOBPS has many strengths:

First, we range across the discipline and interpenetrate within and among varying types of colleges and universities in a much more diverse way than typical members of the discipline. We are faculty in public and private colleges and universities that are historically as well as predominantly black, and in public and private, predominantly white colleges and universities of great differences in size and type.

These types also suggest important differences in the way we view our roles in the profession and the way we respond to and address issues of race and racial politics in our research and teaching.

Second, the location of our members enhances the flow of information in ways that are not ordinarily possible: in the same way the black caucuses on predominantly white campuses can integrate information in ways that very few other organizations can on the campus, a group of black academics can combine, compare, and juxtapose information about resources, discrimination, and other events.

However unwillingly we have faced the event, the experience of not getting tenure is a third strength: it has given many of us exposure to several different types of institutions of higher education, which dramatically increases our expertise and knowledge of how colleges and universities function, compared to those who may have spent their careers located in only one place.

Fourth, the broad range of types of institutions within which we function also allows for and generates some tensions. The perspectives and assumptions of faculty in predominantly white versus predominantly or historically black institutions differ, and these differences offer some opportunities for irritation. On the other hand, I think we have been able to live with, adjust to, and manage these differences rather well over the years.

We have important weaknesses in the following areas:

We are now producing a journal, but we lack the resources at the level of the institution to facilitate the growth and production of research—in other words, most of us have great difficulty in securing funds to travel, for release time, or to acquire the resources to conduct research and publish our results. Those of us in smaller institutions, which have the least resources, suffer the most, but even those in larger public and private colleges and universities are dependent on institutional support rather than resources from private foundations or national funding agencies. Only a very few of us secure external support on a routine basis. This is a critical area on which the organization needs to focus.

Second, gender issues are most often subordinated to racial issues in the organization; from time to time there have been mini rebellions, and women have led the organization in limited time periods. There are far too few black women in the profession and in NCOBPS, and in this organization alone we can identify a number of women with Ph.D.'s or A.B.D.'s—Pauline Terrelonge Stone, Gail Peak, and Freda Wheaton, to name three—who have chosen to shift their professional gears toward (for example) law; we have basically lost them. We need to increase the representation of women in the field.

Those of us who are women and who have lived with the organization can remember the difficult early years of entering and having to fend off advances from some of the male members. Not a one of us is puritanical, but as we seek to recruit new women members and younger scholars this can be a problem.

Third, we need to ask what kind of organization NCOBPS will be as it enters its third and fourth decades of existence; at the start, the core of the organization was centered in black colleges and universities in the South. Its founders were located at Southern and Atlanta and Howard. Those of us who were here twenty years ago all remember the differences between black institutions, and between blacks from southern, black institutions and blacks from northern, white institutions. The background assumptions during those early years were that legitimacy was found only in predominantly black institutions.

The organization cannot grow and develop either if it ignores these foundations, or if it attempts to operate based only on its first principles, on its founding fathers and mother. Because they reflect the shifts in college and university attendance by blacks from predominantly black to nonblack institutions, black political scientists in small numbers are now located all over the country; far too many of them are unknown to us, and too many of them know nothing about NCOBPS. During my presidency, I had calls from people at St. Lawrence University in Canton, New York, and California State University at Fresno, among others, seeking membership information. If NCOBPS is incapable of identifying, locating, and attracting them and welcoming them, whether they are in California, Massachusetts, Texas, Utah, or at Ole' Miss, our membership will inevitably stabilize, eventually grow smaller, and fall into decline.

We need to help in the growth and development of new members; *each one* of us should try to bring at least one undergraduate or graduate student to the conference each year to expose them to the fact that we are not singular in our interests. Many of you do bring students, but not all of us do each year. I think it is fairly clear that the Jewel Limar Prestage model, the intrusive model of the laying on of hands, to encourage students to enter the profession and to give them a great deal of positive reinforcement, is the model to follow. It is quite successful, as is clear from the number of you here today who have had exposure to Professor Prestage directly or indirectly through one of her students.

This organization carries the memories of earlier generations of black political scientists, of institutional discrimination, of challenges to the profession, of the absolutely critical role of race in American political life and history. We do this to an extent unmatched in any other part of the profession. If we do not transmit these rich memories, interests, and understandings of how the discipline has functioned in a highly discriminatory fashion, and of how American political institutions have organized political life according to the racist preferences of American slave owners and commercial beneficiaries of the slave trade in the past and of their descendants in the present, new generations of black political scientists will enter the field and either be absorbed alone in an uncritical manner, or find themselves unwelcome but unable to understand the whys and wherefores. New white political scientists will be unsocialized by our influence. And generations of American students, black as well as white, will have no knowledge or understanding of the politics of race that we have worked so carefully to understand and to publish, because it will have gone untransmitted.

Moreover, there is, as we all know, a great deal of work to be done in the profession, whether we wish to characterize it as political science, politics, or black politics. Much of it will have to be done by us; others are typically uninterested, or are interested in ways that misinterpret what is happening.

Organizational Structure

Next I want to make some specific comments about the structure of the organization in its present state and make some closing recommendations about issues that need to be addressed. In this year of my presidency, I appointed the Twentieth Anniversary Commission to address the current state of NCOBPS and to seek some advice from the collective wisdom of a group of you on these issues. Many of you will have heard some of my observations before about how the organization functions, but I think it cannot hurt to state them again.

The President and President-Elect

We have created these two offices as closely related to each other. I think it very important that we consider whether it is appropriate to have a president-elect who is responsible for the conference program (an extraordinarily demanding job as the twenty of us who have done this know all too intimately), and who then immediately becomes responsible for policy-making for the larger body. The very natural response to the completion of the job of program chair/president-elect is to lower one's sights to the problem of survival until the presidency is over. The first few presidents commented on this with their lively presidential addresses. I now understand what made them so lively.

There are some definite advantages to the current arrangement, however: the most important is that the program chair/president-elect gets to know all sorts of people in the organization that he or she would not otherwise know, because people are constantly calling to get on the program or with some question about the conference in that year.

However, I think the Twentieth Anniversary Commission (and it will continue beyond this meeting) ought to consider whether it is time to make the program chair a free-standing position, not necessarily leading to higher office. We could continue to have a president-elect and president, but this would free these two top officers in the association to consider organizational management, growth, and development in the areas I have outlined above.

Council

The Council is not currently a very active body, partly because of the extent to which the president-elect is overburdened with organizational responsibilities, and partly because the president (and I count myself in this group) is less active in programmatic development because he or she is recovering from the previous year. The Council and other officers ought to meet more often, at least three times a year. Three times a year is what is required by our constitution, although I'd bet very few of you knew that; I didn't until last week myself. The council ought to be more involved in the governance of the organization; this could be facilitated first by having individual members head committees to handle some specific areas of responsibility in conjunction with one of the other officers. These might include, for example, an Internal Financial Committee, a Professional Development Committee, a Recruiting Committee, and an External (Resource) Development Committee. If we want to make the Council a more active body, we ought also to see how we might fund the costs of the members' travel to meetings.

Executive Director

This role will inevitably become considerably more significant over the years because the incumbent, at present Lois Hollis, will develop the greatest depth of knowledge about the organization. Some responsibilities which are not presently located there will and should gravitate to that office: membership is one possibility and publication of the newsletter is another; work with each successive local-arrangements committee will be very valuable. Of course, as we increase the responsibilities of the office, we should plan to increase the remuneration involved. We cannot pay our executive director all she is worth, but we should not take it for granted that she will do it for little or nothing.

Twentieth Anniversary Commission

While this group met for the first time at the 1989 conference, it should continue its task into the 1989–90 academic year and plan to report to the body well before the 1990 meeting so that, if any amendments to the constitution are required, the officers can circulate them prior to the annual conference. [The 1989 Business Meeting later in the evening voted to require the commission to convey any recommendations to the officers and the Council by 15 November 1989.]

National Political Science Review

The NPSR is a welcome, long-awaited addition to the list of NCOBPS activities. I would like to thank editor Lucius Barker and to congratulate him for the work he put in to produce the first issue. However, I cannot say strongly enough that without the participation and timely involvement of all NCOBPS members in the submission of articles, in the writing of book reviews and review essays, and in the review process for articles themselves, it will become a journal of the broader political science profession, which is overwhelmingly dominated, of course, by whites. As NCOBPS, a predominantly black organization, is the body that supports the NPSR, its members should expect, and I would expect, that any editor of the journal would also want to see the members and their views reflected in the pages of the journal. However, in a peer review journal, this is possible only to the extent that NCOBPS's members submit articles, respond to invitations to submit articles, and participate in the review process in a timely fashion.

Because we cannot at present afford to publish on more than an annual basis, late submissions cannot be rolled over into the next publication in three or four months. A delay of a year and some months may, and probably will, make some of the materials seriously outdated.

I also expect that the officers of the journal will make their criteria for evaluation clear to the members, and that these are always to be consistently applied; the Council and officers have directed that the editor will report to the Council and to the membership on the operation of the journal. That began at this meeting and will continue on an annual basis in the future.

Conclusions

My expectation and my great hope for NCOBPS is that we will continue to exist in cooperative and creative tension. As a group of blacks in the profession, there are too few of us to survive in bifurcated or divided cohorts. The larger profession continues to offer too little integration and too little acceptance of our collective sense of our mission as political scientists interested in the status of blacks in the United States for NCOBPS not to be of great value to all of us for the foreseeable future. I think our greatest test over the next twenty years will be in our ability to identify and to create new resources, and to ensure that these new resources will benefit all of us in a relatively equal fashion, or as they are needed. If we are unable to do this none of us will fare as well as I think the first twenty years of NCOBPS has enabled us to. I thank you.

Appendix

Barnett, Marguerite, and James Hefner, eds. 1976. *Public Policy for The Black Community.* New York: Alfred Publishing Company.

Barker, Lucius J. 1988. *Our Time Has Come.* Urbana: The University of Illinois Press.

Barker, Lucius, and Ron Walters. eds. 1989. *Jesse Jackson's 1984 Presidential Campaign.* Urbana: The University of Illinois Press.

Githens, Marianne, and Jewel Prestage, eds. 1977. *A Portrait of Marginality.* New York: Longman.

Jones, Franklin D., Michael O. Adams, with Sanders Anderson, Jr., and Tandy Tollerson, eds. 1987. *Readings in American Political Issues.* Dubuque, Iowa: Kendall/Hunt Publishing Company.

McClain, Paula, and Albert Karnig, eds. 1988. *Urban Minority Administrators: Politics, Policy and Style.* New York: Greenwood Press.

Morris, Lorenzo. 1979. *Elusive Equality.* Washington, D.C.: Howard University Press.

Morris, Lorenzo, Charles Jarmon, and Arnold Taylor, eds. 1990. *The Social and Political Implications of the Jesse Jackson Presidential Campaign.* New York: Praeger.

Pinderhughes, Dianne. 1987. *Race and Ethnicity in Chicago Politics,* A Reexamination of Pluralist Theory. Urbana: The University of Illinois Press.

Preston, Michael. 1984. *The Politics of Bureaucratic Reform.* Urbana: The University of Illinois Press.

Preston, Michael B., Lenneal Henderson, and Paul Puryear, eds. 1987. *The New Black Politics.* New York: Longman.

Reed, Adolph, Jr. 1986. *The Jesse Jackson Phenomenon.* New Haven: Yale University Press.

Rice, Mitchell, and Woodrow Jones, eds. 1984. *Contemporary Public Policy Perspectives and Black Americans; Issues in an Era of Retrenchment Politics.* Westport Conn: Greenwood Press.

———. 1987. *Health Care Issues in Black America: Policies, Problems and Prospects.* New York: Greenwood Press.

Rich, Wilbur. 1989. *Coleman Young and Detroit Politics.* Detroit: Wane State University Press.

Somerville, Carolyn. 1986. *Drought and Aid in the Sahel.* Boulder, Colorado: Westview Press.

Smith, Robert. SUNY Series

Smith, J. Owens. 1987. *The Politics of Racial Inequality.* Westport, Conn.: Greenwood Press.

Smith, J. Owens, Mitchell Rice and Woodrow Jones, eds. 1987. *Blacks and American Government: Politics, Policy and Social Change.* Dubuque, Iowa: Kendall/Hunt Publishing Company.

Walters, Ronald. 1988. *Black Presidential Politics in America: A Strategic Approach.* Albany: State University of New York Press.

Walton, Hanes Jr. 1985. *Invisible Politics.* Albany: State University of New York Press.

―――― . 1988. *When The Marching Stopped.* Albany: State University of New York Press.

Wilson, Basil, and Charles Green. 1989. *The Struggle for Black Empowerment in New York City.* New York: Praeger.

Feature Articles

Racial Belief Systems, Religious Guidance, and African-American Political Participation

Michael C. Dawson
Ronald E. Brown
Richard L. Allen

The University of Michigan
Eastern Michigan University
The University of Michigan

Building on previous work, a schema-based approach to belief systems is used to model an African-American racial belief system. This belief system is used with socioeconomic status, exposure to black media, and religious guidance, as a predictor of individual African-American political participation. A LISREL measurement and causal model are used to estimate the theoretical model. As predicted, the various cognitive schemata of the racial-identity belief system are shown to predict political participation. Further, religious guidance is shown to be a stronger predictor of some forms of political participation than socioeconomic status. Overall, socioeconomic status and religious guidance are shown to be the strongest predictors of political participation. Using a national sample of African Americans, we found that those with a higher socioeconomic status and/ or with a higher degree of religious guidance in their lives were more likely to participate in the political process.

Authors' Note: This work is part of a continuing research project. All authors contributed equally to this paper. Preparation of this manuscript was supported in part by the Rockefeller Foundation and National Science Foundation Grant #SES87–10307. We gratefully acknowledge the assistance of Leitha Chudiha and Che-Wei Tan in the data analysis, and James Jackson, Steven Rosenstone, Richard Bagozzi, Bazel Allen, and Cathy Cohen for comments and suggestions on a draft of this manuscript. Of course, all errors in this endeavor are completely the authors' responsibility.

A frican-American voters have been a decisive factor in many elections in the 1980s. The 1983 and 1987 Chicago mayoral elections, the 1986 Southern Senate elections, and the 1988 Democratic party primary process have all been heavily influenced by high black voter turnout (Kleppner, 1985). In some cases, the presence of black candidates such as the late Harold Washington of Chicago or the Reverend Jesse Jackson has helped lead to higher black turnout (Cavanagh, 1985; Kleppner, 1985). In other cases, such as the 1986 mid-term elections when few black candidates were on the ballot, the decisive role of black voters cannot be explained by the presence of black candidates. In this article we will establish that a cognitive schema-based model of racial identity, the importance of religious guidance in the lives of African Americans, and mass media exposure help to explain the varying levels of African-American political participation.

Group Consciousness and Political Participation

A persistent theme in the political-science literature is that low socioeconomic resources correlates with low levels of political interest and involvement in political matters. Poor people are more likely to feel alienated from the political system than upper-status people and, therefore, less likely to become involved. Black Americans are a low-social-status group but demonstrate much higher levels of political participation than one would expect. Social and political learning in a racially stratified society has produced a sense of racial group consciousness among black Americans (Shingles, 1981). This group-based attitude is a powerful predictor of black political participation. It has been shown to influence voter choice and turnout (Cavanagh, 1985; Kleppner, 1985), campaign activism (Verba and Nie, 1972; Miller et al., 1981; Shingles, 1981), and contacting of public officials (Miller et al., 1981). Although racial consciousness is a strong correlate of African-American political participation, research on this subject has not yet explicated the process through which racial consciousness influences the decision to be a political activist. In this paper we will establish that a cognitive schema-based model of racial consciousness influences black political involvement because of the important socializing role of black religion and black media on racial identification.

Even though racial consciousness has been shown to be an important group-based resource for political mobilization (Verba and Nie, 1972; Miller et al., 1981; Shingles, 1981), research on this subject needs to be extended. Previous work has indicated that racial consciousness is a multidimensional construct (Allen, Dawson, and Brown, 1989). We propose that the linkage between theoretical conceptualizing of the various aspects of racial consciousness and political behavior can be improved by the development and testing of more comprehensive models that explicitly link micro-level psychological constructs with the propensity to engage in certain political behaviors. A second related problem is that the relative effects of schemata that comprise racial consciousness on political action have not been tested. Thus, very little systematic information is available about the relative predictive power of these constructs.

A final problem is that little is known about the process through which racial consciousness influences the decision to be a political activist. For example, work by Shingles (1981) shows that racial consciousness was far more important in explaining the political actions of poor blacks than it was for middle-class blacks. Given the debate in the literature concerning the declining relevancy of race in the lives of middle-class blacks (Frazier, 1957; Wilson, 1988; Kilson, 1983), it is imperative that we investigate the relative effect of socioeconomic status on the propensity to be racially conscious. By specifying which forms of racial consciousness are more likely to vary by social class, we will be in a better position to describe the form of racial consciousness that best predicts the political participation rates of middle-class and working-class blacks. Along similar lines, some argue that because of the centrality of the black church in the struggle for black rights, blacks who are religious may have a higher degree of racial consciousness (Allen et al., 1989). Therefore, we would anticipate a causal linkage between religiosity, racial consciousness, and political participation. Finally, exposure to black media is thought to be correlated with racial consciousness and political action because of its role in conveying information that is in the interest of the group (Allen and Hatchett, 1986; Allen and Bielby, 1979a, 1979b).

In this investigation we attempt to address these issues by (a) estimating a model of racial consciousness that takes into account the multidimensionality of the construct and (b) modeling the social process through which these dimensions of racial consciousness influence political participation.

Racial Belief Systems and African-American Political Participation

Much of the extensive research on African-American racial group-based attitudes and beliefs has tended to focus on the centrality of group identification and consciousness. We argue elsewhere (Allen, Dawson, and Brown, 1989), that the African-American racial belief system is composed of multiple cognitive schemata, and that these schemata are distinctive but interrelated cognitive constructs that vary across individuals in their degree of intensity within the black population. As we have argued previously, this belief system is the cognitive manifestation of the often-conflicting and different political and social heritages of white and black Americans. We presented five cognitive schemata: (1) black autonomy, (2) the propensity to adopt positive stereotypical beliefs about African Americans, (3) the propensity to adopt negative stereotypical beliefs about African Americans, (4) closeness to the black masses, and (5) closeness to black elites.

Cognitive heuristics help us explain the origins of an African-American racial belief system. We assert that, to the extent that black life chances have been historically dominated by the ascriptive factor of race, individual African Americans have been able to use the heuristic of an evaluation of what is "good" or "bad" for the race as a proxy for maximizing individual utility. As long as the *perception* remains that race is more important than other factors such as social class or gender in influencing life chances, one would expect relatively homogeneous group behavior and beliefs. This perception and the associated heuristic would facilitate the processing of information through the racial-identity belief system.

This racial-identity belief system would enhance African-American political participation by strengthening the belief that political participation would lead directly to group benefits. Due to the group-benefit heuristic, this perceived gain in group advantage becomes translated for individual African Americans into perceived individual utility enhancement. Political candidates who invoke African-American racial identity in their campaigns either explicitly or implicitly, ceteris paribus, can expect increased political mobilization from a black community that collectively and individually perceives increased group benefits from the results of a successful campaign.[1] Conversely, candidates who base their campaigns in part on what are perceived as attacks on the black community will also invoke the racial-identity belief system in African Americans, thus amplifying black countermobilization to a candidate who is perceived to threaten the group interests of African Americans. This phenomenon appears to explain the increased voter turnout evidenced in many black communities in the 1982 mid-term elections (Kleppner, 1985; Cavanagh, 1985).

Candidates seeking to benefit from increased black political participation turn to one key institution for aid—the black church. In the next section we explore why religious guidance influences, and, we assert, enhances African-American political participation.

Religious Guidance and African-American Political Participation

During the twentieth century, the African-American church has been the critical institution in the reproduction of African-American beliefs and values, *and* a prominent social and political institution in the black community. As the major autonomous organization throughout black America, the church has played a key role in black politics and political mobilization (Morris, 1984; Cone, 1986; Kleppner, 1985).

It is sometimes argued that religion provides a spiritual refuge from a sociopolitical reality that is often perceived as being too individualistic and alienating (Wald, 1987; Chidester, 1988). Therefore, religious communities are places where people seek comfort and develop communal ties that help them cope with the world around them. For African Americans, racial oppression produces a religious community in which members gather and attempt to interpret their status as second-class citizens (West, 1982).

In the context of this paper, we consider African Americans who engage in Bible reading, praying, and watching religious programs to have a strong sense of religious guidance. We hypothesize that religion creates a sense of self and group spiritual well-being that increases emotional or affective ties toward the group and the motivation to engage in political actions to promote group interest.

In sum, we predict the following relations between religious guidance and the various media, belief, and participation constructs. We expect that higher levels of religious guidance in respondents will lead to more exposure to both black print and black broadcast media, greater levels of racial identity (although with higher levels of support for both positive and negative racial stereotypes), and higher levels of political mobilization.

Socioeconomic Status, the Black Media and Black Political Action

Socioeconomic status (SES) has long been recognized as a predictor of political participation (Verba and Nie, 1972; Wolfinger and Rosenstone, 1980). However, group consciousness has also been shown to increase African-American political participation. In our previous work, we explain why SES has a major effect on the African-American racial-identity belief system, being inversely correlated with the black-autonomy construct, black television, and negative stereotypical beliefs, but positively associated with black print media and the other belief-system schemata. Consistent with previous participation research, we expect SES to be positively associated with both voting and political involvement.

In this section we describe why exposure to black media, that is, print and television programming, should be correlated with racial group identification. We first begin by discussing the relevancy of media in the political arena and then move to a more detailed discussion of the influence of black media on racial group identification and political action.

The relevancy of media to the political process is due to the fact that the majority of American citizens gain information about political events, candidates, and parties from media sources (Allen and Kuo, 1988; Kessel, 1988). For most citizens, television news is the major source of political information. Nonetheless, those citizens whose primary sources are magazines and newspapers are more likely to be politically informed and interested in politics (Kessel, 1988). Moreover, newspaper exposure in comparison to television exposure has been found to be more typically and strongly associated with a variety of political activities (Allen and Kuo, 1988). A growing number of investigations indicate that those who rely only on television for political information tend not to be political activists because television leads to vicarious rather than actual participation (Allen and Kuo, 1988).

Black print media outlets are a vehicle for mobilizing group solidarity and support. Even though black print media have been shown to be a positive socialization agent in the reinforcement and the transmission of cultural values and norms, some maintain that the black print media are not at the cutting edge of the social and political change. However, those who are exposed to black print media may also have a higher propensity to be political activists, because they are in a communication network with people who tend to have more information about how the political system can be used to promote the group's interests.

It is interesting to note that highly religious blacks tend to expose themselves to black media (Allen, Dawson, and Brown, 1989). Hence, religious blacks may have a high level of racial identity and therefore be more likely to be political activists because of their attempts to seek out positive information about the racial group. Highly educated blacks are also more likely to expose themselves to black print (Allen and Bielby, 1979b; Allen and Hatchett, 1986; Allen, Dawson, and Brown, 1989). Thus, the attentive public in the black community tends to be religious or educated.

Television is said to act as a promoter of the dominant culture (Gerbner, Morgan, and Signorielli, 1980). Its role as a dominant cultivator and its tendency to deactivate citizens leads us to posit that black-oriented television will at best have a weak effect on the propensity to be a political activist. Thus, whereas exposure to black-oriented television may be more important in the communication and transmission of cultural orientations, it is exposure to black print that motivates black Americans to be political activists.

Model Specification

Sample

Employing notations in accordance with the conventions of path analysis as suggested by Joreskog and Sorbom (1984), we labeled parameters with Greek letters as follows: ξs (ksis) refers to the exogenous latent variables; ηs (etas) are latent endogenous variables. βs (betas) and γs (gammas) are the structural coefficients or direct causal effects linking the latent variables, ξs and ηs. The ζs (zetas) indicate errors in the equations. Although not shown in the figure, the error variances for the media constructs, the error variances for the belief constructs, and the error variances for the political participation constructs are specified to be correlated (ψs [psis]). By correlating these error variances, we assumed that the variances left unexplained in each of these correlated constructs were due to common antecedents. The λs (lambdas) are the factor loadings or the coefficients of the indicators regressed on the observed dimensions. To establish the unit of measurement for each factor, the factor loading of one of its indicators is constrained to 1. Finally, the εs (epsilons) denote measurement errors associated with the Y observable indicators; the δs (deltas) denote measurement errors associated with the X observable indicators.

Research Design

The 1980 National Survey of Black Americans provided the data for this project. This study was conducted by the Program for Research on Black Americans (PRBA) at the Survey Research Center at the University of Michigan during 1979 and 1980. The sample was drawn according to a multistage area probability procedure designed so that every black household had an equal probability of being selected for the study. The sample was based on the 1970 census distribution of the black population; seventy-six primary areas were selected, stratified by racial composition (number of black households) and region. Within each selected black household, one person was chosen randomly to be interviewed from those who were eligible for the study. Eligibility was restricted to persons eighteen and older, self-identified as black, and U.S. citizens.

The final sample consisted of 2,107 completed interviews; the response rate was 67 percent. The national cross-sectional sample was fairly representative of the black population as reported in the 1980 census. If the cross-sectional survey had living family members from at least two other generations, interviews were attempted with one randomly selected representative from each of those two generations. Cross-sectional respondents were reinterviewed with a form of the three-generation instrument. Of the 2,107 respondents in the cross-section study, 1,122, or roughly 52 percent, were eligible for the Three Generation Study. Reinterviews were obtained from 865 of these respondents, for a 77 percent response rate for the reinterviews with the original respondents. This study is based on data from the Reinterview Study, since it contained the variables of interest.

Measures

We used multiple indicators to represent the two exogenous latent variables.[2] The socioeconomic status construct was composed of three indicators. Education was measured by an item that assessed the number of years of formal training the respondent received (X_1). Total family income was measured by an item that assessed the income, from all sources, of all persons living in that household (X_3). Occupational prestige was measured by an item that assessed the type of work in which the individual was engaged (X_2).

The other exogenous latent variable, religious guidance, was composed of five items. These items were

1. How often do you read religious books or other religious materials? (X_4).
2. How often do you watch or listen to religious programs on TV or radio? (X_5).
3. How often do you pray? (X_6).

4. How often do you ask someone to pray for you? (X_7).
5. How religious would you say you are? (X_8).

The two media exposure constructs were each composed of one indicator. The black print exposure construct was represented by an item that asked the respondent to indicate the frequency of reading black literature (books, magazines, and newspapers) (Y_1). The black-television-exposure construct was represented by an item that asked the respondent the frequency of watching black television programs (Y_3).

We used the five constructs to represent the cognitive schematic of African-American racial beliefs—closeness to black mass groups, closeness to black elite groups, black autonomy, positive stereotypical beliefs about African Americans, and negative stereotypical beliefs about African Americans.[3]

The construct of closeness to black mass groups was represented by one indicator (Y_3). This indicator was constructed from the sum of yes responses to items asking the individual whether he or she felt close to poor blacks, religious blacks and church-going blacks, young blacks, middle-class blacks, working-class blacks, and older blacks.

The construct of closeness to black elite groups was represented also by one indicator (Y_4). This indicator was constructed from responses to a five-point scale asking the individual the degree to which he or she felt close to the following groups: black elected officials, black doctors, black lawyers, and other black professionals.

The black autonomy construct contained four indicators. These items were

1. Black children should study an African language (Y_5).
2. Blacks should always vote for black candidates when they run (Y_6).
3. Black people should shop in black-owned stores whenever possible (Y_7).
4. Black parents should give their children African names (Y_8).

The construct of positive stereotypical beliefs was indicated by four items. They included

1. Most blacks are hard working (Y_9).
2. Blacks do for others (Y_{10}).
3. Blacks are honest (Y_{11}).
4. Blacks are strong (Y_{12}).

The construct of negative stereotypical beliefs was indicated by five items. They were

1. Most blacks are lazy (Y_{13}).
2. Most blacks neglect their families (Y_{14}).

3. Most blacks are lying and trifling (Y_{15}).
4. Most blacks give up easily (Y_{16}).
5. Most blacks are weak (Y_{17}).

Finally, the dimensions of black political participation were represented by two constructs. First, black vote participation was measured by a construct that included the following two indicators:

1. Did you vote in the last presidential election? (Y_{18}).
2. Did you vote in any state or local election during the last year? (Y_{19}).

Second, black political involvement was measured by a construct that included the following two indicators:

1. Have you ever worked for a political party or campaign? (Y_{20}).
2. Have you ever called or written a public official about a concern or a problem? (Y_{21}).

To estimate parameters and test hypotheses, we used the structural equation methodology, LISREL, developed by Joreskog and Sorbom (1984). This procedure estimates unknown coefficients in a set of linear structural equations, and was used to obtain maximum likelihood estimates of the parameters in Figure 1. LISREL is composed of two parts: the measurement model and the latent variable model. The measurement model specifies how the hypothetical constructs are measured in terms of the observed variables. The latent variable model specifies the causal relationships among the latent variables and may be used to describe the causal effects and the amount of unexplained variances (Bollen, forthcoming).[4]

Results

Overall Fit

As structural-equations models are generally quite complex with respect to assumptions, measurement models, and theoretical hypotheses, and because no omnibus criterion exists, we will provide several standards and assessments (Bagozzi and Yi, 1987). Starting with the overall fit of the model, there are several measures that may be used to evaluate its goodness-of-fit. (The major ones as well as the results from the causal model are displayed in Table 2.)

Given that the likelihood-ratio test is very sensitive to sample size, almost no theoretical structure will adequately account for the observed covariances or correlations in large samples (Bentler and Bonett, 1980). With a sample size similar to ours, Wheaton et al. (1977) used a relative χ^2 and its degrees of freedom to assess the goodness-of-fit. This index ostensibly takes sample size into account, and a ratio of 3 or less has

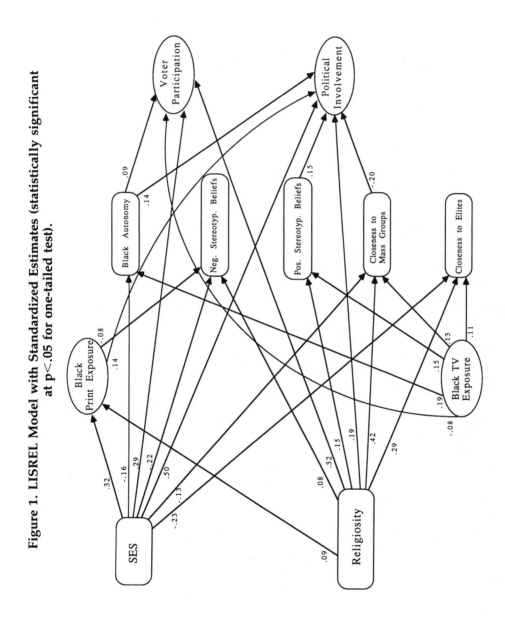

Figure 1. LISREL Model with Standardized Estimates (statistically significant at p<.05 for one-tailed test).

been considered quite adequate (Carmines and McIver, 1981). Applying this measure of fit, our model exhibits a good fit with a relative χ^2/df of 2.02.

The sensitivity of χ^2/df measure to sample size has led to the suggestion that other fit measures be used (Bollen, 1989). Another overall-fit measure that may be used is the Goodness-of-Fit Index (GFI). It indicates the relative amount of variance explained by a model. Its values range from 0 to 1. The GFI for our model was .949, which suggests a good fit. Since GFI does not adjust for degrees of freedom, we employed a modified version of this measure called the "Adjusted Goodness-of-Fit Index (AGFI)" developed by Joreskog and Sorbom (1984). This index is independent of sample size and relatively robust against departures from normality. Again, AGFI ranges from 0 to 1, and values equal to or greater than about .90 suggest a meaningful model from a pragmatic view (Bagozzi and Yi, 1987). The AGFI for our model is .931.[5]

Measurement Model

The overall measures of fit address the adequacy of a model but do not provide explicit information about the nature of individual parameters and other aspects of the internal structure of a model. It is possible that the overall measures of fit signify a satisfactory model, but certain parameters relating to hypothesized relations may be nonsignificant, and/or measures low in reliability may exist. The results from measurement model are presented in Table 1.

We begin our examination of the internal structure or component fit measures by examining the measurement parameters, namely, λ_X, λ_Y, and ζs. The factor loadings for the five indicators of the religious guidance construct ranged from .571 to .669. The factor loadings for the three indicators of the socioeconomic construct ranged from .532 to .826. For both of these constructs, all the factor loadings were substantial and statistically significant.

For the Y indicators of black autonomy, the factor loadings ranged from .453 to .503. For the Y indicators of negative stereotypical beliefs, the factor loading ranged from .576 to .755. For the Y indicators of positive stereotypical beliefs, the factor loadings ranged from .565 to .614. For the Y indicators of voter participation, the factor loadings were .869 and .748, and for political involvement the factor loadings were .453 and .655. All of the above indicators seem to be adequate reflections of their respective constructs and were statistically significant. The constructs black print exposure, black television exposure, closeness to mass groups, and closeness to elites groups were each composed of one indicator and, thus, fixed to a factor loading of 1, and so no measure of statistical significance was possible for these four constructs.

All of the measurement errors for the X and Y indicators (λ_X's and λ_Y's) were statistically significant. For the constructs with only one measure, the measurement errors were fixed to 0.

The composite reliability of the multiple-indicator constructs were as follows: .70 for socioeconomic status, .77 for religiosity, .54 for black autonomy, .81 for negative stereotypical beliefs, .67 for positive stereotypical beliefs, .79 for voter participation, and .48 for political involvement.

Table 1. Measurement Coefficients for African-American Racial-Belief System and Political Participation

Construct	Item	Unstandardized λ^a	Standardized λ	errors
Socioeconomic status(ξ_1)	X_1	1.00^b	.83	.32
	X_2	.74	.61	.63
	X_3	.64	.53	.72
Religiosity(ξ_2)	X_4	1.00^b	.67	.55
	X_5	.87	.58	.66
	X_6	.99	.66	.56
	X_7	.85	.57	.67
	X_8	.97	.65	.58
Black print media(η_1)	Y_1	1.00^b	1.00	$0.00^{d,e}$
Exposure to black TV(η_2)	Y_2	1.00^b	1.00	0.00^d
Closeness bk. masses(η_3)	Y_3	1.00^b	1.00	0.00^d
Closeness bk. elites(η_4)	Y_4	1.00^b	1.00	0.00^d
Black autonomy(η_5)	Y_5	1.00^b	.46	.80
	Y_6	1.09	.51	.73
	Y_7	1.07	.49	.76
	Y_8	.99	.45	.80
Positive stereotypes(η_6)	Y_9	1.00^b	.57	.68
	Y_{10}	1.09	.61	.52
	Y_{11}	1.02	.58	.67
	Y_{12}	1.01	.57	.67
Negative stereotypes(η_7)	Y_{13}	1.00^b	.72	.48
	Y_{14}	.95	.69	.53
	Y_{15}	1.05	.76	.43
	Y_{16}	.80	.58	.67
	Y_{17}	.91	.66	.57
Voter participation(η_8)	Y_{18}	1.00^b	.87	.25
	Y_{19}	.86	.75	.44
Political involvement(η_9)	Y_{20}	1.00^b	.45	.80
	Y_{21}	1.44	.66	.57

n = 865
[a]$p \leq .0005$ for all free coefficients
[b]Coefficient fixed at 1.00
[c]This and following coefficients θ_δ
[d]Error fixed at 0.0
[e]This and following coefficients θ_ϵ

Causal Model

The most interesting aspect of the results pertains to the causal aspect of our model. The significant results from the causal model are depicted in Figure 1. The full results are reported in Table 2 and Table 3.

Those better placed in the social structure are more likely to attend to black print media and less likely to attend to black television programming. These results indicate a fairly strong, statistically significant, positive relationship between SES and black print media exposure as predicted. While SES had a negative influence on black television exposure as predicted, this relationship was small and statistically nonsignificant. The relationship between religiosity and black print exposure received support, but no statistically significant relationship was found for the relationship of religiosity and black television exposure.

Table 2. Unstandardized Regression Coefficients for African-American Racial-Belief System

Independent variable	Bk. Print	Bk. TV	Cl. Mass	Cl. Elite	Bk. Auto.	Pos. Stereo.	Neg. Stereo.
ξ_1 SES	.39[a,d]	-.06	-.15[a]	-.27[a]	-.09[a]	-.02	-.19[a]
	(.32)[e]	(-.05)	(-.13)	(-.23)	(-.16)	(-.02)	(-.22)
ξ_2 Religious guidance	.13[a]	.03	.63[a]	.44[a]	-.01	.12[a]	.08[b]
	(.09)	(.02)	(.42)	(.29)	(-.01)	(.15)	(.08)
η_1 Black print	--	--	.04	.02	.01	.00	-.06[c]
	--	--	(.04)	(.02)	(.01)	(.01)	(-.08)
η_2 Black TV	--	--	.13[a]	.11[a]	.09[a]	.08[a]	.03
	--	--	(.13)	(.11)	(.19)	(.15)	(.04)

n = 865

| R^2 | | .10 | .00 | .25 | .19 | .07 | .05 | .08 |

Total coefficient of determination .57

Goodness-of-fit index .95

Adjusted goodness-of-fit index .93

Critical N 570

χ^2 657.86

df 326

χ^2/df 2.02

[a]$p \le .01$
[b]$p \le .05$
[c]$p \le .10$
[d]Unstandardized coefficient
[e]Standardized coefficient

Table 3. Unstandardized and Standardized Regression Coefficients for Political Participation

Dependent Variables	Voter Participation	Political Involvement
Independent Variable		
ξ_1 SES	.30[a,d]	.28[a]
	(.29)[e]	(.50)
ξ_2 Religious guidance	.42[a]	.13[a]
	(.32)	(.13)
η_1 Black print	.04	.06[a]
	(.04)	(.06)
η_2 Black TV	-.06[a]	-.02
	(-.08)	(-.05)
η_3 Cl. bk. masses	.04	-.09[a]
	(.05)	(-.20)
η_4 Cl. bk. elites	-.01	-.01
	(-.01)	(-.02)
η_5 Black autonomy	.17[c]	.14[b]
	(.09)	(.14)
η_6 Pos. stereo.	.13[c]	.12a
	(.09)	(.15)
η_7 Neg. Stereo.	-.05	-.03
	(-.04)	(-.04)
n = 865		
R^2	.18	.36

[a]$p \leq .01$
[b]$p \leq .05$
[c]$p \leq .10$
[d]Unstandardized coefficient
[e]Standardized coefficient

Turning to the relationship of SES to various black beliefs, most of the predicted relationships were in the hypothesized direction and statistically significant. Those better placed in the social structure expressed of a sense of black autonomy, felt less closeness with mass group or elite groups, and were less likely to endorse the negative stereotypical beliefs of the group. A small and statistically nonsignificant relationship was found between SES and positive black stereotypes. As predicted, SES had a positive and statistically significant relationship with voter participation and political involvement. The (unstandardized) estimates were .30 and .28, respectively.

With respect to religiosity and black belief structures, the results indicated, as predicted, that those scoring high on the religiosity construct were more likely to endorse notions concerning the positive stereotypical beliefs and the negative stereotypical beliefs about blacks as a group and to express a closeness to both mass and elite groups in the black community. The relationship of religiosity with both negative stereotypical beliefs (.08) and positive stereotypical beliefs (.12) was small. Its relationship with closeness to mass groups and closeness to elite groups was moderate (.63 and .44).

We predicted that positive relationships exist between religiosity and voter participation and political involvement. The results indicate both a strong positive relationship between religiosity and voter participation (.42) and a positive relationship (.13) between religiosity and political participation.

The next set of hypotheses refers to the relationship of black print media and black television exposure and black belief structures. We posited a negative relationship between black print exposure and the endorsement of negative stereotypical beliefs. Although small, this relationship was statistically significant.

We posited a positive relationship between black television exposure and the belief-system constructs. A positive relationship was found to exist between black television exposure and all but one belief-system schema. The relationship between television exposure and negative stereotypical beliefs was not statistically significant.

We also predicted negative relationships between television exposure and voter participation and political involvement. Although both were in the predicted direction, only the former was statistically significant.

The final set of hypotheses pertains to the relationship of racial beliefs on voter participation. The results indicated that individuals with stronger black-autonomy beliefs and those with positive stereotypical beliefs about blacks were more likely to vote. These relationships supported our predictions. However, endorsing negative stereotypical beliefs about blacks or exhibiting closeness to black masses or to black elites all had no effect on voter participation.

As predicted, black autonomy, positive stereotypical beliefs, and closeness to mass groups all had a positive effect on political involvement. Conversely, negative stereotypical beliefs and closeness to elite groups were not related to political involvement.

In summary, the global-fit measures suggest a quite adequate model. Similarly, the component measures of fit yielded, for the most part, impressive estimates. Starting with the measurement parameters, the lambdas or factor loading, with a few deviations, were moderate to high in value, and the error in measurement associated with these λs, as expected, were also statistically significant.

The hypothesized theoretical relationships received substantial support. For example, both socioeconomic status and religious guidance had a substantial impact on seven of the nine constructs in this model. In reference to the mass media, black print-media exposure had a positive relationship with only one of the five black belief constructs, but had a positive impact on the level of political involvement. In contrast, while black television exposure had a relationship with four of the five belief constructs, it had a negative impact on voter participation and no impact on political involvement. Lastly, while only one statistically significant relationship was found between the five black belief constructs and voter participation (and that one statistically marginal), three such effects were found for political involvement.

Discussion

The results further confirm the importance of placement in the social structure on political participation, while also suggesting new lines of research on the importance of religious worldviews and belief systems on different forms of political participation. We found that socioeconomic status, religiosity, exposure to black media sources, and the racial-identity belief system all contribute to increased involvement in the political system by African Americans. Socioeconomic status had the largest effect on campaigning. Religiosity had the largest effect on voting participation. We will now discuss the specific effects of each and their substantive importance.

The results on SES confirmed our expectations. SES predicted both voting and political involvement. Along with religiosity, it was one of the two major predictors of voting. Combined with three of the belief schemata, it helped to predict political involvement as well. Better placement in the social structure continues to endow those citizens with the resources to overcome the barriers to participation in the political process. It is not surprising that SES is the most powerful predictor of political involvement as measured in this study. Both contacting officials and participating in a political campaign are participatory activities that require good contacts, ability to overcome bureaucratic obstacles, or other resources more typically found with those with more education, income, and higher-end occupations. The "cost" of political involvement is more easily borne by those with more resources.

The influence of religious guidance on the political mobilization process reinforces our thesis that religion has powerful significance for African Americans. Indeed, the sustaining power of religion is critical for African Americans in that it provides a mechanism for them to feel positive about themselves, which in turn leads them to socially identify with their racial group. This provides many African Americans with the motivation to engage in actions that would improve the status of the group.

The most surprising finding was that religiosity was a stronger predictor of voter turnout than was socioeconomic status. Religiosity may be a strong predictor of voting for African Americans because black Protestantism has a stronger communal orientation than white Protestantism, which has a strong individualistic tendency (West, 1982). Given the historic role of the black church in the struggle to gain the right to vote, blacks who are religious may perceive voting as extremely important. Another reason for the greater strength of religious guidance is the relative lack of salience of social class for most African Americans. Only 23 percent of the sample of African Americans in the 1988 National Black Election Study reported that social class was a concept that they thought about even fairly often.

The effects of the belief system and the individual cognitive schemata that comprise the belief system on political participation are complex. Belief system schemata such as black political autonomy, closeness to the black masses, and propensity to believe positive stereotypical images about blacks have much more of an effect on political campaigning than on voting. Voting, as we saw in the discussion on SES, religious guidance, and exposure to black media, is less correlated to the sources of political information one possesses, while political involvement is very much tied to one's social and informational resources. Thus, it should not be surprising that the belief-system schemata also have a more substantial effect on campaigning than on voting. Black political autonomy has a significant effect on both voting and campaigning. A greater degree of political identification with African Americans and a positive image of the group lead to more political involvement. Neither closeness to elites nor negative stereotypes, both of which are integral parts of the racial belief system (Allen, Dawson, and Brown, 1989), have an effect on political involvement.

The most puzzling result of all is the moderately strong result that closeness to the black masses has a negative effect on political contacting. It may be that those most integrated into the black community, two-thirds of whom do *not* have middle-class status by the most optimistic standard, find campaigning and contacting elected officials to be relatively inefficacious modes of political participation. If this hypothesis is true, we would expect closeness to black mass groups to positively predict less mainstream modes of political participation such as various forms of protest activity. This result needs further confirmation and investigation. We will be able to test this hypothesis with data from the 1988 national election.

The influence of the media variables on political participation are close to what we had predicted. While exposure to black-oriented television programming had nonsignificant effects on the propensity to be a political activist, exposure to black print was related to political involvement. Black television has a mild narcotic effect that leads to lower levels of voter participation.

What was somewhat surprising is the finding that black print media exposure had little influence on the likelihood of voting. What the data may be suggesting is that those who do read black print media may be more selective about the types of political actions in which they engage. They may perceive voting to yield low utility for the group. Those who are part of the attentive public, that is, readers of black print, may feel that they have little control over the selection of candidates and therefore cannot bring needed pressure on such candidates. Moreover, coverage of candidates on the ballot in black newspapers and magazines may lead readers to the conclusion that voting in and of itself has more symbolic value than real tangible policy benefits. In contrast to voting activism, campaigning and contacting are more selective activities that do correlate with black print-media exposure. Blacks who expose themselves to black print outlets may spend more time and energy deciding for which candidate to work and whom they ought to contact about a public concern. This may be done to ensure that the political activities undertaken are those that will yield the greatest outputs for their racial group.

The differences in the effect of the belief system on different modes of political participation are startling. Voting participation is best predicted by factors that are associated with more information resources and attentiveness to the political world—higher placement in the social structure and religious guidance. Religious guidance, as we argue and show in other work (Allen, Dawson, and Brown, 1989), is indicative of involvement in a black religious community as well as a communalistic worldview very different from individualistically oriented white Protestant traditions. In contrast, political action, which is concerned more directly with mobilization of the black community, is associated more strongly with racial identity. Both campaigning and contacting elected officials are activities often organized by black community groups organizing consciously around racial themes (Kleppner, 1985).

In general, our results confirm our hypothesis that a racial belief, which developed historically as a heuristic that substituted group utility for individual utility, tends to increase one's involvement in the political system even after controlling for such powerful forces as one's place in the social structure, religious influence on one's life, and exposure to the black media. There is a direct link between the cognitively based racial-identity belief system of African Americans and the level of political participation in which they engage. This suggests that candidates who need a substantial black vote in order to win, particularly those who are less worried about alienating white voters, can increase the mobilization of African Americans, ceteris paribus, by designing their campaigns to invoke a sense of racial identity. The campaigns of Harold Washington for mayor of Chicago and Jesse Jackson for president help to indicate the strengths and weaknesses of such a strategy. Conversely, a campaign designed to appeal to those who oppose social, political, and economic progress perceived to substantially benefit blacks may also invoke this belief system, which might backfire on such a candidate. Some of the statewide southern races suggest this outcome.

Outside of the electoral arena, those who wish to mobilize African Americans would also be more successful to the degree that they were able to draw on the racial-identity consciousness. Indeed, the most successfully mobilized African-American popular movements, those of Marcus Garvey, the civil rights movement, and the black power movement, could be argued to have directly tapped both the political and positive stereotypical schemata of the racial-identity belief system.

Further analysis will be needed to see if there has been any weakening of the racial-identity belief system, the effect of exposure to black media sources, or the importance of black-oriented religion in the black community over time. In this vein, we plan to test whether religiosity continues to have a strong effect on voter participation when we are able to control for the independent effect of church involvement in our study of political participation using the 1988 National Black Election Study.[6]

However, as long as the racial-identity belief system, black media sources, and the black church continue to influence political participation in the black community, political activists will be able to frame their appeals in order to utilize them to increase the political mobilization of African Americans.

Appendix: Coding of Observed Indicators

SES Indicators

- Education (X_1). Coded 0–17 for years of school completed, with 17 representing all postgraduate training.
- Occupation (X_3). Coded from (1–9), with 1 = service workers, 9 = professionals.
- Total Family Income (X_2). Coded 1–17, with 1 = \$0.0, 17 = \$30,000 or more.

Religiosity Indicators

- How often do you read religious books or materials? (X_4). Coded from 1–5, with 1 = never, 5 = four or more times per week.
- How often do you watch or listen to religious programs on TV or radio? (X_5). Coded from 1–5, with 1 = never, 5 = four or more times per week.
- How often do you pray? (X_6). Coded from 1–5, with 1 = never, 5 = four or more times per week.
- How often do you ask someone to pray for you? (X_7). Coded from 1–5, with 1 = never, 5 = four or more times per week.
- How religious would you say you are? (X_8). Coded from 1–4, with 4 = very religious and 1 = not religious at all.

Black Media Indicators

- The frequency of black print and black TV exposure (Y_1 and Y_2) were both coded on a scale of 1–5, with 1 = less frequent and 5 = more frequent.

The Closeness to Black Masses Construct

- This (Y_3) is a summated construct ranging from 2 = not close at all to 5 = very close.

The Closeness to Black Elites Construct

- This (Y_4) is a summated construct ranging from 2 = not close at all to 5 = very close.

Black Autonomy Indicators

- Black children should study an African language (Y_5). Coded from 1 = strongly disagree to 4 = strongly agree.
- Blacks should always vote for black candidates when they run (Y_6). Coded from 1 = strongly disagree to 4 = strongly agree.
- Black people should shop in black-owned stores whenever possible (Y_7). Coded from 1 = strongly disagree to 4 = strongly agree.
- Black parents should give their children African names (Y_8). Coded from 1 = strongly disagree to 4 = strongly agree.

Positive and Negative Stereotypical Beliefs Indicators

- All of the Stereotypical Belief Indicators (Y_9–Y_{17}) were coded on a four-point scale, with 1 = not true at all, 4 = very true.
- Positive Stereotypical Beliefs:
  – Black people are hard working (Y_9).
  – Black people do for others (Y_{10}).
  – Black people are honest (Y_{11}).
  – Black people are strong (Y_{12}).
- Negative Stereotypical Beliefs:
  – Black people are lazy (Y_{13}).
  – Black people neglect their families (Y_{14}).
  – Black people are lying or trifling (Y_{15}).
  – Black people give up easily (Y_{16}).
  – Black people are weak (Y_{17}).

Participation Construct Indicators

- Voting Participation was a construct that included:
  – Did you vote in the last presidential election? (Y_{18}).
  – Did you vote in any state or local election during the last year? (Y_{19}).
  – Coded 1 = not voted in election, 5 = voted.
- Voting Involvement was a construct of
  – Have you ever worked for a political party or campaigned for a political candidate? (Y_{20}).
  – Have you ever called or written a public official about a concern or problem? (Y_{21}).
  – Coded 1 = no, 5 = yes.

Notes

1. This can backfire on the incautious candidate. Our examination of open-ended responses from blacks in a 1986 Michigan poll shows that Lucas received little support because his record and policy stands were perceived to be in contradiction to the racial appeal he made to the black community.
2. The actual coding of all the observed indicators is given in the appendix.
3. For a more thorough development of the racial-identity belief system presented here, see Allen, Dawson, and Brown, 1989.
4. LISREL embodies a number of assumptions. Errors in the equations, ζs, are assumed uncorrelated with the exogenous latent variables, ξs. Second, the measurement errors, are assumed to be independent for all ζs, ϵs, and δs. Finally, since we are using a maximum-likelihood fitting function, the observed indicators, Xs and Ys, are assumed to be distributed multinormally. Under these assumptions, the goodness-of-fit of the hypothesized specification can be evaluated by examining the overall-fit measures. When a certain formulation provides an acceptable fit to the data (the overall fit), the various components of the model may be usefully evaluated.
5. Still another measure of the overall fit of a model is the Coefficient of Determination (TCD). The TCD demonstrates how well the structural equations (i.e., hypothetical theoretical relations) account for the N variables. Although more experience is needed to ascertain when the TCD is large or small, the .570 estimate that we obtained for this model seems adequate.

   The fifth criterion for evaluating the overall fit of a model used in this study is the Critical N (CN) index (Hoelter, 1983). This estimate permits the assessment of the fit of a model relative to an identically hypothesized model estimated with different sample sizes. Hoelter suggests that a CN greater than 200 for a single sample might be a tentative rule of thumb for deciding whether the discrepancy between the observed and implied variance-covariance matrix is trivial or not. Our CN value was 570.
6. Religious guidance may very well covary with involvement. We have found in preliminary results from the 1988 National Black Election Study that a large number of black churchgoers were encouraged to vote through their churches. It will be interesting to see if religious guidance continues to be a very strong predictor of voter participation when we will be able to control for both effects in the 1988 study.

References

Allen, Richard L., and William T. Bielby. 1979a. "Blacks' Attitudes and Behaviors Toward Television." *Communication Research* 6:437–62.

——— . 1979b. "Blacks' Relationship with the Print Media." *Journalism Quarterly* 56:488–96.

Allen, Richard L., Michael C. Dawson, and Ronald E. Brown. 1989. "Toward a Schema Based Model of an African American Racial Belief System." *American Political Science Review* (June).

Allen, Richard L., and Shirley Hatchett. 1986. "The Media and Social Reality Effects: Self and System Orientations of Blacks." *Communication Research* 13:97–123.

Allen, Richard L., and Chang Kuo. 1988. "The Impact of Symbolic Social Reality on Political Orientations." Unpublished manuscript.

Bagozzi, Richard P., and Youjae Yi. 1987. "On the Evaluation of Structural Equation Models." Unpublished manuscript.

Bentler, Peter M., and Douglas G. Bonett. 1980. "Significance Tests and Goodness of Fit in Analysis of Covariance Structures." *Psychological Bulletin* 88:588–606.

Bollen, Kenneth. 1989. *Structural Equations with Latent Variables*. New York: John Wiley & Sons.

Carmines, Edward G., and John P. McIver. 1981. "Analyzing with Observed Variables: Analysis of Covariance Structures." Pp. 65–115 in George W. Bohrnstedt and Edward F. Borgatta, eds., *Social Measurement*. Beverly Hills: Russel Sage.

Cavanagh, Thomas E. 1985. *Inside Black America: The Message in the 1984 Elections*. Washington, D.C.: Joint Center for Political Studies.

Chidester, David. 1988. *Patterns or Power: Religion and Politics in American Culture*. Englewood Cliff, N.J.: Prentice Hall.

Cone, James H. 1986. *Speaking the Truth: Ecumenism, Liberation, and Black Theology*. Grand Rapids: William B. Eerdmans Publishing Co.

Frazier, E. Franklin. 1957. *Black Bourgeoisie*. New York: Free Press.

Gerbner, George, Michael Morgan, and Nancy Signorielli. 1980. "The Mainstreaming of America: Violence Profile No. 11." *Journal of Communication*, 30:10–29.

Hoetler, Jon W. 1983. "The Analysis of Covariance Structures: Goodness-of-Fit Indices." *Sociological Methods & Research* 11:324–44.

Joreskog, Karl G., and Dag Sorbom. 1984. *LISREL VI: Analysis of Linear Structural Relationships by the Method of Maximum Likelihood*. 3rd ed. Mooresville: Scientific Software, Inc.

Kessel, John H. 1988. *Presidential Campaign Politics: Coalition Strategies and Citizen Response*. Chicago: The Dorsey Press.

Kilson, Martin. 1983. "The Black Bourgeois Revisited." *Dissent*, (Winter):85–96.

Kleppner, Paul. 1985. *Chicago Divided: The Making of a Black Mayor*. DeKalb, Ill.: Northern Illinois University Press.

Miller, Arthur H., Patricia Gurin, Gerald Gurin, and Oksana Malanchuk. 1981. "Group Consciousness and Political Participation." *American Journal of Political Science*, 25:494–511.

Morris, Aldon D. 1984. *The Origins of the Civil Rights Movement: Black Communities Organizing for Change*. New York: The Free Press.

Shingles, Richard. 1981. "Black Consciousness and Political Participation: The Missing Link." *American Political Science Review,* 75:76–91.

Verba, Sidney, and Norman H. Nie. 1972. *Participation in America: Political Democracy and Social Equality.* New York: Harper and Row.

Wald, Kenneth. 1987. *Religion and Politics in the United States.* New York: St. Martin's Press.

West, Cornel. 1982. *Prophecy Deliverance! An Afro-American Revolutionary Christianity.* Philadelphia: The Westminster Press.

Wheaton, Blair, Bengt Muthen, Duane G. Alwin, and George F. Summers. 1977. "Assessing Reliability in Panel Models." In Donald R. Heise, ed., *Sociological Methodology.* San Francisco: Jossey-Bass.

Wilson, William J. 1988. *The Truly Disadvantaged: The Inner City, the Urban Underclass, and Public Policy.* Chicago: The University of Chicago Press.

Wolfinger, Raymond E., and Steven J. Rosenstone. 1980. *Who Votes?* New Haven: Yale University Press.

White/Black Perceptions of the Electability of Black Political Candidates

Linda F. Williams

Joint Center for Political Studies

Since passage of the Voting Rights Act in 1965, blacks have made substantial progress in winning public office. In 1965, it was estimated that there were fewer than five hundred black elected officials in the United States; by 1970, there were 1,469 black elected officials in the nation. In January 1989, the number of black elected officials had risen to 7,225 (*Roster*, 1989).

Despite this salutary development, three alarming facts are concealed in the overall growth in the number of black elected officials. First, blacks (who constitute 11 percent of the nation's total voting-age population) still compose only 1.4 percent of all elected officials in the nation. Second, state-by-state comparisons reveal that blacks do not hold offices proportionate to their numbers in the voting-age population in any state. Third, the annual rate of growth has slowed considerably since the mid-1970s. From 1970 to 1976, the annual rate of growth in the numbers of blacks elected to public office was always in the double digits. Since 1976, the annual rate of growth has been always a single-digit rate. Between 1987 and 1988, for example, the rate of growth was only 2.2 percentage points (*Roster*, 1989). In sum, blacks are far from reaching proportionality in their election to public office, and the low rate of growth is a dismal sign for the future.

The relatively small number of black elected officials is attributable in part to tactics such as districting plans that reduce black influence (Davidson, 1984). Black candidates apparently do less well in at-large elections because they are unable to attract sufficient white voters. In fact, in most cases, black candidates have been unable to capture more than 25 percent of the white vote (Hahn, Klingman, and Pachon, 1976:308; Karnig and Welch, 1980:46). Consequently, the number of blacks holding

45

office occurs disproportionately in areas having a black majority (Bul lock, 1984). Yet, it is unlikely that blacks will substantially or rapidly increase their numbers in public office (especially in higher offices) in a nation whose voting-age population is still approximately 85 percent white unless much more of what is often called racial "crossover" voting occurs. Despite the critical interaction between a black candidate's chances for victory and white crossover voting, however, little is known about the latter aside from the observation that black candidates' shares of the vote will be a product of the crossover of whites, minus the crossover of blacks, plus black turnout and registration (Bullock, 1984).

To fully explore the conditions and factors that encourage white crossover voting, a study would include analysis of demographic factors— especially size of the black population in the electorate; types of electoral systems; black and white voter registration and turnout trends; office being sought, the total number of candidates, and the number of black candidates in an election; campaign strategies, tactics, messages, and financing; candidate strengths, experience, and background; incumbency advantages; media and leadership endorsements; political culture; changing voting patterns over time; the nature of coalition building; and a host of other factors. A good starting place, however, is an examination of white perceptions of black political candidates. If whites hold the same attitudes toward black candidates that they hold toward white candidates, and if they vote on the basis of qualifications rather than race, an important development necessary to increase white crossover voting and thereby black chances of victory is simply the promotion of better, more-qualified black candidates. If whites hold racially biased views toward black candidates, then clearly the task of convincing whites to vote for black political candidates is a far more formidable one.

Whites' perceptions of black political candidates is the central subject of this article. For comparison purposes, the perceptions of blacks toward black political candidates are also presented.

These tasks are made possible by analyzing data from two surveys conducted by the Gallup Organization for the Joint Center for Political Studies (JCPS). The first survey was conducted in August, 1987, and asked a range of questions aimed at (1) finding out whether or not whites negatively stereotype black candidates' personal attributes or their abilities to achieve societal goals when nothing more is known about a candidate than his or her race; (2) establishing whether whites are more unwilling to vote for black candidates for higher rather than lower offices; and (3) finding out whether whites believe there is racial bias in voter preferences and choices. The number of whites and blacks in the August, 1987, survey were 916 and 918 respectively.

The second survey was conducted in August, 1988, and asked a range of questions aimed at (1) analyzing white perceptions of the qualifications of any black candidate for president; (2) analyzing the likelihood of whites voting for any black presidential contender; and (3) analyzing attitudes toward Jesse Jackson as a presidential contender. The number of whites and blacks in the August, 1988, survey were 695 and 643 respectively.

Both surveys were modified-probability samples conducted by in-person interviews. Both surveys have a margin of error of +/–4 percentage points.

The research that follows presents both a simple bivariate analysis to demonstrate differences between white and black perceptions of black political candidates and logistic regression analysis to report the effects of various independent variables on white perceptions of black political candidates.

Racial Stereotypes of Political Candidates among Whites

That voters will support the candidate with whom they share skin color and/or ethnicity is well known (Lorinskas, Hawkins, and Edwards, 1969; Hahn and Almy, 1971; Pettigrew, 1972; Murray and Vedlitz, 1978). As a result, it has been argued that it is understandable that some voters turn to race as a simple, readily available cue if they find the competitors' policy stands equally attractive (Bullock, 1984). Such an argument, however, hardly counters the conclusion that voting becomes a product of racism if, even before voters become attentive to candidates' policy positions (and especially if they never do), they have decided a priori that one candidate is superior in his or her abilities and personal attributes simply on the basis of shared racial identity.

To see whether white political candidates were likely to benefit and black candidates were likely to suffer from such race-based predispositions, respondents in the 1987 JCPS/Gallup survey were asked whether a black or a white politician would be more likely to achieve ten societal goals: reducing drug abuse, improving the quality of public education, reducing taxes, reaching an arms agreement with the Soviets, reducing the federal budget deficit, helping U.S. farmers, reducing imports from foreign countries, helping the poor and needy, reducing teenage pregnancy, and increasing U.S. economic growth.

As Table 1 demonstrates, by and large, whites (knowing nothing more about candidates than their race) reported that politicians of their own race would be more likely to achieve the goals than black politicians. Thus, for example, 44 percent of white respondents reported that a white candidate would be more likely than a black candidate to reach an arms agreement with the Soviets, while only 4 percent thought a black candidate would be more likely to reach an arms agreement. Similarly, 42 percent of whites reported that a white candidate would be more likely to increase economic growth, compared to only 4 percent of whites who thought blacks would do better. Only in one category did more whites report that a black candidate would probably be more successful at achieving the goal than a white candidate: 40 percent of the white respondents reported that a black candidate would be more likely than a white candidate to help the poor and needy, while only 15 percent of the white respondents reported that a white would be more likely to help the poor.

It should be noted that when asked which of these goals concerned them most, helping the poor and needy ranked ninth out of the ten goals in whites' list of concerns—only above reducing teenage pregnancy—in the 1987 survey. Thus, one could infer that even the better evaluation of black candidates on this dimension might be relatively meaningless in influencing white voter preferences and support, since it ranked low on whites' list of pressing concerns.

In addition, the data reveal a pattern in the kinds of goals whites are *most* likely to report that white political candidates would achieve versus those where they are more likely to report that black political candidates are equally as likely or more likely to achieve. When one combines the

Table 1. White Evaluations of a White Candidate versus a Black Candidate—Selected Goals and Attributes

QUESTION: Now, I'm going to read a list of goals that politicians sometimes hope to achieve. For each, please tell me whether you think a white politician or a black politician would be more likely to meet this goal.

Goal	White Candidate	Black Candidate	Race Does Not Make a Difference
Reducing drug abuse	25.5%	13.5%	51.7%
Improving the quality of public education	36.0	12.3	45.3
Reducing taxes	34.6	9.9	46.6
Reaching an arms agreement with the Soviets	43.9	3.7	44.7
Reducing the federal budget deficit	36.0	4.6	50.1
Helping U.S. farmers	43.8	7.4	41.3
Reducing imports from foreign countries	34.2	5.7	50.6
Helping the poor and needy	14.9	39.8[a]	39.2
Reducing teenage pregnancy	22.5	18.0	50.6
Increasing U.S. economic growth	41.7	3.7	47.1
Mean	33.3	11.4	46.7

QUESTION: Next, I'll read a list of phrases that are sometimes used to describe political candidates. For each phrase, please tell me whether you think it is more likely to describe a white candidate or more likely to describe a black candidate.

Phrase	White Candidate	Black Candidate	Race Does Not Make a Difference
Intelligent	34.5%	1.4%	58.0%
Compassionate	19.8	13.8	58.8
A strong leader	35.3	5.3	54.2
Knowledgeable	33.9	2.1	58.6
Hard-working	23.6	7.5	62.8
Exciting	19.0	13.9	56.1
Gets things done	33.6	2.7	56.4
Clear on issues	28.7	6.0	56.5
Fair	21.7	6.6	64.0
Good judgement in a crisis	34.6	1.0	56.5
Religious	10.5	26.8[a]	56.4
Trustworthy	24.5	3.4	63.3
Liberal	20.6	22.1[a]	49.6
Experienced	50.4	0.7	43.6
Mean	27.9	8.1	56.8

Source: JCPS/Gallup Survey, 1987.
[a]Blacks ranked more favorably on item.

proportions of whites who responded that race does *not* make a difference with those who reported that white candidates versus black candidates were more likely to achieve a goal, the goals in which black candidates appear to have a more favorable image relative to other goals are all in areas that afflict blacks disproportionately (poverty, teenage pregnancy, and drug abuse). Conversely, black political candidates fared poorest in whites' perception when the goals were related to pressing national issues such as peace and prosperity (e.g., reaching an arms agreement with the Soviet Union, reducing the federal budget deficit, and increasing economic growth).

A similar question was asked about fourteen personal attributes related to leadership characteristics. Respondents were asked whether the following phrases were more likely to describe a black or a white political candidate when the only fact known about the candidate was his or her race: intelligent, compassionate, a strong leader, knowledgeable, hard-working, exciting, gets things done, clear on issues, fair, good judgement in a crisis, religious, trustworthy, liberal, and experienced.

Among those who reported that race made a difference, whites reported that a candidate from their own racial group was more likely to have the attribute in every category except being "religious" and "liberal" (Table 1). For example, 35 percent of whites surveyed reported that a white candidate was more likely to be "intelligent" or to have "good judgement in a crisis" compared to only 1 percent of whites who reported a black candidate was more likely to possess these characteristics. Whether being religious or liberal helped or hurt a black candidate among whites is unclear. On the one hand, the "L word" does not appear to be a central factor hurting black political candidates among whites, since almost identical proportions of whites reported that black candidates are more liberal as reported that white candidates are more liberal. Of whites, 21 percent reported that white candidates were more likely than black candidates to be liberal, while practically the same proportion (22 percent) reported that black candidates were more likely to be liberal. On the other hand, the perception of black candidates as being more liberal could be a drag on white support for blacks among conservative whites. Self-identified conservatives and Republican-party identifiers were roughly twice as likely as moderates and liberals and Democrats and Independents to report that a black candidate was more likely to be liberal than a white candidate.

In sum, among whites who reported the likelihood of differences among black political candidates and white political candidates when only the race of the candidate was known, whites provided positive stereotypes for white candidates and negative stereotypes for black candidates.

Racial Stereotypes of Political Candidates among Blacks

Blacks, too, held racial stereotypes generally favoring political candidates of their own race. Yet, particularly in terms of the likelihood of goals achievement, blacks were substantially less likely than whites to give the advantage to candidates of their own race (Table 2). Thus, while

Table 2. Black Evaluations of a White Candidate versus a Black Candidate—Selected Goals and Attributes

QUESTION: Now, I'm going to read a list of goals that politicians sometimes hope to achieve. For each, please tell me whether you think a white politician or a black politician would be more likely to meet this goal.

Goal	White Candidate	Black Candidate	Race Does Not Make a Difference
Reducing drug abuse	13.2%	31.8%	44.6%
Improving the quality of public education	20.7	29.9	42.2
Reducing taxes	24.0	24.9	42.3
Reaching an arms agreement with the Soviets	33.6[a]	17.5	37.1
Reducing the federal budget deficit	23.9	19.7	44.7
Helping U.S. farmers	21.0	31.4	39.6
Reducing imports from foreign countries	30.9[a]	17.2	41.3
Helping the poor and needy	7.4	52.7	33.9
Reducing teenage pregnancy	9.0	35.1	45.6
Increasing U.S. economic growth	23.9[a]	18.4	46.6
Mean	20.8	27.9	41.8

QUESTION: Next, I'll read a list of phrases that are sometimes used to describe political candidates. For each phrase, please tell me whether you think it is more likely to describe a white candidate or more likely to describe a black candidate.

Phrase	White Candidate	Black Candidate	Race Does Not Make a Difference
Intelligent	14.6%	20.4%	58.6%
Compassionate	6.7	43.6	42.5
A strong leader	15.7	29.6	47.3
Knowledgeable	20.0	22.0	51.9
Hard-working	4.8	42.7	47.3
Exciting	7.0	35.8	46.6
Gets things done	18.4	23.6	50.4
Clear on issues	15.7	25.6	51.0
Fair	5.9	37.6	48.7
Good judgement in a crisis	12.3	24.7	53.7
Religious	2.6	50.8	39.9
Trustworthy	6.3	31.3	53.5
Liberal	13.6	31.8	44.6
Experienced	32.1[a]	14.6	45.6
Mean	12.6	31.0	48.7

Source: JCPS/Gallup Survey, 1987.
[a]Whites ranked more favorably on item.

black respondents who stereotyped candidates by race reported that black candidates were more likely to achieve six of the ten goals, they reported that white candidates were more likely to reach an arms agreement with the Soviet Union, reduce the federal budget deficit, reduce imports, and increase economic growth. In short, blacks' perceptions of likelihood of goal achievement showed a pattern similar to whites' perceptions: black candidates were considered to be probably much better at achieving those goals in policy areas disproportionately important to blacks; white candidates were considered to be probably better at achieving economic and foreign-policy-related goals.

Blacks, who provided a racial advantage when nothing was known but a candidate's race, also reported that a candidate from their own racial group was more likely to have each personal attribute in every category except being "experienced." Of blacks, 32 percent reported that a white candidate was more likely than a black candidate to be experienced, compared to slightly less than half that many (14 percent) who provided the advantage to a black candidate.

As a simple summary statistic, the mean of each racial group's perception of black and white candidates was computed. On the average, three times as many whites reported that white candidates were superior to black candidates in both goals achievement and personal attributes (Table 1). While almost two-and-one-half times as many blacks reported that black candidates were superior in terms of personal attributes, only slightly more blacks gave black candidates rather than white candidates the edge in goals achievement: on the average, 28 percent gave blacks the advantage compared to 21 percent who gave whites the advantage (Table 2).

In sum, large proportions of both blacks and whites hold stereotypes favoring political candidates of their own race. While relatively equal proportions of blacks and whites give the advantage vis-à-vis personal characteristics to candidates of their own race, whites are substantially more likely than blacks to report that politicians of their own race will achieve important political goals. The data imply that a black candidate begins his or her campaign disadvantaged in terms of perceptions of his or her ability to achieve goals among about one out of every three whites. Meanwhile, in terms of the perception of who is more likely to achieve important national economic goals, if nothing more is known about a candidate than his race, black political candidates begin campaigns disadvantaged even among blacks.

White Voters and Black Candidates for Higher Office

Another way to analyze the extent of racial antipathy toward black political candidates is to examine whether whites may be more willing to vote for blacks running for certain political offices than for others. In general, the data show that the higher the office, the more likely it is that whites report that they would not vote for a black candidate. Thus, only 3 percent of whites reported in the 1987 survey that they would not vote for a black candidate for school board, but 8 percent reported they would not vote for a black for governor, 11 percent reported they would not vote for a black for vice president, and 20 percent reported they would not vote for a black for president (Table 3). In short data in Table 3 indicate that white crossovers may be less prevalent for the more important offices. White opposition to black candidates is greatest in top executive offices.

The 20 percent of whites reporting they would not vote for a black for president are analogous to the proportion of whites found in the standard question used to measure white backlash against the presence on the presidential ballot of black candidates. Since 1958, Gallup has asked: "If your party nominated a generally well-qualified man for president and he happened to be black, would you vote for him?" The responses indicate a clear trend of declining white hostility toward blacks as presidential candidates. In 1958, 53 percent of the white respondents said they would not support a qualified black for president, whereas 38 percent said they would (Cavanagh, 1985:64). In the Gallup survey conducted for the JCPS in 1988, only 16 percent of the white respondents said they were opposed to a qualified black candidate, whereas 77 percent professed support.

Those data, although showing a dramatic improvement over time, are nonetheless frequently misinterpreted. The "no" response indicates automatic opposition to a black candidate purely on racial grounds, and it

Table 3. Support for Black Candidate by Office

QUESTION: There are many different types of elected officials in this country. Please look at this list and tell me if you would refuse to vote for a qualified black person to fill any of these offices.

Type of Official	Whites in percent	Blacks in percent
School board member	3.4	1.2
City council member	2.5	1.5
Mayor	5.2	1.7
County officials	2.7	0.8
State legislature	3.6	1.1
Lieutenant governor	3.7	1.3
Governor	7.5	1.6
Congressman in the U.S. House of Representatives	4.3	1.4
U.S. Senator	5.6	0.5
Vice President	10.5	1.4
President	19.7	3.0
N	918	916

Source: JCPS/Gallup Survey, 1987.

seems reasonable to assume that many or most of those who express "no opinion" have feelings of opposition but are too embarrassed to admit their prejudice to a pollster. (It has been widely observed in mayoral races involving black candidates that the "undecided" vote usually breaks overwhelmingly for a white opponent on the day of the election. Moreover, data in the 1988 survey indicate that reports of white respondents on this question are affected by interviewer bias. For example, 87 percent of whites reported to black interviewers they would vote for a qualified black for president; only 4 percent said they would not, and 9 percent had "no opinion.") Thus, the 16 percent "no" response in 1988 added to the 7 percent "no opinion/don't know" response yields a total of 23 percent, or almost a quarter of the white electorate that would probably automatically oppose a black candidate. This 23 percent handicap leaves 77 percent of the white electorate from which a black candidate would have to assemble a winning coalition. To secure a majority, then, a black presidential candidate would have to win the votes of 65 percent of that part of the electorate that did not automatically reject black candidates (including roughly 60 percent of the white vote). Yet, no presidential candidate since the dawn of the two-party system has won more than 61 percent of the entire vote, racist and nonracist (Cavanagh, 1985).

Moreover, the situation may be even more difficult than simply the "no" and "no opinion" responses in the standard question imply. A "yes" response to the question of whether one would vote for a "well-qualified black" for president also may be essentially meaningless, because a person can rationalize opposition to a given black candidate on the grounds that such a candidate was not "well qualified." To examine whether this was the case, the 1988 survey asked as a follow-up: "Is there a black man or woman in politics today that you personally consider to be well qualified to be president?" Only 26 percent of the white respondents reported that any black on the current political scene was qualified to be president, while 56 percent said no black was qualified, and 18 percent reported they had "no opinion." In short, slightly more than three-quarters of the white electorate might automatically oppose a black candidate for president or, even in the best possible scenario, take a lot of convincing. A black candidate for higher office begins with the bias among many (and in the case of the presidency, most) whites that he or she is not qualified.

Perceptions of Racial Bloc Voting

To examine whether blacks and whites believe there is racial bias in voter preference, the 1987 survey asked respondents whether they thought most blacks and whites vote for the most qualified candidate or for the candidate of their race. Table 4 shows that more than half of the white respondents reported that they think people (black and white) vote more on the basis of race than qualifications. Thus, whites reported that 56 percent of blacks and 54 percent of whites would vote on the basis of race in an electoral contest between a white and a black candidate. Similarly, whites reported that they would expect only 33 percent of blacks and 38 percent of whites to vote on the basis of the candidates' qualifications.

More (54 percent) of the black respondents were likely to think that whites vote on the basis of race than to think that blacks vote on the basis of race (39 percent). Instead, half of the black respondents reported that they thought most blacks vote on the basis of qualifications, but they would expect only 34 percent of whites to vote on the basis of qualifications. Thus, white and black expectations about *white* bloc voting

Table 4. Perceptions of Racial Bloc Voting

QUESTION: Suppose a black candidate and a white candidate are running against each other for mayor of your city. Do you think that most black voters will tend to vote for the black candidate regardless of qualifications, or do you think most black voters will vote for the most qualified candidate regardless of race?

Black Voters in White vs. Black Mayoral Race	Whites	Blacks
Vote for black	55.5%	38.8%
Vote for most qualified	32.6	50.2
It depends (volunteered)	5.1	7.6
Don't know	6.8	3.4
N	916	918

QUESTION: How about white voters? Do you think most white voters will tend to vote for the white candidate, regardless of qualifications, or do you think most white voters will vote for the most qualified candidate regardless of race?

White Voters in White vs. Black Mayoral Race	Whites	Blacks
Vote for white	53.6%	53.9%
Vote for most qualified	38.4	34.1
It depends (volunteered)	4.5	7.0
Don't know	3.5	5.0
N	916	918

Source: JCPS/Gallup Survey, 1987.

were virtually the same, while whites were more likely than blacks to expect blacks to bloc vote as well.

In short, large proportions of whites not only provide more favorable stereotypes to white candidates, but many also report that they would refuse to vote for a black candidate for higher office, especially for president. Indeed, white opposition to a black presidential candidate—whoever he or she may be—is currently monumental. Finally, many more whites than blacks also believe that racial bloc voting among both groups is the order of the day.

When these findings are viewed in the context of the large size of the white electorate, it is no wonder that the number of black elected officials and the rate of growth in their number remain disproportionately low.

The Demographics of White Support for Black Candidates

Some whites, of course, do vote for black candidates and figure prominently in determining their victories. For example, exactly half of the forty-eight larger cities (that is, those with populations of 25,000 or more) represented by black mayors are white-majority cities. In some of these cities (for example, Philadelphia), black voters were a substantial-enough proportion of the electorate to require only about 20 percent of the white vote for the black mayoral candidate to win. In other cities, whites were a substantial part of the winning coalition (for example, Los Angeles). Other evidence of support from whites for black candidates is found in the election of five statewide elected administrative officials and eight judges of state superior courts. Since blacks composed no more than 31 percent of the voting-age population in any state, clearly blacks who won statewide offices did so with substantial white support. Similarly, two black members of the United States House of Representatives come from districts that are more than 70 percent white; they, too, have repeatedly won with large proportions of the white vote. A critical question, then, is which whites are most willing to vote for black political candidates.

By conducting logit analysis, the white constituencies most and least opposed to a black political candidate can be highlighted. For the logit analysis, answers to several questions in the surveys were used as dependent variables: high or low scores on a scale created with the responses on the goals achievement items; support for or opposition to a well-qualified black candidate for president; and agreement or disagreement that there is a black on the current political scene qualified to be president. Each of these dependent dichotomous variables were tested for the effects of a set of independent demographic variables as well as for the effects of several attitudinal variables.

The independent demographic variables are gender, age, region, size of place, education, occupation, membership in labor unions, and income. Gender is a dichotomy of male/female; age is a continuous variable; region is a four-way classification of East, Midwest, South, and North; size of place is a three-way classification of central city, suburb, and rural areas; education is a four-way classification of less-than-high-school graduate, high-school graduate, some college education, and college graduate or postgraduate; occupation is recoded into a dichotomous variable of white-collar and blue-collar; membership in labor union is a dichotomy of labor household or non-labor household; and income is also a four-way classification of less-than-$12,500 household income; $12,500–$24,999 household income; $25,000–$39,999 household income; and $40,000-or-more household income.

The political/attitudinal variables used in the analysis were chosen to test the extent to which views toward other race-related issues and partisanship were important predictors of views toward black political candidates. The independent political/attitudinal variables used in the analysis were partisan identification (Democrat, Republican, Independent), agreement or disagreement that whites have a right to keep blacks out of their neighborhoods, support for or opposition to a law guaranteeing that a homeowner cannot discriminate in selling his or her house, agreement or disagreement that societal factors are responsible for black poverty, agreement or disagreement that whites have a lot of common interests with blacks in their social class, agreement or disagreement that many or most whites dislike blacks, and agreement or disagreement that the federal government should do all it can to aid minorities. Only those relationships found to be significant are reported in the tables.

Table 5 presents the findings on determinants of the view that black candidates would be equally or more likely to achieve societal goals. While the pseudo R^2 of logistic regression cannot be viewed in "variance explained" terms, it does have the useful quality of ranging between 0 and 1, approaching 1 as the quality of the fit improves. Thus, the results of this analysis demonstrate that the model fits well (.64); that is, that ten variables (age, region, education, income, membership in a union, partisanship, view about the causes of black poverty, perceived racial hostility, view about a homeowner's right to discriminate, and view about whether blacks and whites of the same social class share common interests) are strongly related to whites' perceptions of candidates' ability to achieve goals when only their race is known. More specifically, as the negative signs before the coefficients indicate: whites age fifty years old or older, whites who never graduated from high school, whites whose household incomes are less than $12,500 annually, white Republicans, whites who fault blacks themselves for the fact that many blacks remain in poverty, whites who report that many or most whites dislike blacks, and whites who oppose a housing law enforcing nondiscrimination are all less likely to report that a black candidate would be equally or more likely to achieve goals. On the other hand, whites who are 30 to 49 years old, western whites, white college graduates, whites who belong to unions, white Democrats, whites who report that few whites dislike blacks; and whites who report that they share a lot of common interests with blacks in their social class are more likely to report that most whites vote on the basis of qualifications (Table 5).

Table 5. Maximum Likelihood (Logit) Estimates of White Agreement That a Black Candidate Would Be Equal to or More Likely Than a White Candidate to Achieve Goals

Variable	Coefficient Estimate	Standard Error	Coeff./ SE	x^2	Number of Cases
Intercept	.546	.071	7.69	59.14[b]	
Age: 30 - 49	.279	.114	2.45	6.00[a]	371
Age: 50 and over	-.303	.129	2.35	5.52[a]	351
West	.296	.118	2.51	6.30[a]	187
Less than high school	-.414	.171	2.42	5.86[a]	167
College graduate	.566	.222	2.55	6.50[a]	217
Less than $12,000	-.301	.147	2.05	4.20[a]	168
Labor Household	.245	.111	2.21	4.88[b]	181
Democrat	.278	.104	2.67	7.13[a]	300
Republican	-.430	.116	3.71	13.76[b]	277
Reasons for black poverty:individual factors	-.409	.203	2.02	4.08[a]	460
Perceived racial hostility lots	-.452	.223	2.03	4.12[a]	153
Perceived racial hostility little	.308	.147	2.10	4.41[b]	229
Homeowner can decide not to sell to blacks	-.465	.178	2.61	6.81[b]	355
Share a lot of common interests with blacks in same social class	.358	.136	2.63	6.92[b]	170

Source: JCPS/Gallup Survey, 1987.

[a]less than .05
[b]less than .01
$R^2 = C/(N + C) = .64$

Data in the next two tables reveal similar findings. In Table 6, the logit estimates indicate that several demographic factors are determinants of white support for a well-qualified black presidential candidate: age, region, education, and income. Thus, whites who are under fifty years old, who live in the west, who are college graduates, and who have household incomes of $40,000 or more were disproportionately likely to report that they would support a qualified black candidate for president. Whites who were fifty years old or older, southern whites, whites who never graduated from high school, and whites whose household incomes were less than $12,000 were disproportionately likely to report that they would *not* vote for a well-qualified black for president. In addition, the data also demonstrate the importance of attitudes toward racial issues in general in determining support for or opposition to a qualified black presidential candidate. Thus, whites who report that poor blacks remain caught in the mire of poverty because of societal factors such as discrimination and whites who support federal efforts to help minorities are more likely to report that they would support a well-qualified black candidate for president. Finally, whites who report that they share a lot of common interests with blacks in their social class are also more likely to report that they would support a qualified black candidate.

The results of the logit analysis to predict support for the view that there is a black qualified to be president are presented in Table 7. Here the list of determinants are age, region, size of place, education, occupation, income, partisanship, and views toward racial issues. Those whites who are most likely to answer yes, there is a black man or woman in politics today that they personally consider to be well qualified for the presidency are whites between the ages of thirty and forty-nine years old, western whites, whites who live in central cities, white college graduates, whites with white-collar occupations, whites with household incomes of $40,000 or more, white Democrats, whites who support federal aid to help minorities, and whites who report they share a lot of common interests with blacks in their social class. Meanwhile, southern whites, whites who never attended college, whites with blue-collar occupations, white Republicans, and whites who fault blacks themselves for black poverty are the least likely to report that there is a black who is qualified to be president.

In general, data in tables 5, 6, and 7 demonstrate that racist opposition, or the handicap factor, is most apparent among southern whites, low-income whites, whites who never graduated from high school, whites age fifty and older, whites who are conservative on racial issues. Opposition is lowest among western whites, college-educated whites, whites in the middle-age cohort (thirty to forty-nine years old), and whites who are liberal on racial issues.

Thus, the Archie Bunker or southern redneck stereotype is not far off the mark as a description of the average racist voter, while the Berkeley yuppie profile describes the white voter most likely to give a black candidate a sympathetic hearing.

Finally, it should be noted that there were no significant differences by one independent variable tested: gender. While there may be a gender gap on many political issues, white women are no more likely than

Table 6. Maximum Likelihood (Logit) Estimates of Determinants of Support for a Qualified Black Presidential Candidate among Whites

Variable	Coefficient Estimate	Standard Error	Coeff/ SE	x^2	Number of Cases
Intercept	-.059	.310	0.19	0.04	
Age: 18 - 29	.284	.124	2.29	5.25[a]	115
Age: 30 - 49	.291	.120	2.43	5.91[a]	245
Age: 50 and over	-.250	.114	2.19	4.80[a]	330
South	-.279	.094	2.97	8.82[b]	192
West	.347	.118	2.94	8.64[b]	128
Less than high school	-.433	.178	2.43	5.91[a]	140
College graduate	.508	.164	3.10	9.61[b]	172
Less than $12,000	-.410	.160	2.56	6.55[a]	102
$40,000 or more	.390	.153	2.55	6.50[a]	155
Reasons for black poverty: societal factors	.443	.168	2.64	6.97[b]	217
Federal government should aid minorities	.362	.146	2.48	6.15[a]	190
Share a lot of common interests with blacks in same social class	.283	.126	2.25	5.06[a]	134
There is a black qualified to be president	.514	.114	4.51	20.33[b]	179

Source: JCPS/Gallup Survey, 1988.

[a]less than .05
[b]less than .01
$R^2 = C/(N + C) = .64$

white men to report different attitudes vis-à-vis black political candidates.

Implications for Jesse Jackson

Application of this analysis to the Jesse Jackson campaign of 1988 yields several interesting insights.

First, Jesse Jackson has often been plagued by the press about why he cannot win the white vote. The above analysis demonstrates that not

Table 7. Maximum Likelihood (Logit) Estimates of Agreement with View That There Are Blacks Qualified to be President

Variable	Coefficient Estimate	Standard Error	Coeff./SE	x^2	Number of Cases
Intercept	-.496	.335	1.48	2.19	
Age: 30 - 49	.443	.144	3.08	9.49[b]	245
South	-.258	.120	2.15	4.62[a]	192
West	.263	.111	2.37	5.62[a]	128
Central City	.250	.113	2.21	4.88[a]	185
Less than high school	-.343	.117	2.93	8.59[b]	140
High school	-.325	.114	2.85	8.12[b]	258
College graduate	.427	.206	2.07	4.29[a]	172
White Collar	.225	.104	2.16	4.67[a]	265
Blue Collar	-.271	.123	2.20	4.84[a]	112
$40,000 and more	.267	.130	2.05	4.20[a]	155
Democrat	.401	.200	2.01	4.04[a]	257
Republican	-.346	.148	2.34	5.48[a]	214
Reasons for black poverty: individual	-.377	.145	2.60	6.76[b]	408
Federal government should aid minorities	.422	.158	2.67	7.13[a]	190
Share a lot of common interests with blacks in same social class	.326	.129	2.53	6.40[a]	134

Source: JCPS/Gallup Survey, 1988.

[a]less than .05
[b]less than .01
$R^2 = C/(N + C) = .64$

only Jackson but any black candidate has the propensity to be negatively stereotyped by white Americans, especially as regards his or her ability to achieve goals. From the start, the candidate has an uphill struggle, particularly in those policy areas that more white Americans identify as the most important problems. Similarly, a large majority of whites simply do not believe there is any black candidate qualified to be president. The issue, then, is not so much why Jackson could not win the white vote, but why whites stereotype blacks unfavorably.

Second, as the logit analyses demonstrate, attitudes toward racial issues unsurprisingly correlate highly with attitudes toward black candidates. Thus, rather than creating or abetting the racial divide as some have accused Jackson of doing, a black candidate is more or less a victim of it. Those whites who do not support fair-housing laws, who do not support federal aid for minorities, and who believe they share few common interests with blacks in their class also report that black political candidates are less likely to achieve important goals and/or that no black, whomever he or she may be, is qualified to be president.

Third, although Jackson's emphasis on a class-based lower-income coalition touches the heart of objective needs of black and white working-class America, it appears that it has the ironic effect of targeting his message at precisely the group of white voters least likely at the present historical conjuncture to respond to a black candidate. The state of working-class white consciousness today appears to nearly mitigate cooperation on the electoral front when the candidate is black. Less affluent, less educated, and blue-collar whites tend to be the most opposed not only to federal efforts to aid minorities but to report that they share few common interests with blacks in their class, and concomitantly less likely to support black political candidates. (Colasanto and Williams, 1987). In contrast, younger, more upwardly mobile whites tend to be more progressive on social justice issues, more likely to report they share many common interests with blacks in their social class, and more likely to report they would support black candidates.

Other data in the survey show a pattern indicating that the latter are precisely the type of whites who reported voting for Jackson in the Democratic primaries and caucuses in 1988. Among the small number of whites who reported voting for Jackson in the 1988 Democratic nomination contest (17 percent of all white Democratic primary and caucus voters), Jackson did disproportionately well among whites thirty to forty-nine years old (28 percent of this group), midwestern (28 percent) and western whites (26 percent), college-educated whites (26 percent), whites in white-collar occupations (29 percent), and whites with household incomes of $25,000 or greater (24 percent). By comparison, Jackson did worst among whites fifty years old and older (8 percent), whites who lived in the south (10 percent), whites who never graduated from high school (2 percent), whites in blue-collar occupations (11 percent), and whites with household incomes less than $12,500 (9 percent).

Fourth, data in the survey demonstrate that, so far, the threshold for white support for black political candidates hovers around 20 to 25 percent. Thus, about 20 percent more whites stereotype white candidates more favorably than stereotype black candidates more favorably in terms of goals achievement and personal attributes; about 20 percent of whites report they would refuse to vote for a black candidate for president, and only about 25 percent report that there is any black who is qualified to be president. Jackson in 1988 came close to this 20 percent threshold in white support. Going beyond it is likely to remain difficult.

Fifth, the only clue from the data about how a black political candidate might seek to win over skeptical, if not just plain racist, whites is that he or she should emphasize his or her ability to achieve important goals. Thus, as some black statewide officials (for example, Virginia's Lieutenant Governor L. Douglas Wilder and Alabama State Superior Court Judge Oscar Adams) have characterized their campaigns, a black candidate seeking white support must develop a "PIES" strategy; that is, they must emphasize pragmatism, independence, experience, and skills. By implication, undoubtedly Jackson's quest for the presidency was harmed by his inability to harken back to experience in electoral office. In addition, since whites tend to negatively evaluate black political candidates' ability to achieve inclusive national goals, the black political candidate must increasingly articulate political methods, goals, rhetoric, and symbols that are *unmistakably inclusive* and not viewed as the special province of any particular interest group. As a former Dukakis campaign staffer, Donna Brazile, puts it,

> Jesse always did well with white voters when he was talking about his message—jobs and economic justice. When Jesse started talking about process— "I've been discriminated against; I don't have enough delegates, Michael Dukakis didn't call me"—he started losing white voters. When black candidates talk about issues of common interest, you can gain support in the white community. But when you talk about process—"blacks need this seat on the city council"—you lose white voters real quick. They don't support black power. (Brazile, 1989)

Conclusion

Black political candidates still suffer from negative stereotypes and white bloc voting. Not only do whites perceive blacks as less capable of achieving goals, less likely to possess important personal attributes, and less qualified for the presidency, but a majority of whites also agree that most whites vote on the basis of race rather than qualifications. While many blacks also stereotype white candidates negatively, they are far less likely to do so in terms of a white candidate's ability to achieve important societal goals and far more likely to report that blacks vote more on the basis of qualifications rather than race. Even if blacks held the same views of whites candidates that whites hold of black candidates, perhaps, it would not be as meaningful. After all, blacks compose only 11 percent of the voting-age population in the United States and are minorities in every state, while whites compose 85 percent of the voting-age population in the nation and are the majority in every state. As the dominant group in the electorate, whites are much more likely to determine election results in most jurisdictions. Thus, negative perceptions of black political candidates among whites can be far more damaging to the prospects of black political candidates than analogous perceptions among blacks can be for white candidates.

For the most part, alliances with white working-class voters remain difficult to build. Not only are blue-collar, less-affluent, and less-educated whites less likely to vote at rates comparable to higher-status whites, but the extent to which they are more likely than whites at the top of the economic ladder to compete directly with blacks for scarce resources in an economy that, in the last decade, reduced the share of the pie for all the poor, undoubtedly mystifies the common-objective economic interests they share with many black Americans and mobilizes them against black political candidates. Thus, while blue-collar whites remain disproportionately likely to support the same white candidate supported by blacks in many instances, this coalition may come apart when the candidate is black. Only efforts to alter the racial consciousness of the white working class in general are likely to mitigate poor-white opposition to black candidates.

Today, however, upwardly mobile whites are more likely than poor whites to support social justice issues and black political candidates. Meanwhile, coalitions with upwardly mobile whites have the potential for falling apart, the more economic issues dominate the political agenda. In short, a coalition with either class of whites remains fragile and difficult to maintain.

Perhaps the most optimistic finding of this analysis is that in every instance, education was an important determinant of support for black political candidates. A more-educated populace, then, should produce one less biased against black candidates. In the meantime, given the negative perceptions of black political candidates held by large proportions of whites, the percentage of blacks in a political jurisdiction will remain the most important contributing factor to a black candidate's prospects for success. Given the current state of white perceptions of black political candidates, it's little wonder that racial polarization in voter behavior remains the order of the day, and widespread white crossover voting is still simply a goal.

References

Black Elected Officials: A National Roster. 17th ed. 1989. Washington, D.C.: Joint Center for Political Studies Press.

Brazile, Donna. 1989. Quoted in "Race and Politics, Part VIII: Jackson's Future." *Political Hotline.* Washington, D.C.

Bullock, Charles S., III. 1984. "Racial Crossover Voting and the Election of Black Officials." *Journal of Politics,* 46:239–51.

Cavanagh, Thomas. 1985. *Inside Black America: The Message of the Black Vote in the 1984 Elections.* Washington, D.C.: Joint Center for Political Studies Press.

Colasanto, Diane, and Linda Williams. 1987. "The Changing Dynamics of Race and Class." *Public Opinion,* 9:50–54.

Davidson, Chandler, ed. 1984. *Minority Vote Dilution.* Washington, D.C.: Howard University Press.

Hahn, Harlan and Timothy Almy. 1971. "Ethnic Politics and Racial Issues: Voting in Los Angeles." *Western Political Quarterly* 24:719–30.

Hahn, Harlan, David Klingman, and Harry Pachon. 1976. "Cleavages, Coalitions and the Black Candidate: The Los Angeles Mayoralty Election of 1969 and 1973." *Western Political Quarterly* 29:508.

Karnig, Albert K., and Susan Welch. 1980. *Black Representation and Urban Policy.* Chicago: University of Chicago Press.

Lorinskas, Robert A., Brett W. Hawkins, and Stephen Edwards. 1969. "The Persistence of Ethnic Voting in Rural and Urban Areas: Results from the Controlled Election Method." *Social Science Quarterly* 49:891–99.

Murray, Richard, and Arnold Vedlitz. 1978. "Racial Voting Patterns in the South: An Analysis of Major Elections from 1960 to 1977 in Five Cities." *Annals* 439:29–39.

Pettigrew, Thomas F. 1972. "When a Black Candidate Runs for Mayor: Race and Voting Behavior." In Harlan Hahn, ed., *People and Politics in Urban Society.* Beverly Hills, CA: Sage.

Roster. 1989. See *Black Elected Officials: A National Roster.*

Electoral Politics, Affirmative Action and the Supreme Court: The Case of Richmond v. Croson

W. Avon Drake
Robert D. Holsworth

Virginia Commonwealth University

This paper is an attempt to come to grips with some of the important questions raised as a result of the Supreme Court's decision in Richmond v. Croson. *The essay attempts to specify where the Court now stands on affirmative action, especially with regards to race. We do this by examining the voting records and the opinions of the membership of the Court from the time of* Bakke *to* Richmond v. Croson. *The final section of the essay probes some of the broader political implications of the case. We show how the decision about the Richmond set-aside ordinance is connected to an attempt to redefine the meaning of civil rights and to reinterpret the meaning of the civil rights movement by conservatives. We then demonstrate the practical effects that such a redefinition has on the policy options and strategies available to black elected leadership in American cities.*

Justice Marshall's dissent in *Richmond v. Croson* called the majority's decision overturning the Richmond set-aside ordinance a "deliberate and giant step backward in this Court's affirmative action jurisprudence. Cynical of one municipality's attempt to redress the effects of past racial discrimination, the majority launches a grapeshot attack on race conscious remedies in general."[1] In the body of his argument, Marshall paid particular attention to the manner in which the Court had interpreted the Equal Protection Clause of the Fourteenth Amendment and to what its decision implied about the state of racial discrimination today. He accused the majority of adopting a standard of review in which "remedial classifications" are "equated with the most brute and repugnant forms of state-sponsored racism."[2] Moreover, Marshall maintained that the Court's decision actually implied that "racial discrimination is largely a phenomenon of the past, and that government bodies need no longer preoccupy themselves with rectifying racial injustices."[3]

In the weeks that followed the decision not all commentators adopted Marshall's position about the implications of the majority's opinion, and they took pains to argue that the Court had not denied the possible validity of affirmative action in municipal economic policy, but had only contended that Richmond went about it incorrectly. Yet it seems to us that Marshall's argument needs to be taken very seriously, largely because it identifies the central legal and political issues raised by the decision in the Richmond case. On the most immediate level, there are constitutional questions about how the Equal Protection Clause of the Fourteenth Amendment ought to be interpreted. The decision also raises questions about what civil rights should mean today. Finally, the Court's decision has serious implications for the approach that black political officials have taken to promote the economic interests of their constitutents.

This paper is an attempt to come to grips with some of these questions. We begin by describing the evolution of the case from the time that a black majority gained control of the Richmond City Council and a set-aside policy was passed, through the development of the controversy in the lower federal courts and to the arguments in the United States Supreme Court. The second part of the essay attempts to specify where the Court now stands on affirmative action, especially with regard to race. We do this by examining the voting records and the opinions of the membership of the Court from the time of *Bakke* to *Richmond v. Croson*. The final section of the essay probes some of the broader political implications of the case. We show how the decision about the Richmond set-aside ordinance is connected to an attempt to redefine the meaning of civil rights and to reinterpret the meaning of the civil rights movement by American conservatives. We then demonstrate the practical effects that such a redefinition has on the policy options and strategies available to black elected leadership in American cities.

The argument of the paper suggests that the decision in *Richmond v. Croson* is critically important. In the first place, the Court maintained that the precedent in *Fullilove v. Klutznick*, which Richmond and other municipalities believed to legitimate their set-aside programs, did not apply to localities but only to Congress. Moreover, we demonstrate that the voting pattern on the present Court is configured in such a manner that affirmative action policies will not easily receive Court approval in the future. In fact, the Court is probably one vote away from overturning affirmative action in almost any conceivable circumstance. Finally, we note that the Court's interpretation of civil rights further sharpens the dilemmas that confront African-American political leadership in improving the economic condition of their constituency. We suggest that the decision may well intensify the need for a serious reconsideration of the strategies employed to promote black economic progress.

In this vein, we hope that our analysis of affirmative action will also contribute to the discussion about the political role of the Supreme Court in the American constitutional system. During the 1950s and 1960s, in the heyday of the Warren Court, observers frequently spoke about the Court's role as a protector of minorities and as educator of the American public in the area of race relations. In fact, the commitment of the Warren Court to the protection of minorities had been seen as one of the notable exceptions to Robert Dahl's widely quoted argument that the Court largely reflected and reinforced majority norms in American society. (This point is made in Barker, 1973). The popular depiction of the Warren Court may well have exaggerated its commitment to and capacity for reordering racial priorities in the nation.[4] But it was true that the Court was one of the few places where black Americans could even possibly receive a fair hearing. In the terms that John Hart Ely has employed, the Court was the one national institution committed to rectifying the problems of representation in the practice of American democracy.[5]

Throughout the 1970s and 1980s, commentators noted that while the Burger Court had not overturned the landmark civil rights decisions, it had tempered the Court's commitment to the issue and had eschewed the educative function that had been critical to the Warren years. (See Barker, 1973, for an early statement of this position.) The Rehnquist Court is certainly reinforcing Burger's tendency to limit the use of litigation as a method for black Americans to achieve policy goals. (For a fuller discussion of this topic, see Barker and Combs, 1989.) Indeed, many of the affirmative action cases represent an attempt by conservative forces (particularly those in the executive branch) to utilize the courts in order to contest policies that black leadership pursued either as a result of electoral success or as a consequence of negotiations with corporate America. The decision in *Croson* thus may signify more than a tempering of the Warren Court's commitment to civil rights. We suggest that it represents an explicit use of the discourse of civil rights to oppose the policies endorsed and pursued by contemporary black leadership.[6]

The Evolution of *Richmond v. Croson*

Although the population of Richmond was nearly 50 percent black by the end of the 1960s, political control remained firmly in the hands of whites until 1977. Richmond's political establishment was tenacious in its effort to retain its position and was aided by members of the state legislature fearful of the changes that might accompany a black political victory in the former capital of the confederacy.[7] During the mid-1960s, the white power structure embarked on a controversial annexation plan that incorporated part of a surrounding county. Publicly justified by the city's need for undeveloped land and a broader tax base, many blacks saw the proposal as a way of reducing the growing political influence that their numbers might provide. Their suspicions were well grounded, as the city's negotiations took place almost entirely in secret and without consulting the black community. In fact, the mayor at the time was reported to have said, in a meeting with representatives from the county, "We don't want the city to go to the niggers. We need 44,000 white bodies" (Moeser and Dennis, 1982:93).[8]

The Richmond annexation plan was challenged in the courts for diluting black voting strength and, in the ensuing litigation, the city was prevented from holding a city council election for almost seven years. It was only able to do so after the United States Supreme Court approved a compromise that allowed the annexation to stand but coupled it with the replacement of the at-large method for selecting council members by a ward-based system. In the special election of 1977, blacks were able to gain majority control of the city council. Since Richmond's version of the council-manager form of government calls for the mayor to be elected from the council by its members, the election also resulted in the selection of Richmond's first black mayor, Henry L. Marsh III, a civil rights activist, a lawyer, and a member of the council for the past ten years (Moeser and Dennis, 1982:178–83).

The black majority that was elected in 1977 and was returned in the regular election of 1978 immediately demonstrated its commitment to changing Richmond politics. The result was a "series of conflicts that saw council votes sharply divided along racial lines" (Moeser and Dennis, 1982:183). The new city council replaced the white city manager, it adopted a redistricting plan that prompted white politicians and business leaders to complain to the Justice Department about racial discrimination against whites, and its appointments to various boards and commissions were enveloped in controversy. In addition, the new council paid more attention to neighborhood development than its predecessors had and broadened the practice of historic preservation to include poor and middle-class black residential areas, not only affluent white ones. The conservative editorials of the city's daily newspapers and certain spokespersons for the old regime claimed that the city was being destroyed by racialist policies (Moeser and Dennis, 1982:183–85; Silver, 1984:315–20).

Yet the bitter clashes on council and the baleful commentaries in the local dailies exaggerated the extent of the changes that were undertaken. The new black city manager had served as assistant city manager prior to 1977 and he pursued relatively conservative fiscal policies that embroiled him in ongoing controversy with the more liberal members of council. And when members of the white business establishment threatened to take their offices (and their taxes) "to the counties," black council members demonstrated their willingness to reach a rapprochement. In fact, the new majority gave what one commentator has called "unflagging support" to the questionable strategy of making a hotel/convention center complex the focus of downtown development (Silver, 1984:318). The anchor unit in the center city was a "festival mall" built under the auspices of James Rouse as a means of luring tourists and suburbanites to Richmond, hardly a revolutionary economic policy. In general, black leaders came to the conclusion that promoting their own agenda required that they frequently work with and not against the business establishment in matters of economic development.

Any lingering thoughts about the revolutionary consequences of the new political configuration in Richmond were put to rest in the elections of 1982. Emerging class and ideological divisions in the black community, a long-standing personal feud, and a nearly unanimous white vote led to the replacement in one of the wards of Willie Dell, a member of the Marsh faction, by Roy West, a relatively conservative black school principal. West had been involved in a running dispute with Henry Marsh from the time that the man whom Marsh had supported for superintendent of schools had transferred West from a high-school to a middle-school position during a period of consolidation. Perhaps more importantly, West's criticisms of the Marsh faction, his promise to bridge the racial gap on council, and his reputation as a no-nonsense disciplinarian in the schools enabled him to garner a sizeable minority of the black vote and almost total support from the 20 percent of his ward that was white. West's election became even more significant when, in a stunning maneuver, he agreed to become mayor by voting for himself and accepting the support of the four white council members.

In 1983, when the Richmond set-aside ordinance was passed, the city council was numerically led by a black majority. But it certainly was not a monolithic one. On a number of issues—school policy, budgetary allocations to neighborhoods, and appointments to city boards and commissions—there were bitter divisions between the black council members elected in 1977 and Roy West. The Marsh faction publicly accused West of siding with its old political enemies and privately was even harsher in its judgement. The new mayor, for his part, rarely passed up an opportunity to question the intelligence of the man he replaced and to emphasize that Marsh no longer held the reigns of power. Yet it is noteworthy that the set-aside ordinance was one of the few major issues on which the Marsh faction and Roy West agreed. Members elected in 1977 viewed the ordinance as fulfilling their mandate to carry out the economic aspects of the civil rights vision. In their minds, it was another step in remedying the discrimination that had permeated Richmond politics. For Roy West, endorsing the set-aside ordinance helped to legitimate his argument that he cared about issues that really helped blacks and that he did not waste his time mouthing empty rhetoric that had no practical consequences. West took his position a step further and publicly chastised the Marsh faction for waiting more than five years to do anything about the issue.

The decision to develop a set-aside ordinance was based on an examination of city contracts that revealed a striking discrepancy in the contract dollars going to white and black firms. During the five years prior to 1983, minority businesses had received only .67 percent of the city's construction contracts, which had totaled more than 124 million dollars.[9] When this statistic was combined with the previous exclusion of blacks from the mainstream of Richmond's political and business life and with knowledge of the discrimination that had historically been practiced in the construction trades, it seemed evident to the majority of council that it had a moral and political responsibility to redress the inequity.

In 1983, the council thought that its desire to do so stood on a firm legal basis as well. Members were aware that other large cities had established set-aside programs. In addition, they believed that the Supreme Court's *Fullilove v. Klutznick* decision had provided a legal foundation for their effort to redress the inequities in city contracting. *Fullilove* was concerned with a challenge to the minority-business-enterprise provision of the 1977 Public Works Employment Act, which required, absent an administrative waiver, that at least 10 percent of federal funds granted for local public-works projects must be used by the state or local grantee to procure services or supplies from businesses owned by minority-group members.[10] The major claim of those protesting the law was the argument that it violated the Equal Protection Clause of the Fifth Amendment. The Court rejected the challenge and concluded that Congress had the authority to redress the present effects of past discrimination so long as the method of redress was narrowly focused and limited in size, impact, and duration. It asserted that the 10 percent set-aside was a reasonable figure insofar as it represented a midway point between the percentage of minorities in the population at large and the percentage of minority contractors in the nation.[11]

The six members of the Richmond City Council who supported the bill believed, along with the city's legal advisors, that they were simply applying the principles of *Fullilove* to the local level. The key part of the Richmond ordinance was that, absent a waiver, "all contractors awarded construction contracts by the city shall subcontract at least 30 percent to the contract of minority business enterprises."[12] In fact, in almost all of its significant features, the city attorney's office tailored the bill to what it believed *Fullilove* permitted. It felt that the legality of the set-aside provision itself had been established in the case. Its definition of minorities (which returned to haunt the city in 1989) to extend beyond the black community to include "Spanish-speaking, Orientals, Eskimos, or Aleuts" was arrived at simply by replicating the language of the Congressional law. And, in the selection of 30 percent as the set-aside target, the city was choosing a point nearly midway between the percentage of contracts awarded to minorities in 1983 and the percentage of minorities in the general population of the city, precisely what it felt Congress had done in 1977.

The principal legal challenge to the city ordinance commenced within five months of its initial passage. On 30 September 1983, J. A. Croson, an Ohio-based corporation, received bid documents from the city to install stainless-steel plumbing fixtures in the Richmond City Jail. In this particular contract, Croson concluded that the city's regulation could only be met if a minority contractor supplied the fixtures because these alone would consume 75 percent of the contract's value. On the same day, a representative from Croson testified that it contacted several minority businesses to inform them of the project and requested that they submit quotes on the fixtures if they were interested. On October 12, the last day to submit bids, Croson testified that it again contacted the minority businesses to see if any would be quoting it a price. None were able to do so, and Croson submitted a bid of $126,530 using a quote provided by a nonminority firm.[13]

On October 12, however, Melvin Brown of the minority-owned firm Continental Metal Hose Incorporated did inform Croson's representative that he wanted to participate in the bid and that he had not been contacted previously. Brown attempted to obtain a price quote for the fixtures but was rebuffed when the distributor claimed that his company had not established its worthiness for credit. At the bid opening the following day, Brown told Croson's representatives that his company would still attempt to supply the fixtures. But on October 19 Croson requested a waiver from the city's minority-utilization requirement on the grounds that there was no qualified minority supplier available. On October 27, the day that Brown learned of Croson's request, he called the city's Director of Purchasing and Planning and noted that he had obtained a price for the fixtures, though his markup was $6,183.29 higher than the quote Croson was using from the nonminority supplier.[14]

After reviewing the various documents and arguments, the city advised Croson that it was cancelling the bid and rebidding the contract. Croson attempted to appeal the decision but the city had no provision for an appeal when a contract was rebid. Croson then filed suit alleging that the city's program violated several state laws and protections inherent in the Fourteenth Amendment to the U.S. Constitution. Croson maintained that the set-aside ordinance violated a Virginia law that local procurement policies had to be based on "competitive principles."[15] More important for our purposes, Croson contended that the ordinance violated the Equal Protection Clause of the Fourteenth Amendment by endorsing a race-conscious remedy for which there was no compelling government interest and which was not narrowly tailored.[16] In this regard, it should be noted that while the Croson suit was an explicit challenge to the Richmond law, it was also part of a more general series of challenges to set-aside policies that were being brought to the courts of the nation under the auspices of the Associated General Contractors of America.[17]

The case was heard in the U.S. District Court by Judge Robert Merhige. Merhige was no stranger to civil rights litigation concerning the city of Richmond. In the 1970s, Merhige had been a key figure in the controversy over integration and school bussing. He had actually ordered consolidation of the Richmond system with the surrounding counties. His plan had been overturned by the Circuit Court of Appeals, and the court's decision was upheld when the Supreme Court had a four-to-four tie vote when Lewis Powell abstained because he had been chairman of the Richmond School Board. Merhige also presided over the challenge to Richmond's annexation plan and ruled, over the city's objections, that it was racially motivated and that it could not be upheld until the city changed its methods of selecting council. Seen by segments of the black community as one of its few potential allies in official government, Merhige was villified in some white circles, and at one time anonymous death threats compelled him to request police protection for his own home.

Merhige's decision in 1984 was grounded in an interpretation of the applicability of *Fullilove* to the city's program. Recognizing that the Supreme Court decision in that case had not provided a "clear, easily applied test" evaluating set-aside programs, Merhige employed an approach developed by the Eleventh Circuit Court of Appeals in South Florida that had attempted to distill from the majority's position a common set of concerns.[18] This approach required (1) that the governmental body have the authority to construct the plan, (2) "that the governmental body adopting a remedial plan make adequate findings to ensure that it is remedying the present effects of prior discrimination and not advancing one racial group's interest over another," and (3) that the "use of racial classifications not extend further than established need of remedying the effects of past discrimination."[19]

On all these grounds, Merhige upheld the Richmond program. He maintained that Croson provided no evidence to demonstrate that a city council does not have the power to develop set-aside programs. Merhige also contended that Richmond provided adequate findings of the need for a remedial program. In this regard, Merhige pointed to the lack of minority businesses in Richmond, the city's claims about the historical discrimination in the construction industry that went unrefuted at the trial, and the evidence cited by Congress itself in passing the Minority Business Enterprise Act that was challenged in *Fullilove*.[20] Merhige also concurred with the city's claim that its program did not extend too far. As evidence, he cited the inclusion of a waiver provision and the temporally limited duration of the plan. Merhige specifically addressed the argument that the percentage of the set-asides in Richmond was set at an arbitrary and unreasonably high level. He maintained that the city was acting reasonably in putting forward the 30 percent set-aside figure insofar as a number of lower-court decisions had implied that "the percentage of minorities in the community's general population, not the percentage of minorities in the area's business community, is the appropriate benchmark for evaluating the reasonableness of a set-aside figure."[21]

Croson appealed the decision to the Fourth Circuit Court of Appeals. Once again, the city's plan was upheld when a two-to-one majority rejected Croson's arguments and affirmed both the reasoning and conclusions outlined in Judge Merhige's opinions, particularly his interpretation of the applicability of *Fullilove*. At the same time, the dissent by Judge Harvie Wilkinson laid the foundation for what would eventually become the reversal of the city's plan. In his dissent, Wilkinson maintained that the city's plan actually violated state law, which demanded that procurement policies be consistent with competitive principles.

Using reasoning drawn from the free-market critiques of affirmative action policies, Wilkinson argued that the Richmond plan predetermined results "in a way that does not comport with savings in the public fisc or quality in the public product."[22] More significantly, Wilkinson contended that the factual findings of discrimination were inadequate and that the 30 percent set-aside figure "emerged from a vacuum."[23] Wilkinson's summary maintained that although he recognized the need to "overcome the legacy of discrimination," his colleagues on the circuit court had actually harmed civil rights by approving "the casual adoption of a crude numerical preference that can only impair the ideal that all stand equally before the law and postpone the day of human fellowship that transcends race."[24]

Wilkinson was a Reagan appointee and his strong dissent left Croson with a basis for hope that its appeal to the Supreme Court might result in a different outcome. These hopes were enhanced when the justices remanded the case to the circuit court with specific instructions to reconsider its decision in light of the *Wygant v. Jackson* case that the Supreme Court had recently heard. *Wygant* arose from a collective-bargaining agreement between a city in Michigan and a teachers union after the city of Jackson was threatened with a suit for discrimination in employment procedures. The agreement provided that "if it became necessary to lay off teachers, those with the most seniority would be retained, except at no time would there be a greater percentage of minority personnel laid off than the current percentage of minority personnel employed at the time of the layoff."[25] When a budget crunch forced the school district to engage in layoffs, some nonminority teachers were laid off while minority instructors with less seniority were retained. When the appeal by the nonminority teachers reached the Supreme Court, their position was upheld and the Court overturned the collective-bargaining agreement on the grounds that it penalized innocent nonminority parties and that findings calling for such a drastic remedy had not been adequately demonstrated.[26]

On the face of things, the instruction to reconsider *Croson* in the light of *Wygant* was odd, because the two cases appeared to be dissimilar. The Richmond set-aside ordinance did not prevent any individual from having a job, while the other clearly prevented at least some individuals from temporarily practicing their vocation. But what the Court appeared to be doing by its instruction was challenging the entire basis of the Richmond ordinance, namely, the applicability of *Fullilove* to local programs. It was telling the circuit court that it should examine the set-aside policy in light of its recent decisions, which did admit the possible legality of affirmative action, but which had been tightening requirements about the type of findings necessary to prove discrimination and about the kind of statistical evidence that was acceptable.

The significance of the Supreme Court's instruction was evidenced by the circuit court's reversal of its own decision upon reconsideration. With Judge Hall of the three-member appeal panel changing his vote, Wilkinson's position now became the majority opinion. Wilkinson argued that for set-asides to be justified, adequate findings of identifiable discrimination must be made and that the set-aside percentage cannot be based on comparisons with the entire population of the area. In Wilkinson's mind, the Richmond program was now illegitimate in conception inasmuch as its findings were based on notions of societal discrimination. He claimed that it was too sweeping in its application insofar as there was no justification for the 30 percent set-asides and because the definition of minorities included people—Aleuts and Eskimos—who had never resided in Richmond in substantial numbers.[27] Ultimately, Wilkinson felt that the liabilities of the Richmond program opened it to possible abuse as nothing more than a racial pork barrel. As to *Fullilove*, Wilkinson acknowledged that some aspects of the plan followed it "to the letter." Yet the city's premise "was in error" because he contended that the Congress has much broader power in addressing violations of the Fourteenth Amendment than city governments.[28]

The city of Richmond appealed the circuit court's decision to the Supreme Court, but most observers who had watched the development of the case recognized that the city was fighting a losing battle. Richmond's brief before the Supreme Court emphasized once again its contention that *Fullilove* was the controlling case and that it was misguided to apply *Wygant* in circumstances that were so completely different.[29] The city was joined in its efforts by amicus briefs from a number of organizations, including the National League of Cities. Their arguments, along with those put forward by Brennan, Blackmun, and Marshall, failed to persuade a majority of the Court. Justice O'Connor's opinion (joined by Rehnquist, White, and Kennedy), echoed Wilkinson's dismissal of *Fullilove* as the controlling precedent by noting that it was a special case applicable only to the United States Congress as a coequal branch of the national government, and not to municipalities. O'Connor also repeated most of the major arguments that Wilkinson had made. She contended (1) that the Richmond plan was not justified by a compelling governmental interest, since the record revealed no prior discrimination by the city itself in awarding contracts, and (2) that it was almost impossible to ascertain whether the Richmond plan was narrowly tailored because it was not related to identified discrimination.[30]

Affirmative Action and the Supreme Court

Observers of the Supreme Court would not suggest that its treatment of affirmative action in the past decade has been a model of lucid exposition and logical analysis. Since it first addressed the issue by declaring that Allan Bakke was unfairly denied entrance to medical school by the University of California's use of racial quotas, while simultaneously maintaining that race-specific remedies could possibly be constitutional, the Court has been sharply divided. It has argued about whether affirmative action is permissible and, if it is, what kind of findings of discrimination are necessary to legitimate a policy of race-conscious relief.

Opinions have disputed which statistical measures are really an adequate indication of serious discrimination. Even in cases where the Court has agreed that race-conscious relief might be justified, members have disagreed about whether the program under consideration is legitimately remedial and narrowly tailored. There has been controversy about whether the same criteria should be employed to evaluate programs mandated by governmental units and those undertaken by private employers. And, at least until *Croson*, the justices could not agree on the level of judicial scrutiny that should be applied to its examination of affirmative action claims. But it is important that we try to make some sense out of these divisions if we are to come to a genuine understanding of *Croson*'s implications.

Yet the difficulty of accomplishing this has been aggravated by a number of factors. In the first place, affirmative action cases that have come before the Court have frequently resulted in a proliferation of opinions that have not permitted a definitive interpretation of the decisions. In the *Bakke* case alone, six separate opinions were published. Matters are further complicated when it is recognized that, although most justices hold fast to the position they originally adopted, the stance of others has undergone a considerable evolution. Justice Stevens, for example, believes that the precedents established in *Bakke* and *Weber* ought to be respected, even though he personally did not agree with the constitutional interpretations made in those cases. On the other hand, Justice White now writes that he would vote to overturn *Weber*, even though he was a member of the majority that approved the affirmative action program that was contested at the time. Finally, the Court's decisions in particular cases have been rendered, at times, on relatively narrow grounds that have not always explicitly addressed the major legal and constitutional questions raised by affirmative action. Indeed, in *Bakke*, five justices felt that constitutional issues were involved, while four others believed that they need not address them.

Yet these difficulties do not make it impossible to bring clarity to the discussion of the Court's treatment of the issue. With the exception of Anthony Kennedy and Antonin Scalia, the justices have each voted on affirmative action plans in at least seven cases. An examination of the voting patterns in affirmative action cases can demonstrate that the Court's disagreement is not random but is structured in ways that have significant political implications.[31] In addition, the very proliferation of opinions that have made it difficult to interpret the meaning of any individual decision may, in fact, enable us to specify the Court's pattern of disagreement with more accuracy than if the majority and dissenting opinions on every case had spoken univocally. In the course of the past ten years, most of the justices have explained their positions on the more general or theoretical aspects of affirmative action. They have, for example, commented on whether they believe that the Equal Protection Clauses of the Fifth and the Fourteenth Amendments permit affirmative action; on whether the Civil Rights Act of 1964, especially its Title VII provisions, allow employers to develop plans that give preferential treatment to minorities; and about what level of scrutiny should be given to affirmative action plans. The justices have also expressed their positions on the methods that have been employed to apply race-conscious relief and what the relationship is between their general stance on the constitutionality of affirmative action and the particular applications of it.[32]

Three of the justices that have been on the Court since *Bakke*—Blackmun, Brennan, and Marshall—have voted in favor of affirmative action plans every time that these have been granted certiorari and been the subject of an official opinion. Moreover, they have rarely published separate justifications staking out a distinctive position on the constitutional issues raised by affirmative action policies. When one of these justices does write a separate concurrence or dissent, it is typically used as a vehicle for expressing a personal opinion about a particular aspect of a case and not for developing a position about the constitutionality of race-conscious relief that differs substantively from the other two. In this regard, we might think of Blackmun's dissent in *Croson*, in which his purpose is not to distance himself from Marshall's scathing critique of the majority's outlook, but to express amazement that a Supreme Court in 1989 would overthrow an effort by leaders in the former capital of the Confederacy to make amends for its history of discrimination.[33]

The essence of the Blackmun-Brennan-Marshall position is that eliminating racial subjugation in the real world of contemporary America will require the use of race-conscious policies, or in the words they are fond of using, "in order to get beyond racism, we must first take account of race."[34] The constitutional defense of their position is grounded in a distinction between racial classifications that stigmatize and those that are appropriately remedial.[35] For Blackmun, Brennan, and Marshall, legalized segregation stigmatized; set-asides rectify past discrimination. The implication of the distinction is that affirmative action is perfectly legitimate and does not violate the Equal Protection Clause, which they believe is directed primarily against classifications that stigmatize. In addition, they believe that the Civil Rights Act of 1964 clearly permits the voluntary adoption of affirmative action programs by private employers, and that it is a cruel misreading of its intent to utilize this landmark legislation on behalf of American blacks as a way of prohibiting efforts to remedy racial discrimination.

Blackmun, Brennan, and Marshall thus argue that affirmative action programs should be judged by what they label "intermediate scutiny," that is, whether these plans further an important governmental purpose and whether they are reasonably drawn up so as to fulfill this goal.[36] The use of the intermediate-scrutiny standard has led them to be relatively tolerant about the development of affirmative action programs by local governments and private employers in terms of both the numerical goals employed and its extension beyond the hiring process to promotion and layoff policies and to matters such as economic set-asides. They suggest that other members of the Court who have been willing to overturn these programs on the grounds that adequate findings of discrimination have not been made or that local governments have used improper statistical comparisons in establishing target quotas are willfully naive about how American society has actually functioned and what the continuing effects of discrimination are today. In political terms, it might be said that Blackmun, Brennan, and Marshall echo the standard liberal argument by asserting that affirmative action is a logical extension of the civil rights movement, and that it is an integral element in the "task of moving our society toward a state of meaningful equality of opportunity, not an abstract version of equality in which the effects of past discrimination would be forever frozen into our social fabric."[37]

The voting bloc constituted by Rehnquist, White, and Scalia defines the opposite pole of the Court's thinking. Rehnquist has voted against affirmative action plans in each of the ten cases that have come to the Court. Scalia has denied affirmative action claims in each of the three cases since his confirmation. White's voting pattern is more checkered, because he was actually part of the majority that supported affirmative action in *Weber* and *Fullilove*. Yet it is evident that both his voting and his thinking have changed in recent years. In the last seven cases in which the Court published an opinion, White has voted against affirmative action on each occasion. Perhaps more important, he has also expressed a desire to overturn *Weber* and has suggested that his belief about the meaning of affirmative action turned out to be quite different from the beliefs of those with whom he voted at that time.[38]

The Rehnquist-Scalia-White voting bloc is characterized by the following common features. It holds, first, that affirmative action plans need to be subjected to "strict scrutiny" to ensure that equal protection guidelines are not violated. The standard of strict scrutiny holds that any policy based on racial classifications is inherently suspect and must be subject to the most rigorous judicial examination to determine whether the governmental interest involved is not merely important, but "compelling," and whether the means chosen to implement this interest are "narrowly tailored."[39] In addition, Rehnquist, Scalia, and, more recently, White, have argued that the Civil Rights Act of 1964, especially Title VII, does not permit race-conscious policies in the areas of hiring, promotions, and layoffs. Their opinions often refer to the legislative history of the Civil Rights Act of 1964 to defend their stance that the vision of civil rights legislation was that of a color-blind and not a race-conscious society. Indeed, they suggest that the defenders of affirmative action today have subtly but almost completely transformed the meaning of civil rights so that they are attempting to "replace the goal of a discrimination-free society with the quite incompatible goal of proportionate representation by race and by sex in the workplace."[40] Rehnquist, Scalia, and White also agree that the standards applied to private employers do not substantively differ from those which governmental units must meet, but they draw much less permissive conclusions from this assumption than does the more liberal wing of the Court.

Given these positions on the major theoretical questions raised by affirmative action, it is not surprising that Rehnquist, Scalia, and White have been so critical of the specific plans brought to the Court for judgement. While the Blackmun-Brennan-Marshall group is tolerant of the use of affirmative action as government policy, the most conservative wing of the Court examines its utilization with extraordinary rigor to see if the specific applications of affirmative action are incompatible with the guiding principle of race neutrality. And, in almost every instance, they find that the programs formulated by municipalities, unions, and employers either violate equal-protection guarantees, subvert the meaning of the Civil Rights Act, harm innocent nonminorities, promote legitimate social goals by unjustified means, or provide advantage too widely to the class of nonvictimized minorities.

The theoretical position of the Court's right flank is not as uniform as its voting record. Scalia's position is clearly more extreme than that of White and even Rehnquist. In essence, he does not believe in anything that could be remotely called affirmative action. He argues that relief can only be granted to identified victims of discrimination on an individual basis. He believes that going beyond this to include race-specific measures that benefit members of a group who did not personally experience discrimination is unconstitutional.[41] Rehnquist and White at least minimally assert that activities called affirmative action can be permissible. Rehnquist's opinions suggest that affirmative action policies that are narrowly tailored to remedy past discrimination could possibly be permissible. White concurs and suggests that in particularly egregious cases he could even support affirmative action aid for individuals who are nonvictims.[42] But it also remains true that Rehnquist has never seen an affirmative action plan that he could support, and that White appears to be increasingly less inclined to do so. Analyses such as the one by the *New York Times* reporter who observed that Scalia "is alone on the right flank of the Court" are misleading, because the practical effects of his theoretical isolation are negligible.[43]

Perhaps the critical case to illustrate this point was the 1986 decision in *Local 28 of the Sheet Metal Workers' International Association v. Equal Employment Opportunity Commission.* A local union in New York had attempted to maintain what was essentially a whites-only policy by nepotistic recruitment practices. In 1964, the New York State Commission on Human Rights and the New York State Supreme Court ordered the union to change its method of selecting apprentices. When the union persisted in efforts to circumvent the order, the United States initiated suit against it, and in 1975 the union was found guilty of discrimination in district court in violation of Title VII of the Civil Rights Act. The union was ordered to adopt an affirmative action plan with numerical quotas for membership and a court-appointed administrator was chosen to facilitate achievement of the goal. In 1982, the union was again taken to district court and found guilty of contempt of the 1975 order. The court now "imposed $150,000 fine to be placed in a fund designed to increase nonwhite membership in the apprentice program and the union."[44] At this time, the union filed suit appealing the contempt order, the requirement to initiate the fund, and the original affirmative action plan.

It is hard to believe that a more clearly defined justification for affirmative action or an example of what Justice Powell called "egregious discrimination" would be available to the Court. But while acknowledging the seriousness of discrimination, both Rehnquist and White (Scalia had yet to join the Court) felt that the remedies extended beyond the legitimate reach of the Constitution. White argued that the effects of the court's actions "established not just a minority membership goal but also a strict racial quota that the union was required to attain. We have not heretofore approved this kind of racially discriminatory hiring practice and I would not do so now."[45] Rehnquist's argument was even more restrictive, maintaining that the plan was invalid because Title VII of the Civil Rights Act did not allow the union or the court "to sanction the granting of relief to those who were not victims at the expense of innocent nonminority workers injured by racial preferences."[46] If the facts of this case—twenty years of resisting court orders added to decades of discrimination—were not sufficient for Rehnquist and White to warrant an affirmative action plan with numerical quotas, it is hard to see how the theoretical differences between Rehnquist and Scalia, for example, will have any practical consequences.

Although Justice Kennedy has only ruled on affirmative action in the *Croson* case, his opinion gives evidence that his voting record will likely follow that of the most conservative members of the Court. Kennedy suggests that he is in agreement with Scalia's claim that "the moral imperative of racial neutrality is the driving force of the Equal Protection Clause" and that it might be beneficial to "strike down all preferences which are not necessary remedies to victims of unlawful discrimination."[47] Ultimately, however, Kennedy does not join Scalia's opinion primarily because he believes that its practical effects can be accomplished by a less-sweeping claim that does not actually require the Court to overturn precedents established in the recent past. He notes that he interprets the majority's adherence to the strict-scrutiny standard to already forbid "the use even of narrowly drawn racial classifications except as a last resort."[48]

The swing vote on the Court is presently composed of Stevens and O'Connor, though prior to the addition of Kennedy, Lewis Powell occupied this role as well. In the seven cases regarding affirmative action that she has heard, O'Connor has voted in favor of plans on two occasions, while Stevens has supported these policies in five of the eight times these have come before the Court during his tenure.[49] The replacement of Powell by Kennedy is likely to be extremely important, because it makes the possibility of forming a majority for affirmative action programs significantly more difficult. While Powell was on the Court, proponents of affirmative action needed to receive two of the three swing votes. Today, it appears that they will need to obtain both swing votes to put together a majority.

The evolution of Stevens's position has followed a path almost directly opposite to that of White. Stevens voted against affirmative action plans in *Fullilove* and in *Firefighters v. Stotts.* Moreover, he has written that he disagreed with the interpretation of the Civil Rights Act of the 1964 made by the majority in *Weber*. Yet since 1984, *Croson* has been the only case in which he voted against affirmative action plans. Arguing that the interpretations of the Equal Protection Clause and the Civil Rights Act in *Bakke* have become part of American law, Stevens has been more willing to defer to affirmative action plans by employers and legislatures. In one of his opinions, Stevens even quoted approvingly an article from the *Harvard Law Review* that contended that affirmative action can be a forward-looking policy and need not be justified by referring to previous acts of discrimination.[50] Yet he did vote against *Fullilove* and continued that line of reasoning in *Croson* by arguing that set-asides are neither an adequate remedy for discrimination nor an especially effective plan for helping those most harmed by previous discrimination.

O'Connor has been much less supportive of affirmative action than Stevens, and her opinion for the majority in *Croson* clearly demonstrates this. She believes that "strict scrutiny" needs to be applied to the examination of affirmative action plans. Yet she has been a bit more lenient than Rehnquist and White in the application of the standard, suggesting that certain narrowly tailored plans can be legitimately employed to remedy past discrimination. But it is also indisputable that O'Connor's interpretation of what narrow tailoring means is more rigorous than the Blackmun-Brennan-Marshall understanding, or even that of Justice Stevens and former-Justice Powell. In some of O'Connor's opinions, for instance, she has argued that affirmative action plans that utilize statistical comparisons to prove discrimination by comparing the percentage of minorities in the particular job to the percentage in the population at large are often invalid.[51] In addition, O'Connor has been adamant in insisting that affirmative action cannot be justified as an effort to remedy "societal discrimination" but must instead be premised on tangible and visible examples of discrimination.[52] The reluctance of O'Connor to support affirmative action might best be noted in that, in addition to the egregious discrimination evidenced by the Sheet Metal Workers' Union in New York, she has supported an affirmative action plan on only one other occasion, and this had to do with a plan based on gender and not race. Whereas Justice Powell "swung" in favor of affirmative action plans five times out of nine occasions, O'Connor's record shows that she "swings" much less frequently.

Prior to the decision, most commentators on the Court's treatment of affirmative action issues emphasized its continued willingness to acknowledge its constitutionality. They pointed especially to its decision in cases such as *Paradise v. the United States* and *Johnson v. Transportation Agency, Santa Clara*. As late as 1988, a noted scholar of constitutional law could maintain that, even with Ronald Reagan's two terms in office, the Court's position on the issue was still best captured by Justice Marshall's remark in *Bakke* that "despite the Court's inability to agree upon a route, we have reached a common destination in sustaining affirmative action against constitutional attack" (Schwartz, 1988:163). Some commentators went even further and claimed that the decisions in *Paradise* and *Johnson* amounted to nothing less than a repudiation of the Reagan perspective on civil rights by a markedly conservative Court.[53]

These commentators were not necessarily mistaken in their claim that the Court had shown that it was willing to uphold certain kinds of affirmative action policies. Yet they did not always explore the full implications of the statistical measures of discrimination that the Court felt were appropriate or the consequences of the manner in which "narrow tailoring" was being interpreted. In addition, they may well have neglected to portray how precarious and vulnerable the Court's support for affirmative action really was. They rarely, if ever, mentioned the evolution of White's position or compared O'Connor's record on the issue to the other swing votes. Nor did they always mention how a single change on the bench could easily reverse the outcome in a number of important cases. The decision in *Croson* should, at a minimum, prompt a serious reconsideration of where the Court is moving.

Supporters of affirmative action might possibly take solace by noting that, in *Croson*, a majority of the Court did not rule out the possibility that race-conscious relief could be constitutional. Even O'Connor's scathing critique of the Richmond plan was careful to note that all forms of government-sponsored affirmative action were not being condemned. In the immediate aftermath of the decision, leaders in some municipalities and in the civil rights organizations tried to place the Court's rejection of affirmative action in a positive light. They argued that they had supplied more positive proof of discrimination than Richmond had furnished, or that their programs were more narrowly tailored. Even in Richmond, Councilman Henry Marsh, one of the principal backers of the original ordinance, spoke confidently about reconsidering and rewriting the set-aside program so that it would be compatible with the Court's decision.[54]

Such an interpretation may well be overly optimistic. With the addition of Kennedy, the Rehnquist-Scalia-White voting bloc probably has four solid votes against affirmative action programs, regardless of the case. Even if Stevens continues to vote more frequently with the Blackmun-Brennan-Marshall flank of the Court, this will not do much for the pro–affirmative action position. In any event, race-specific plans in the immediate future will need to receive the support of Justice O'Connor, and this is unlikely to be forthcoming in most instances. O'Connor has continually argued against anything that might resemble an expansive interpretation of affirmative action. Yes, race- and gender-specific relief is likely to be upheld in certain cases as a narrowly tailored remedy, though not as frequently as when Justice Powell, who never really made a "last resort" claim, was on the Court. But it is not very likely to be approved as a routine policy undertaken by state and local governments. In this regard, supporters of affirmative action might also recall that the lower federal courts, which will hear the inevitable array of challenges to established plans, are populated by a majority of judges, such as J. Harvie Wilkinson, who were appointed during the Reagan era.

Political Implications

The Meaning of Civil Rights

The decision in *Croson* was widely perceived as a victory for the Reagan administration and its effort to move the Court in a more conservative direction. Besides attempting to appoint justices who shared the President's conservative ideological stance, the Reagan administration had utilized its rhetorical and institutional resources to push the president's philosophy in the judicial system. Civil rights policy was of special importance to the president's agenda. It is important to recognize that the Reagan administration did not merely oppose the specific policies of black elected officials. It went much further to claim that it actually had a more appropriate understanding of the meaning of civil rights than did black leaders. Opposing affirmative action programs was now described as a means of upholding the legacy of Martin Luther King, Jr. In fact, members of the Reagan administration and commentators who concurred with its outlook tirelessly quoted a single remark of King's, to the effect that he could not wait for the day when people would be judged in this country by the "content of their character and not by the color of their skin." It was as if the administration believed that the entire meaning of the civil rights movement could be encapsulated by that single statement.

This perspective was forcefully presented in the speeches, writings, and policies of William Bradford Reynolds, assistant attorney general, Civil Rights Division. In an article in the *Yale Law Journal*, Reynolds maintained that there was a pervasive tendency in the 1970s and 1980s to discuss questions that were properly social-policy matters as if these were simply civil rights issues. Reynolds argued that "civil rights" were primarily protections that *individuals* possessed against government discrimination (emphasis ours). For Reynolds, this conception entailed a governmental commitment to "official color blindness and equal opportunity for all individuals" (Reynolds, 1984:998). Reynolds contended that in recent years the traditional understanding of civil rights had been submerged by a school of thought that focused on obtaining "group entitlements" for racial minorities and, regrettably, Reynolds suggested, this position was now being advanced most forcefully by the "same men and women who were in the vanguard of the great civil rights movement of the 1950s and 1960s" (Reynolds, 1984:996).

On the Supreme Court, Justice Rehnquist had been advancing a similar position through an interpretation of what the civil rights movement itself had for its goals. His dissent in *Weber* argued that the majority's endorsement of affirmative action went against the explicit language of the Civil Rights Act. In his opinion, Rehnquist returned to the debate in Congress during passage of the bill to argue that the legislative intent (what the majority called the "spirit of the bill") also prohibited private employers from utilizing the kind of race-conscious decision making that later became known as affirmative action. Rehnquist pointed to the response of the bill's supporters to questions posed by its southern opponents, such as Alabama senator John Sparkman, to contend that the congressional understanding of the Civil Rights Act was to enshrine color blindness as a policy and to avoid all hints of race-conscious remedies. He drew particular attention to Hubert Humphrey's proclamation that "nothing in the bill would permit any official or court to require any employer or labor union to give preferential treatment to any minority group."[55]

The position of the Reagan administration thus implied that the practice of civil rights in the 1980s was most threatened by the philosophy and policies associated with the African-American political community. Whereas most black leaders had come to assert that the promotion of economic interests in policies such as set-aside programs was the logical continuation of the civil rights vision, the Reagan administration asserted that the manner in which these interests were pursued jeopardized civil rights and undermined the philosophy of Martin Luther King, Jr. In the 1980s, it claimed, civil rights could only be protected by placing them against blacks or, at a minimum, against the expressed outlook of spokespersons for the African-American community. In the world in which the MX was a peacekeeper, civil rights was now the vehicle for blocking the political agenda of black elected officials.

Implementation of this perspective was vigorously pursued by the Solicitor General's Office. A number of accounts have pointed to the manner in which this relatively obscure but important part of the government was politicized in the Reagan years (see Caplan, 1988; Graham, 1989). It became less concerned with providing impartial assessments of the legal issues involved in cases in which the government had an interest and more dedicated to promoting the policy agenda of the administration in office. With affirmative action, the Solicitor General's Office, particularly under Charles Fried, pushed as hard as possible to convince the Court to issue decisions based on the principles enunciated by William Bradford Reynolds. A study of the Solicitor General's role has indicated that, in eight major civil rights cases from 1984 on, the Solicitor General's Office submitted five amicus briefs, all opposed to what previously had been considered the civil rights position (Graham, 1989:119). But in many instances, even where the Court voted with the administration's position, it did not adopt its entire logic.

One measure of *Croson*'s significance is that the Court has now come much closer to supporting the viewpoint of the Reagan administration about the meaning of civil rights. To be sure, the Court did not approve the extreme position of Reynolds and Scalia that civil rights applies only to individual, identified victims of discrimination. Yet for the traditional supporters of civil rights, this is small consolation. By adopting the strict-scrutiny standard to judge affirmative action policies, the Court is suggesting that these programs be viewed in the same light as the racial classifications that once constituted the structure of segregation in American history. It is small wonder that Mr. Fried would respond gleefully to the decision and tell a reporter from the *New York Times* that the Court's opinion "made his four years in the job 'worth it' even if it had accomplished nothing else" (quoted in Greenhouse, 1989).

The effort by Rehnquist, Reynolds, and members of the Reagan administration to define the true meaning of the civil rights movement is hypocritical to the extent that a number of people who never supported the goals of the movement now profess to have plumbed its true intent. As Randall Kennedy has noted, it was not "color blindness" that animated the marchers and freedom riders who put their lives at stake, but the concrete hope that the movement could improve the lives of black citizens in this country (Kennedy, 1986). Yet even when hypocrisy is not at issue and the disagreement about the meaning of civil rights is sincere, this interpretation of the movement's meaning tends to be based on a selective reading of history. The people who are fond of quoting King's statement about judging people by the content of their character rarely mention his criticisms of the American economy and his call in *Why We Can't Wait* for a Bill of Rights for the Disadvantaged that looks suspiciously similar to what is labeled affirmative action today. Moreover, contemporary conservatives who argue that equal opportunity for individuals is the essence of civil rights have to ignore the communitarian dimensions of King's liberalism that stressed the importance of personal service, social responsibility, and the development of a more humane economic system.

The effort to redefine the meaning of civil rights is a manifestation of the continuing historical battle to define the appropriate application of the Fifth and Fourteenth Amendments. For most of the nineteenth and for the first half of the twentieth centuries, these amendments were employed to justify discrimination and to limit the capacity of government to rectify it. For a few decades in the middle of this century, the civil rights movement was able to reinterpret their purpose in a manner that served the interests of the black community burdened by legalized segregation. In recent years, however, a new struggle is taking place in which certain members of the Court and powerful American conservatives are using the ideology of civil rights to overturn public policy in black-run cities. In Richmond, the conservative editorial page of its afternoon paper, the *Richmond News Leader,* gained national prominence in the 1950s for its defense of massive resistance. In 1989, the editorial page of the same paper salutes the *Croson* decision for taking a stand on civil rights that brings us "almost home—home to the nation Martin Luther King envisioned" ("Almost Home," 1989).

The Dilemma for Black Politicians

Judge Wilkinson's dissent when the court of appeals first considered *Richmond v. Croson* noted that the Supreme Court had not forbidden all remedial programs, but had instead flashed an "amber light." But by rejecting affirmative action as a routine policy, the Supreme Court's decision in *Croson* sent a more dramatic signal. To continue with Wilkinson's analogy, we might say that the Court has done more than flash an amber light or place a proceed-with-caution sign in front of black leadership; the Court has begun to dig a wide and deep trench across the very road on which black leaders were traveling. The decision ultimately raises serious questions for black elected officials about whether it is feasible and reasonable for it to continue to follow the path it has been taking.

The legal and political victories of the civil rights movement in the 1950s and 1960s were obviously major accomplishments. But it soon became evident that dismantling officially segregated education, removing legal barriers to voting, and refusing to uphold restrictive covenants in housing did not directly confront the basic fact of economic inequality. This was particularly true of the large urban areas of the Northeast and the Midwest, but it was evident elsewhere as well. Indeed, black officials had hardly been elected before scholars were noting that, at least with respect to economic progress, the mere fact of holding political power might be a relatively hollow victory. It soon became a commonplace to note that the fulfillment of the civil rights vision required corresponding gains in the economic arena.

The difficulty centered on discovering a strategy for promoting economic advance. Although leaders of the civil rights movement had frequently spoken of full employment and the need to eradicate poverty, they had never developed a well-developed outlook that was relevant to the conditions of urban America. In this regard, it exhibited weaknesses common to American liberal reformism. Moreover, by the end of the 1960s, much of the liberal-left was either beaten, exhausted, assassinated, or rent by internal strife. The Nixon administration came to office publicly espousing "black capitalism" as its answer to the economic difficulties of urban America, while privately endorsing the views of Edward Banfield that benign neglect of the cities might be the best possible stance for it to take. The need to address economic development was clearly not matched by a compelling and imaginative program for accomplishing it.

Black mayors devised a variety of ad hoc strategies to deal with the problem. In Gary, Indiana, Richard Hatcher attempted to use an aggressive tax policy to extract resources for development from the business community. In Detroit, Coleman Young pursued a more conciliatory approach. In Richmond, we have noted that the black-majority city council came to office voicing the rhetoric of change but pursued a strategy of economic development framed largely by existing business interests. It accepted the Rouse festival marketplace as the centerpiece of downtown development, but then demanded that a certain percentage of businesses in the mall be owned and operated by blacks.

Affirmative action set-aside policies might be best viewed in a context in which economic advance was considered to be a paramount necessity, but the means available to accomplish it were severely limited. To some degree, set-aside policies represented an unwritten compromise with the major corporate interests in American cities. Given the lack of control that they actually exercised over the economies of metropolitan America, black elected officials utilized the limited influence they did possess to funnel a modest amount of resources to their own constituencies. Banks, downtown insurance companies, and the major retailers eventually decided that, so long as their version of economic development was not threatened, they could certainly live with set-aside policies in city contracting. In Richmond and in many other cities, it has only been the one particular segment of business that has something to lose—the construction industry—that has raised objections to this kind of affirmative action program.

Black politicians have typically justified set-aside programs as part of their moral and political responsibility to remedy the discrimination that prevented their constituencies from obtaining their fair share of economic resources. The evidence presented in Richmond about the disparities in city contracting certainly validates this claim. At the same time, it should also be recognized that the development and continuation of economic set-aside programs also served the political interests of black elected officials. It enables them to demonstrate that "progress" is being made on the economic front, and that more progress will occur in the future. It also allows them to distinguish themselves in a favorable manner from more radical activists who do not demonstrate a capacity to "deliver the goods."

The decision in *Croson* should prompt a reconsideration of the options that are available to promote economic progress. On one hand, black elected officials might continue to pursue their civil rights agenda by tailoring their economic initiatives to the new standards imposed by *Croson*. They can possibly devise policies that will promote "goals" instead of "quotas." Municipal governments that engage in affirmative action will probably also perform much more extensive research than Richmond did to demonstrate the existence of discrimination. The initial remarks of officials in Atlanta and Chicago after the *Croson* decision suggested that this is a path that will be taken. In addition, black politicians will likely develop more sophisticated ways of tackling the problems posed by the historical discrimination in the construction industry. City governments, for example, might not set numerical quotas, but may attack the bonding requirements that have prevented minority businesses from becoming competitive.

On the other hand, the *Croson* decision might prompt black leadership to reconsider its strategy of carving out modest gains within an accommodationist mode. In this regard, two considerations are especially relevant. First, we have noted that during the Warren years, the courts were relatively sympathetic to efforts that promoted black equality. In the past two decades, however, the courts have adopted a much more ambivalent posture and, in fact, have been sympathetic to conservative challenges to the policies that black leadership implemented as a result of electoral success. Consequently, in the post-*Croson* era black leaders must decide to what extent they can continue to rely on the courts to press the policy concerns of African Americans.

Second, the dilemma for black leadership is magnified when it is recognized that electoral victories in urban areas have not been necessarily translated into widespread economic gains. In recent years, there has been a growing consensus among scholars that the aggregate state of black America is not improving, and that American metropolitan conditions are deteriorating. Scholars as diverse in their orientation as William Julius Wilson, Harold Cruse, and Adolph Reed, Jr., have pointed to the deindustrialization of black-dominated cities, the changing demographic structure of urban areas, and the daunting social problems that have become manifest. While these scholars do not all necessarily believe that affirmative action is misguided, they argue that it is not especially relevant to the most serious problems confronting the black community.

The solutions that have been proposed vary considerably. Wilson believes that we need a federal policy that will be directed at conditions in urban areas, particularly joblessness, without being race specific. Harold Cruse argues for a black pluralist perspective, in which the black leadership operates within the capitalist system to produce more gains for its own racial group and attempts to rebuild an independent economy and political party. Some neo-Marxists recommend the development of an explicitly class-based politics that recognizes capitalism as the enemy and attempts to foster a mass-based movement among its victims. There is one common theme contained in these diverse positions: namely the inability of the traditional liberal/civil rights approach to cope with the disintegration of the urban economy.

We will enter this debate ourselves in our book on set-asides and affirmative action. For now, however, we would note that the Court's treatment of affirmative action is a relatively narrow one, and that it does not place it within the context of the changing American economy. Yet it cannot be denied that a decision that claims that set-asides violate civil rights further restricts the capacity of black elected officials to address the economic problems of their constituents. *Croson* can thus only reinforce the need to discuss and debate alternatives to the traditional liberal approach.

Notes

1. City of Richmond v. J. A. Croson, U.S. Supreme Court, Number 87–998, cited in *United States LAW WEEK*, January 24, 1989, p. 4149.
2. *Ibid.*, p. 4155.
3. *Ibid.*
4. Robert McCloskey has noted that the Court's tendency to enlarge civil rights and civil liberties has always been "cross threaded by many doubts and pauses and vacillations" (McCloskey, 1972:4).

5. See Ely, 1980, especially Chapter 4, "Policing the Process of Representation: The Court as Referee," pp. 73–104. See Horowitz, 1977, for a skeptical view of the Court's capacity to make and to enforce social policy.

6. Our argument about the conservative use of civil rights discourse is an example of Kimberle Williams Crenshaw's claim that the "civil rights constituency cannot afford to view antidiscrimination doctrine as a permanent pronouncement of society's commitment to ending racial subordination. Rather, antidiscrimination law represents an ongoing ideological struggle in which the occasional winners harness the moral, coercive, consensual power of law." See Crenshaw, 1988:1, 335.

7. The political conditions in Richmond are described in Moeser and Dennis, 1982. Our description of the context of Richmond politics on the next two pages draws heavily upon their work.

8. The man who was the Richmond mayor at the time denied making this statement. Yet Moeser and Dennis provide corroboration of similar statements by him from three other witnesses in addition to the one who heard the statement quoted here.

9. This statistic is cited in District Judge Robert Merhige's opinion in *Croson v. Richmond*, United States District Court for the Eastern District of Virginia, Richmond Division, No. 84–0022–R, page 28. This opinion will be cited hereafter as Merhige, U.S. District Court.

10. *Fullilove v. Klutznick, Supreme Court Reporter,* 100A, p. 2758.

11. *Ibid.,* p. 2793.

12. Richmond City Ordinance, No. 82–294–270, p. 10.

13. Testimony in U.S. District Court revealed a disagreement between Croson and the city of Richmond about the sincerity of Croson's effort to contact minority firms. See Merhige, U.S. District Court, p. 6.

14. See Merhige, U.S. District Court, p. 9.

15. Ibid., pp. 16–17.

16. Ibid., p. 15. See also *Richmond v. Croson,* U.S. Supreme Court, Brief on Behalf of the Apellee, p. 11. This is cited herafter as U.S. Supreme Court, Croson's Brief.

17. The stance of the Associated General Contractors of America is described in Williams, 1989.

18. Merhige, U.S. District Court, pp. 26–27.

19. Ibid.

20. Ibid., p. 28.

21. Ibid., p. 29.

22. J. A. Croson v. Richmond, United States Court of Appeals for the Fourth Circuit, No. 85–1002, pp. 48–49.

23. Ibid., p. 60.

24. Ibid., p. 62.

25. Wendy Wygant v. Jackson Board of Education, *Supreme Court Reporter,* 106A, p. 1,845.

26. Ibid., p. 1848 and 1852.

27. J. A. Croson v. Richmond, United States Court of Appeals for the Fourth Circuit, No. 85–1041 (On Remand from the U.S. Supreme Court), p. 15.

28. Ibid, p. 11.

29. Richmond v. Croson, U.S. Supreme Court, 1988, Reply Brief of Appellant City of Richmond, pp. 3–7.

30. Richmond v. Croson, U.S. Supreme Court, No. 87–998, cited in *United States LAW WEEK,* January 24, 1989, pp. 4139–4143.

31. There are some obvious limitations to examining voting patterns of Supreme Court justices. As we have noted, justices may not agree on the issues raised by a particular case, and so their votes on any single case may not be properly comparable. In addition, scholars have sometimes argued that certain justices may sometimes vote with the winning side, not because they believe in the principle articulated but in order to tone down the majority's argument. We do not think that these limitations are decisive in examining the affirmative action cases because of the number of votes that have actually been cast and because of the number of highly individualized opinions that have been published.

32. Besides *Richmond v. Croson*, we use the nine other cases that are typically referred to in the scholarly literature as affirmative action cases in making our analysis. These are *University of California Regents v. Bakke* (76–811), *United Steelworkers of America v. Weber*, (78–432, 78–435, 78–436), *Fullilove v. Klutznick* (78–1007), *Memphis Fire Department v. Carl Stotts*, (82–206), *Wendy Wygant v. Jackson Board of Education* (84–1340), *Local 28 of the Sheet Metal Workers International Association v. Equal Employment Opportunity Commission* (84–1656), *Local Number 93, International Association of Firefighters v. City of Cleveland* (84–1999), *United States v. Paradise* (85–999) and *Johnson v. Transportation Agency, Sanata Clara County* (85–1129).

33. *City of Richmond v. J. A. Croson*, in the *United States LAW WEEK*, pp. 4157–4158.

34. This assertion was first employed by Blackmun in his opinion in *Bakke*. It was then quoted by Marshall in his opinion in *Fullilove*. See *The Supreme Court Reporter*, 100A, p. 2797.

35. Ibid. p. 2795.

36. Ibid., p. 2796.

37. Ibid., p. 2797.

38. White's willingness to overrule *Weber* is stated in his opinion in *Johnson v. Transportation Agency, Santa Clara, Supreme Court Reporter*, 107, p. 1465. ("I also would overrule *Weber*.")

39. An interesting discussion of the evolution of the "strict scrutiny" standard from a guideline used to promote a liberal, activist jurisprudence to the basis of a conservative attack on liberal policies such as affirmative action is found in Cox, 1987:305–7, 317–20. See also Schwartz, 1988: 66–67, 72–75, 85–87, and Baer's discussion of "suspect classifications" (1983:105–52).

40. This statement is in Justice Scalia's opinion in *Johnson v. Transportation Agency, Santa Clara, Supreme Court Reporter*, 107, p. 1466.

41. See Scalia's opinion in *Richmond v. Croson, The United States LAW WEEK*, p. 4,148. "Nothing prevents Richmond from according a contracting preference to identified victims of discrimination. While most of the beneficiaries might be black, neither the beneficiaries nor those disadvantaged by the preference would be identified *on the basis of their race*. In other words, far from justifying racial classification, identification of actual victims makes it less supportable than ever" (emphasis Scalia's).

42. White notes that he could still possibly accept relief for nonvictims in his opinion in *Local 28 of the Sheet Metal Workers' International Association v. Equal Employment Opportunity Commission, Supreme Court Reporter*, 106, p. 3,062. We argue below, however, that it is significant that White judged the affirmative action plan in this case unconstitutional.

43. This analysis appears in Greenhouse, 1989.

44. *Local 28 of the Sheet Metal Workers' International Association v. Equal Employment Opportunity Commission, Supreme Court Reporter,* 106, p. 3,029.
45. Ibid., p. 3062.
46. Ibid., p. 3063.
47. *Richmond v. Croson,* in *United States LAW WEEK,* January 24, 1989, pp. 4145–4146.
48. Ibid., p. 4146.
49. Tallying O'Connor's vote is complicated by the fact that her opinion in *Sheet Metal Workers v. E.E.O.C.* concurred in part with the plurality while not concurring in the judgement. We have counted this as a vote against an affirmative action plan not only because of the refusal to concur in judgement, but also because so much of the opinion is itself directed against the plurality's position.
50. *Johnson v. Transportation Agency, Santa Clara, Supreme Court Reporter,* 107, p. 1460.
51. "In the employment context, we have recognized that for certain entry level positions or positions requiring minimal training, statistical comparisons of the racial composition of an employer's workforce to the racial composition of the relevant population may be probative of a pattern of discrimination. . . . But where special qualifications are necessary, the relevant statistical pool *must be the number of minorities qualified to undertake the task"* (emphasis ours), *City of Richmond v. J. A. Croson,* in *The United States LAW WEEK,* p. 4141. The Court's use (or misuse) of statistics and the curious logic embodied in it could be the subject of an entire article on its own.
52. Ibid., p. 4136.
53. This perspective is argued in Caplan, 1988.
54. Responses by local officials suggesting that their programs might not be effected by the Court's decision are detailed in Tolchin, 1989.
55. *United Steelworkers of America v. Weber, Supreme Court Reporter,* 99, p. 2744.

References

"Almost Home." 1989. *The Richmond News Leader,* (25 January):14.

Baer, Judith A. 1983. *Equality under the Constitution: Reclaiming the 14th Amendment.* Ithaca: Cornell University Press.

Barker, Lucius. 1973. "Black Americans and the Burger Court: Implications for the Political System." *Washington University Law Quarterly,* 1973(4):766–68.

Barker, Twiley W., and Michael W. Combs. 1989. "Civil Rights and Liberties in the First Term of the Rehnquist Court: The Quest for Doctrines and Votes." *New Perspectives in American Politics: The National Political Science Review,* 1:31–57.

Caplan, Lincoln. 1988. *The Tenth Justice: The Solicitor General and the Rule of Law.* New York: Vintage Books.

Cox, Archibald. 1987. *The Court and the Constitution.* Boston: Houghton Mifflin.

Crenshaw, Kimberly Williams. 1988. "Race, Reform, and Retrenchment: Transformation and Legitimation in Antidiscrimination Law." *Harvard Law Review,* 101(7).

Ely, John Hart. 1980. *Democracy and Distrust.* Cambridge: Harvard University Press.

Graham, Barbara Luck. 1989. "Executive Authority, Constitutional Interpretation, and Civil Rights." *New Perspectives in American Politics: National Political Science Review*, 1:114–20.

Greenhouse, Linda. 1989. "Court Bars a Plan Set Up to Provide Jobs to Minorities." *The New York Times*, (24 January):A19.

Horowitz, Donald. 1977. *The Courts and Social Policy*. Washington, D.C.: Brookings Institution.

Kennedy, Randall. 1986. "Persuasion and Distrust: Comment on the Affirmative Action Debate." *Harvard Law Review*, 99(6).

McCloskey, Robert G. 1972. *The Modern Supreme Court*. Cambridge: Harvard University Press.

Moeser, John, and Rutledge Dennis. 1982. *The Politics of Annexation*. Cambridge: Schenkman Publishing.

Reynolds, William Bradford. 1984. "Individualism vs. Group Rights: The Legacy of Brown." *Yale Law Journal*, 93(983).

Richmond City Ordinance, No. 82–294–270, p. 10.

Schwartz, Bernard. 1988. *Behind Bakke: Affirmative Action and the Supreme Court*. New York: New York University Press.

Silver, Christopher. 1984. *Twentieth Century Richmond: Planning, Politics, and Race*. Knoxville: The University of Tennessee Press.

Tolchin, Martin. 1989. "Officials in Cities and States Vow to Continue Minority Contractor Programs." *The New York Times*, (25 January):A18.

Williams, Michael Paul. 1989. "Contractors Took Aim at 'Special Preference.'" *Richmond Times Dispatch*, (29 January):A1.

Political Responses
to Underemployment among
African Americans

Cedric Herring
Gloria Jones-Johnson

Texas A. & M. University
Iowa State University

This paper uses data from the National Survey of Black Americans to examine African Americans' reactions to being underemployed. It tests predictions derived from relative deprivation theory that the underemployed will be less likely than their adequately employed counterparts to participate in conventional political activities, but more likely to be supportive of protest activities and more likely to drop out of the political system. The results indicate that there are differences between the underemployed and those with adequate skill utilization; moreover, there are significant differences among those with different types of underemployment. The modes of political expression that these different groups use, however, do not conform to predictions from relative deprivation theory.

In order to realize their political interests, most citizens must become involved in the political process in some fashion or another. This need for involvement is, if anything, even greater for those actors from dominated groups, whose interests are not routinely served by the normal operation of the political process. On a number of occasions those confronted with economic adversity have mobilized in attempts to bring about political solutions to problems facing them (e.g., McAdam, 1982; Morris, 1984; Gamson, 1975; McCarthy and Zald, 1977). Yet, it is quite

An earlier version of this paper was presented at the 1989 Annual Meeting of the National Conference of Black Political Scientists in Baton Rouge, La. We would like to thank Katherine Tate, Frederick Wright, Lorn Foster, and the anonymous reviewers for their helpful comments and suggestions.

This research was funded, in part, by National Science Foundation Grant SES-8716642.

possible that hardships reduce, rather than enhance, the likelihood of participating politically. Indeed, while most observers have become accustomed to surges of social protest and activism from groups encountering economic disadvantage, they would not be very astonished to hear that these same groups often withdraw in defeat when confronted with policies that run counter to their preferences and needs.

Given this seeming paradox, it is unclear whether unpropitious circumstances mobilize or demobilize potential participants. The literature on political responses to such conditions provides little guidance. On the one hand, it provides support for the idea that being unemployed, impoverished, or unable to utilize one's skills leads to political acquiescence (e.g., Schlozman and Verba, 1979; Piven and Cloward, 1988). On the other hand, it points to occasions in which these very same predicaments lead to mobilization and activism (e.g., Piven and Cloward, 1977).

This paper examines the effects of one kind of economic adversity—underemployment—on the political behavior of African Americans. Using data from the National Survey of Black Americans, it estimates the relationship between types of underemployment on alternate forms of conventional political behavior and readiness to participate in forms of unconventional political behavior.

Underemployment and Political Behavior

Underemployment is a form of economic disadvantage that exists when employment or skill utilization is inadequate according to prevailing norms. A number of social scientists have hypothesized that various aspects of underemployment will have political consequences (e.g., Burris, 1983; Gorz, 1967; Bowles and Gintis, 1976). For example, Burris (1983) suggested that "overeducation" might be related to an affinity toward political leftism or increased levels of political alienation. Marsh (1985) put forth the idea that dramatic increases in unemployment would lead to massive protest. Piven and Cloward (1988) have suggested that low income reduces the tendency to register and vote. And, in perhaps the most extensive study of its kind, Schlozman and Verba (1979) found that unemployment creates psychological strain, leads to greater receptivity to government intervention in the economy, and produces lower levels of political involvement and activity. Still, multivariate empirical research on the numerous kinds of underemployment has not provided much in the way of demonstrating which forms of underemployment promote or hinder which modes of political expression. It is necessary, therefore, to go beyond the underemployment literature, per se, to find a theoretical framework in which to situate a study of political responses to underemployment.

One such framework that puts special emphasis on unconventional modes of political engagement is provided by relative deprivation (RD) theories (Morris and Herring, 1987). As a family of theories, these formulations suggest that political actors are oriented toward peace and the avoidance of conflict. They suggest that citizens will attempt to satisfy their values through peaceful competition, that is, electoral and interest-group politics, as opposed to violent or unruly means. "This disposition toward pacific politics can be blocked and diverted under specifiable and 'special' aberrant conditions" (Eckstein, 1980:142). Individuals resort to unconventional political activities when unusual conditions occur and disrupt their tendency toward "normal" politics. When, for example, people perceive great discrepancies between the power and privileges they possess and the amount they think they ought to have, they experience frustration (e.g., Gurr, 1970; Davies, 1962; Crosby, 1976). Although these theorists differ over the sources and forms of felt deprivation (e.g., progressive/J-curve, aspirational/V-curve, status, decremental, and egotistical) that are important in predicting political behavior, they basically agree that when frustrations and dissatisfactions become too intense, people will demand change (Gurr, 1970; Muller and Jukam, 1983). They also agree that frustrated political actors may become engaged in aggressive activities to remedy their feelings. These aggressive activities can include participation in unconventional politics. Conditions that supposedly increase the likelihood of unconventional political activities include high levels of status anxiety and monetary deprivation, as well as worsening socioeconomic conditions.

Thus, according to the relative deprivation perspective, experience with underemployment or underutilization of one's skills should lead to frustrations and subsequent involvement in unconventional political activities. More specifically, this perspective would predict that most forms of underemployment, especially those in which actors *feel* that they are not utilizing their talents or are not receiving adequate compensation for their efforts, should lead to increased support for protest politics. By the same token, such underemployment should lead to a rejection of conventional modes of political expression, either in the form of increases in the tendency to drop out or as decreases in the tendency to be involved in conventional politcal activities.

Other frameworks also make predictions about who will participate in political activities. For example, Campbell's (1960) "core-periphery" model of political participation suggests that some "core voters" are sufficiently interested in and motivated to participate in virtually all electoral contests. "Periphery voters," in contrast, participate in only high-stimulus elections where there is much media attention. And "chronic nonvoters" hardly ever participate in the electoral process. Although a number of studies have demonstrated that groups with higher socioeconomic statuses are more likely than their lower-status counterparts to participate in conventional politics (e.g., Rosenstone and Wolfinger, 1980; Milbrath and Goel, 1977; Verba, Nie, and Kim, 1978), sociodemographic variables do not do much in distinguishing between core voters and peripheral ones (e.g., Wolfinger, Rosenstone, and McIntosh, 1981). Moreover, the core-periphery framework, while relevant to understanding conventional political participation, does not clearly set forth predictions about who will turn to unconventional modes of participation and under what circumstances.

Another framework that presents clues as to how the underemployed might respond politically is the "political process model of collective action" (e.g., Gamson 1975; Tilly, 1978; McAdam, 1982). Proponents of this model suggest that some groups, because they are excluded from the polity, will lack low-cost, routine access to policymakers. As a consequence, such underdog groups must resort to noninstitutional means of political involvement if they are to realize their political interests. Rather than focusing on the psychological makeup and predispositions of individual actors, this perspective pays far more attention to the constraints that collective actors face. It focuses on the resources and "repertoires of contention" that contending groups have available to them. Nevertheless, while relevant to understanding involvement in social movements and other forms of unconventional collective action, this framework does not provide much in the way of predictions with respect to which individuals will participate in the formal political arena.

The relative deprivation formulation is complementary to the core-periphery model's theorizing with respect to predictions about conventional political behavior. It is antithetical in many respects to political-process predictions about unconventional political involvement. Unlike these other two perspectives, however, it does offer to the analyst the advantage of making theoretically informed predictions about both kinds of political activity.

Empirical research examining the effects of relative deprivation on political behavior has presented mixed results. Gurr and his associates (e.g., Gurr and Duvall, 1973) have found support for key propositions derived from various formulations of the theory. Others have suggested that relative deprivation is neither necessary (e.g., Tilly, 1978) nor sufficient (e.g., Muller, 1979) for explaining various types of political activity. Generally, however, when researchers have operationalized the concepts using individual-level data, as most analysts would agree is appropriate given the nature of the formulations, support for the theory has been lacking (e.g., Herring, 1989).

Nevertheless, some rather straightforward predictions about the political consequences of underemployment can be derived from RD theories: (1) the underemployed are more likely to endorse protest politics or to drop out of political activity altogether than they are to participate in conventional political activities, (2) experiencing underemployment decreases one's involvement in conventional modes of political involvement, (3) underemployment increases one's tendency to endorse protest politics, and (4) adequate skill utilization increases one's participation in conventional politics, but decreases one's inclination to endorse protest. The analysis below focuses on the relationship between underemployment and different modes of political behavior by testing these predictions consonant with relative deprivation explanations. The operationalizations of the key variables used in these formulations are presented first, however.

Methods

The data used in the analysis come from the 1979–80 National Survey of Black Americans. The sample for the survey was drawn according to a multistage area probability procedure, which was designed to ensure that every African-American household in the United States had an equal probability of being selected for the study. Within each household in the sample, one person age eighteen or older was randomly selected to be interviewed from among those eligible for the study. Only self-identified African-American citizens were eligible for the study. Professionally trained African-American interviewers carried out all interviewing. Data from 1,480 respondents who were part of the labor force[1] were used to operationalize discrete political behaviors, types of under-employment, education, family income, sex, marital status, political partisanship, region, urbanicity, and perceptions about changes in personal economic conditions.

Discrete Behavioral Reactions

As Milbrath (1981) points out, there are countless specific political behaviors in which people might engage. For example, some people might join "extremist" social movements, while others might write letters to their congressmen, read literature printed by alternative political parties, withhold their votes, campaign more fervently for those they believe will better serve their political interests, drop out of political activities altogether, or do something completely different. For the most part, such activities can be classified as conventional politics or unconventional politics (see, e.g., Muller, 1979). Modes of conventional political expression include such activities as registering to vote, voting, writing letters to congressmen, writing letters to editors of newspapers and magazines, and signing petitions.

Modes of unconventional political expression incude such activities as sit-ins, demonstrations, protests, and other collective efforts to bring about solutions to national or local problems. Of course, the economically disadvantaged can choose to participate in both conventional and unconventional politics, or they can choose to participate in neither type. In order to summarize (and simplify) these possibilities, one can cross-classify (non)participation in conventional politics by (non)participation in unconventional politics. This cross-classification yields four categories: (1) dropouts, (2) conventionalists, (3) dualists, and (4) protestors.

"Dropouts" participate in neither conventional politics nor unconventional politics.[2] They are identified not only by their failure to register and vote, but also by their lack of participation in such conventional political activities as writing letters to congressmen, writing letters to the editors of newspapers or magazines, and signing petitions. They also abstain from participation in such unconventional political activities as sit-ins, demonstrations, protests, and other collective action. "Conventionalists" continue to participate in the conventional political process (even when they feel that such participation is unfruitful). People in this category do not participate in unconventional politics, however. "Dualists" continue to participate in conventional politics. They are, however, willing to go outside the bounds of the formal political process and to engage in unconventional political actions as well. "Protestors" no longer seek results through conventional politics. Rather, they seek to effect desired results through such unconventional tactics as sit-ins, demonstrations, and other forms of collective protest and problem solving.

In order to determine respondents' appropriate categories, they were asked to respond to the following: (1) "Did you vote in the last presidential election?" (2) "Did you vote in any state or local election during the last year?" (3) "Have you ever worked for a political party or campaigned for a political candidate?" (4) "Have you ever called or written a public official about a concern or a problem?" and (5) "To gain equal rights in this country, black people should . . . one, work through the present system by voting and being active in politics [or] two, use demonstrations, boycotts, and other forms of group protest?"[3] Respondents who participated in any of the conventional political activities (1–4) and rejected use of group protest were coded as "conventionalists." Those who participated in any of the conventional activities and endorsed group protest were classified as "dualists." Those who participated in none of the conventional activities but endorsed group protest were defined as "protestors." And those who participated in none of the conventional activities nor endorsed group protest were classified as "dropouts." A decision matrix that specifies the process used in determining the appropriate classification for respondents is presented in Figure 1.

Underemployment

As mentioned previously, underemployment exists when workers' skills are not adequately utilized. Unlike unemployment, which can be defined in comparatively straightforward terms, underemployment, by definition, must be studied with reference to a normative standard. The gauge against which *under*employment is measured is not *optimal* utilization of talent or skill, but *adequate* employment. The Labor Utilization Framework (LUF) associated with Clogg and his associates (Clogg, 1979; Clogg and Shockey, 1984) and Sullivan and her associates (Sullivan, 1978; Sullivan and Mutchler, 1985) is the most widely used approach to measuring underemployment. While researchers working within this framework generally agree that it refers to underutilization of skills or talents of members of the work force, they have not always agreed on the types or number of types of underemployment. Sullivan (1978), for example, identifies three broad types: (1) inadequate hours of work, (2) insufficient income, and (3) incongruous occupation and skills. Clogg (1979) identifies five forms of underemployment: (1) sub-unemployment, (2) unemployment, (3) part-time (un)employment, (4) underemployment by low income, and (5) mismatch or invisible underemployment. While Clogg and Sullivan (1983) also employed a five-category scheme, Clogg, Sullivan, and Mutchler (1986) identified as many as nine mutually exclusive forms of labor underutilization that can be thought of as underemployment. The strategy here will be to use a modified verison of the LUF that identifies six types of underemployment and a seventh, residual category that is identified as "adequate" labor utilization.

The categories are as follows: (1) the *sub-unemployed* are those would-be workers who are unemployed but have the additional distinction of being discouraged to the point of having given up searching for employment; (2) the *unemployed* are those workers who have quit, been laid off, fired, or dismissed from their jobs but who continue to pursue suitable employment; (3) the *part-time (un)employed* are underemployed by reason of low work hours in the sense that they would prefer to be employed in full-time jobs, but have their employment restricted (involuntarily) to less than forty hours per week; (4) the *intermittently (un)employed* are those workers with temporary, seasonal, or other full-time jobs that involve frequent layoffs; (5) the *low-income* (poverty-wage) underemployed

**Figure 1. Decision Matrix for the Determination
of R's Mode of Political Expression**

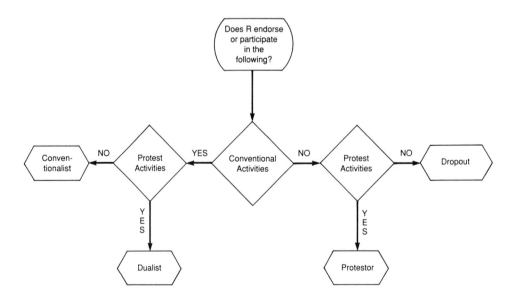

are those workers with full-time employment who, nevertheless, do not receive wages sufficient to raise their personal incomes above 1.25 times the poverty level ($3,619 in 1979); (6) those with *mismatch* (or invisible) underemployment are workers who, having no other forms of underemployment, feel that they have the skills and abilities necessary for better jobs than the ones in which they are currently employed; and (7) the residual category consists of all others in the labor force whose skills and talents are *adequately utilized.* Consistent with the LUF, the underemployment types are ordered in terms of "severity," and respondents are hierarchically assigned memberships in the appropriate categories, such that membership in one category precludes membership in all others. For multivariate analysis, the categories have been dummy-variable coded. A decision matrix that specifies the process used in determining the appropriate classification for respondents is presented in Figure 2.

A departure from the LUF should be noted. Our operationalization, because it is based on survey data, can rely on respondents' own assessments of whether their skills are underutilized (i.e., whether they have mismatch underemployment). This subjective assessment of (mismatch) underemployment is consistent with the notion of relative deprivation.[4]

Control Variables: Some Correlates of Political Participation

Education is the amount of formal schooling or the level of credentialing a person receives. "Less than a grade-school education" was coded 4, "less than high-school education" was assigned a score of 10, "high school or equivalent" was coded 12, "some college" was classified as 14, and "college graduate or more" was given a score of 18.

Family Income is the amount of money from all sources (e.g., wages, profits, and interest) that all members of the respondent's family earned in 1978. Each respondent was assigned a score that corresponded to the midpoint of his or her income category. A Pareto curve estimate was used to derive midpoints for respondents whose incomes fell in the highest, open-ended income categories. Codes ranged from 0 through 43333.

Sex was divided between males and females. Respondents were assigned the score of 0 if they were *male,* and 1 if they were *female.*

Marital Status was dichotomized between those who were *married* or cohabitating (coded 1) and those who were not married (coded 0).

For the urbanicity variable, respondents were categorized as *urban* (1) if they lived in self-representing urban areas. They were coded 0 (nonurban) if they did not.

Political partisanship was split between *Democrats* (coded 1) and non-Democrats (coded 0).

Region of current residence was collapsed into two categories: *South* and non-South. Respondents were coded 1 (South) if they lived in Alabama, Arkansas, Delaware, the District of Columbia, Florida, Georgia, Kentucky, Louisiana, Maryland, Mississippi, North Carolina, Okla-

Figure 2. Decision Matrix for the Determination of R's Underemployment Status

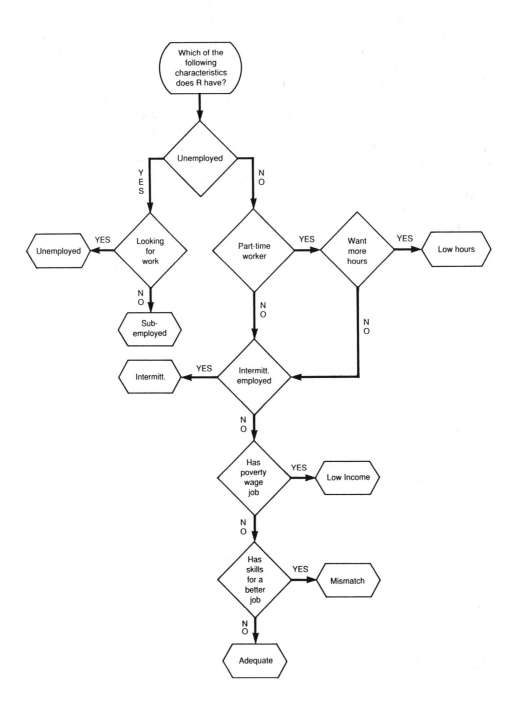

homa, South Carolina, Tennessee, Texas, Virginia, or West Virginia. They were coded 0 (non-South) if they lived in any other state.

Respondents were also asked whether they belonged to any organizations or took part in any activities that represent the interests and viewpoints of African-American people. Those who said that they did *Belong* to such organizations were coded 1. Others were coded 0.

And finally, respondents were asked whether they and their families were better off or *Worse Off* financially at the time of their interviews than they had been the year before. Those who reported that they were worse off were coded 1. Those who were not worse off were coded 0.

Data Analysis and Results

As mentioned previously, there are still disputes about just how the underemployed react to their circumstances. Figure 3 presents evidence that suggests that as a group, adequately employed African Americans do differ in terms of their modes of political expression from most of those who are underemployed. It shows that, generally, a lower percentage of those with adequate skill utilization drop out of the political system than do those who are underemployed. In particular, about one out of four (26 percent) of those with adequate employment are political dropouts. This compares with 42 percent of those who are sub-unemployed, 37 percent of the unemployed, 42 percent of those employed only part-time, 38 percent of those with poverty-level incomes, and 31 percent of those unemployed intermittently. Those workers with mismatch underemployment are, however, *less* likely than the adequately employed to be political dropouts, as 20 percent of this group drops out politically.

About 9 percent of the part-time underemployed, poverty-level workers, and the intermittently unemployed endorse the sole use of protest. This is in contrast to 5 percent of the adequately employed. It should be noted, however, that not all forms of underemployment have the predicted effect on support for protest. For example, less than 5 percent of the unemployed and the mismatch underemployed support resorting to protest activity. Similar patterns emerge with respect to those who engage in political dualism. The proportion of those with adequate employment who engage in political dualism (6 percent) falls within the extremes. Less than 5 percent of the part-time underemployed and poverty-wage workers are dualists, but roughly 12 percent of the unemployed, the intermittently unemployed, and the mismatch underemployed are dualists. There are statistically significant differences among the categories at $p < .01$ ($\chi^2 = 86.3$, $df = 18$). It should be noted, however, that the relative frequencies of the different types of underemployment do not support the relative deprivation theory, as for all types of underemployment, conventional political responses are more prevalent than dropping out or endorsing protest. This is counter to what relative deprivation theory predicts.

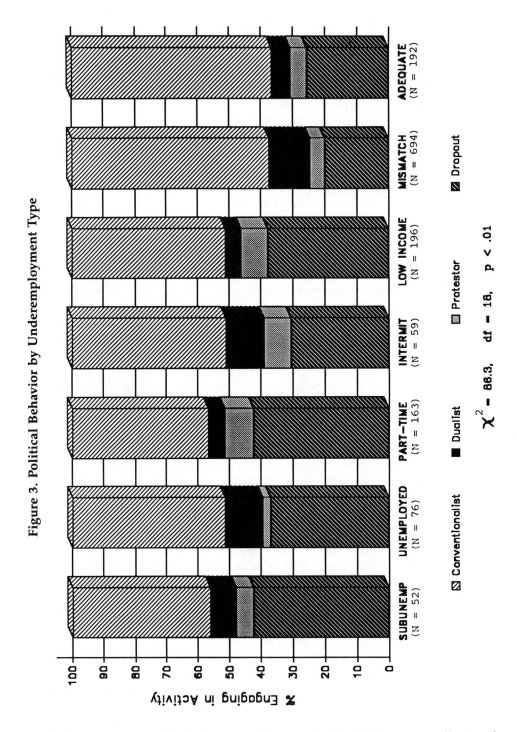

Figure 3. Political Behavior by Underemployment Type

Table 1 presents a logistic regression analysis of the gross effects of underemployment on the modes of political expression among African

Americans.[5] Sub-unemployment, unemployment, low hours, low in come, intermittent employment, and mismatch underemployment are contrasted to adequate employment for each of the types of political expression. Generally, this table shows that the effects of underemployment on political behavior are small but statistically significant. Specifically, consistent with relative deprivation theory is the finding that the underemployed are less likely than the adequately employed to engage in conventional political activities. (Again, the mismatch underemployed appear to be an exception on this.) While these factors account for less than 4 percent of the variance, the overall model is statistically significant at $p < .01$.

With respect to support for protest activities, Table 1 shows that the underemployed do not differ significantly from the adequately employed. This outcome is counter to what relative deprivation theory predicts. Moreover, the overall model explains about 1 percent of the variance and does not achieve statistical significance.

The gross effects of underemployment on political dualism are also presented in Table 1. Workers with mismatch underemployment appear to be more likely than the adequately employed to pursue this type of political involvement. Others among the underemployed are not significantly different from the satisfactorily employed. The overall model does not attain statistical significance, and it helps explain less than 1 percent of the variance.

The final relationship in Table 1 involves underemployment and dropping out politically. Consistent with the expectations of relative depriva-

Table 1. Gross Effects of Underemployment on African Americans' Modes of Political Expression

Independent Variables	Conventionalist	Protestor	Dualist	Dropout
Constant	5.346^c	3.375^c	3.422^c	4.342^c
Sub-unemployed	$-.491^b$	.051	.152	$.464^b$
Unemployed	$-.379^b$	-.313	.395	$.322^b$
Part-time	$-.508^c$	.297	-.076	$.465^b$
Intermittent	$-.367^b$	.251	.396	.148
Low income	$-.372^c$	.264	-.108	$.346^c$
Mismatch	-.019	-.044	$.429^c$	$-.188^b$
R^2 Analog[a]	$.037^c$	.012	.008	$.037^c$
N	1432	1432	1432	1432

Note: Coefficients are unstandardized logistic regression coefficients. A constant of 5 has been added to each intercept (constant) term. For the dummy (binary) variable coefficients, significance levels refer to the difference between the omitted dummy variable category and the coefficient for the given category.

[a]The R^2 Analog statistic is the proportion of reduction in a baseline model X^2 (a model fitting only the constant term) attributable to the model shown. It is calculated as follows:

R^2 = (Baseline model X^2 - Selected model X^2)/Baseline model X^2.

[b]$p < .05$
[c]$p < .01$

tion theory is the general finding that underemployed workers are significantly more likely than those with sufficient employment to cease political involvement altogether. There do appear to be a couple of exceptions, however. The intermittently employed are not significantly different from the adequately employed, and those with mismatch underemployment appear to be *less* likely than the adequately employed to drop out politically. Again the overall model accounts for less than 4 percent of the variance, but achieves statistical significance at $p < .01$.

The gross effects of underemployment on the political participation of African Americans are small, and at times, they appear to be in the opposite direction from what relative deprivation theory anticipates. It is, however, possible that these effects are masked by variables left out of the models. Table 2 presents the effects of the different forms of underemployment on political behavior, net of a host of sociodemographic variables and the perception that economic conditions are worsening.

Table 2 suggests, for the most part, that the effects of underemployment on political behavior are attenuated by the inclusion of other correlates of political behavior. In particular, with respect to dropping out and engaging in political dualism, all of the significant differences between the forms of underemployment and adequate employment vanish when other factors are held constant. Virtually the same pattern emerges with respect to endorsing protest activities and dropping out altogether. The only respondents who are more likely than the adequately employed to endorse protest or to drop out are those who work on a part-time basis. Such results do not provide much in the way of support for the hypotheses derived from relative deprivation theory.

The only mode of political expression that conforms to the expectations of the relative deprivation formulation is that of conventional activities. Net of the correlates of political behavior, the underemployed remain less likely than adequately employed workers to participate in orthodox political activities. Even in this model, however, not all kinds of underemployment have effects on conventional political behavior that differ significantly from the effects of having sufficient employment. In particular, the intermittently unemployed and the mismatch underemployed do not appear to be significantly different from the adequately employed in their inclinations toward conventional political behavior. Again, while there are differences between the underemployed and their adequately employed counterparts, not much support is provided for relative deprivation explanations.

Discussion

This research has sought to determine what effect, if any, underemployment has on the political participation of African Americans. In doing so, it used insights from relative deprivation theory not only to ask whether the underemployed behave differently from their adequately employed counterparts, but it also attempted to shed light on those ele-

Table 2. The Net Effects of Underemployment on African Americans' Modes of Political Expression

Independent Variables	Conventionalist	Protestor	Dualist	Dropout
Sub-unemployed	-.402[b]	.280	.258	.261
Unemployed	-.321[b]	-.039	.311	.261
Part-time	-.493	.561[b]	-.054	.379[b]
Intermittent	-.161	.401	.227	-.030
Low income	-.247[b]	.418	-.066	.178
Mismatch	-.126	.252	.281	-.059
Education	.011	-.008	.044[c]	-.031[c]
Family income	.000	.000	.000	-.000
Female	.166	-.122	-.110	-.131
Married	.104	-.089	-.043	-.041
Democrat	.737[c]	-.603[c]	.130	-.684
Belong	.400[c]	.367[b]	.128	-.684[c]
Urban	-.034	.026	.117	-.003
South	-.194	-.030	-.200[b]	.339[c]
Worse off	.042	-.138	.129	-.074
R^2 Analog[a]	.153[c]	.214[c]	.132[c]	.163[c]
N	1240	1240	1240	1240

Note: Coefficients are unstandardized logistic regression coefficients. A constant of 5 has been added to each intercept (constant) term. For the dummy (binary) variable coefficients, significance levels refer to the difference between the omitted dummy variable category and the coefficient for the given category.

[a]The R^2 Analog statistic is the proportion of reduction in a baseline model X^2 (a model fitting only the constant term) attributable to the model shown. It is calculated as follows:

$$R^2 = (\text{Baseline model } X^2 - \text{Selected model } X^2)/\text{Baseline model } X^2.$$

[b]p< .05
[c]p< .01

ments that lead to differential reactions among those with different kinds of underemployment.

It is clear from the foregoing analysis that, in terms of their modes of political expression, there are statistically significant differences between the adequately employed and those who are not so fortunate. In other words, underemployment does, indeed, have political consequences. It is also clear from the analysis that there are gross differences among the underemployed that lead them to have different reactions to their circumstances. However, relative deprivation predictions about the relative frequency of different kinds of political activity were not borne out, as the underemployed are more likely to continue participating in the political system than they are to drop out, and they are more likely to participate in the formal process than they are to endorse protest. In other words, not only do the underemployed vary from the adequately employed, but also they vary substantially among themselves; yet, their

variations do not conform strictly to the expectations of relative deprivation formulations.

Relative deprivation theory, while relevant to understanding the nature of underemployment, does not appear particularly useful for understanding the *responses* to such economic disadvantage. Mobilization of
the underemployed for participation in both conventional and protest
politics apparently requires more than a disadvantaged economic position.

The political-process perspective on collective action points out that
some (especially underdog) political challengers are denied routine access to policymakers. These actors, they suggest, will use those tactics
that they believe will be most likely to produce the kinds of political
policies they favor, even if such tactics are disruptive, unruly, or unconventional. In order to realize their interests, therefore, they resort to actions that fall outside the formal political process. Decisions to pursue
political interests via protest, riots, strikes, or even brick throwing rather
than through the ballot box have more to do with tactical choices, resource availability, repertoires of contention, structural arrangements,

**Table 3. Net Differences Among Underemployed African Americans in
Modes of Political Expression**

Independent Variables	Conventionalist	Protestor	Dualist	Dropout
Sub-unemployed	-.283	.080	-.052	.319
Unemployed	-.180	-.295	.013	.306[b]
Part-time	-.369[c]	.320	-.346[b]	.437[c]
Intermittent	-.035	.149	-.060	.031
Low income	-.116	.179	-.370[b]	.231[b]
Education	.010	.001	.041[b]	-.033[c]
Family income	.000	.000	.000	.000
Female	.199[c]	-.151	-.151	-.132
Married	.214[c]	-.144	-.084	-.127
Democrat	.741[c]	-.606[c]	.158	-.686[c]
Belong	.417[c]	-.368[b]	.131	-.624[c]
Urban	-.053	.004	.109	.016
South	-.162[b]	-.015	-.222[b]	.314[c]
Worse off	.116	-.119	-.008	-.112
R^2 Analog[a]	.146[c]	.213[c]	.144[c]	.150[c]
N	1277	1277	1277	1277

Note: Coefficients are unstandardized logistic regression
coefficients. A constant of 5 has been added to each intercept
(constant) term. For the dummy (binary) variable coefficients,
significance levels refer to the difference between the omitted dummy
variable category and the coefficient for the given category.

[a]The R^2 Analog statistic is the proportion of reduction in a baseline
model X^2 (a model fitting only the constant term) attributable to the
model shown. It is calculated as follows:

$$R^2 = (\text{Baseline model } X^2 - \text{Selected model } X^2)/\text{Baseline model } X^2.$$

[b]p< .05
[c]p< .01

and other objective conditions than emotions, psychological predispositions, or personality traits.

Because the underemployed generally are not in positions to make demands by disrupting or threatening to disrupt the normal operation of
the system, it is a bit credulous to expect that they will realize their political interests through mass protest alone. Also, because some types of
underemployment appear to reduce participation through conventional
means, the underemployed are not likely to have their policy preferences
translated into public policy, as their status makes them even more marginal to the operation of the polity.

In the future, analysts who wish to sort out the effects of underemployment on the political participation of African Americans will need to
consider the options available to such citizens. If economic opportunities
continue to contract and African-American workers become increasingly
marginalized, understanding such issues will become even more crucial.

Notes

1. This study excludes from the analysis respondents who were retirees, house-
   wives, and students, as they are not ordinarily considered regular members
   of the labor force.
2. Because the data used in this study are cross-sectional, it is not possible to
   disentangle the temporal order of "dropping out" and being underemployed. "Drop outs," therefore, include not only those respondents who
   once participated in conventional political activities or supported protest activities but subsequently decided not to do so, but this category also includes
   those people who have *never* participated in conventional politics and who
   have never supported protest politics.
3. Obviously the authors would prefer to have data on actual participation in
   protest politics rather than indicators of support for or endorsement of such
   activities. Unfortunately, no such indicators were available in this data set.
4. Because mismatch underemployment comes closest to the kind of subjective
   interpretation of one's conditions that is consistent with the relative deprivation framework, it should most clearly demonstrate the pattern of political
   behaviors hypothesized by the relative deprivation approach.
5. Logistic regression analysis, a technique appropriate when using discrete dependent variables, is fairly analogous to Ordinary Least Squares (OLS) regression analysis. Unlike OLS regression analysis, however, the "dependent
   variable" is the probability that members of a population have a particular
   combination of characteristics. More precisely, this technique models log
   odds; that is, the natural logarithm of the ratio of two probabilities. Using
   this technique, an analyst can isolate the relationship between a discrete dependent variable and an independent factor of interest while holding constant the effects of other, possibly confounding variables.

   Logistic regression models yield parameter estimates for the log of the
   odds of the expected cell frequencies for the dependent variable. Log odds
   coefficients of 0 indicate that no relationship exists; coefficients less than 0
   indicate that an inverse relationship exists; and coefficients greater than 0
   indicate direct covariation between variables.

References

Bowles, Samuel, and Herbert Gintis. 1976. *Schooling in Capitalist America*. New York: Basic Books.

Burris, Val. 1983. "The Social and Political Consequences of Overeducation." *American Sociological Review*, 48:454–67.

Campbell, Angus. 1960. "Surge and Decline: A Study of Electoral Change." *Public Opinion Quarterly*, 24:397–418.

Clogg, Clifford C. 1979. *Measuring Underemployment: Demographic Indicators for the United States*. New York: Academic Press.

Clogg, Clifford C., and James W. Shockey. 1984. "Mismatch Between Occupation and Schooling: A Prevalence Measure, Recent Trends, and Demographic Analysis." *Demography*, 21:235–57.

Clogg, Clifford C., and Teresa A. Sullivan. 1983. "Demographic Composition and Underemployment Trends, 1969–1980." *Social Indicators Research*, 12:117–52.

Clogg, Clifford C., Teresa A. Sullivan, and Jan E. Mutchler. 1986. "Measuring Underemployment and Inequality in the Work Force." *Social Indicators Research*, 18:375–93.

Crosby, Faye. 1976. "A Model of Egotistical Relative Deprivation." *Psychological Review*, 83:85–113.

Davies, James C. 1962. "Toward a Theory of Revolution." *American Sociological Review*, 27:5–19.

Eckstein, Harry. 1980. "Theoretical Approaches to Explaining Collective Political Violence." Pp. 135–66 in T. R. Gurr, ed., *Handbook of Political Conflict: Theory and Research*. New York: Free Press.

Gamson, William A. 1975. *Strategy of Social Protest*. Homewood, Ill.: Dorsey Press.

Gorz, André. 1967. *Strategy for Labor*. Boston: Beacon Press.

Gurr, Ted R. 1970. *Why Men Rebel*. Princeton, N.J.: Princeton University Press.

Gurr, Ted R., and Raymond Duvall. 1973. "Civil Conflict in the 1960s: A Reciprocal Theoretical System with Parameter Estimates." *Comparative Political Studies*, 6:135–69.

Herring, Cedric. 1989. "Acquiescence or Activism?: Political Behavior among the Politically Alienated." *Political Psychology*, 10:135–53.

Marsh, Catherine. 1985. "Political Responses to Unemployment in Britain." Paper presented at the annual meeting of the American Sociological Association in Washington, D.C.

McAdam, Doug. 1982. *Political Process and the Development of Black Insurgency, 1930–1970*. Chicago: University of Chicago Press.

McCarthy, John D., and Mayer N. Zald. 1977. "Resource Mobilization in Social Movements: A Partial Theory." *American Journal of Sociology*, 82:1,212–39.

Milbrath, Lester W. 1981. "Political participation." *Handbook of Political Behavior*, 4:197–240.

Milbrath, Lester W., and M. L. Goel. 1977. *Political Participation*. 2nd ed. Chicago: Rand McNally.

Morris, Aldon. 1984. *Origins of the Civil Rights Movement*. New York: Free Press.

Morris, Aldon D., and Cedric Herring. 1987. "Theory and Research in Social Movements." *Annual Review of Political Science*, 2:137–93.

Muller, Edward N. 1979. *Aggressive Political Participation*. Princeton: Princeton University Press.

Muller, Edward N., and Thomas O. Jukam. 1983. "Discontent and Aggressive Political Participation." *British Journal of Political Science*, 13:159–79.

Muller, Edward N., Thomas O. Jukam, and Mark A. Seligson. 1982. "Diffuse Political Support and Anti-System Political Behavior: A Comparative Analysis." *American Journal of Political Science*, 26:240–64.

Piven, Frances F., and Richard A. Cloward. 1977. *Poor People's Movements: Why They Succeed, How They Fail*. New York: Vintage.

———. 1988. *Why Americans Don't Vote*. New York: Pantheon.

Rosenstone, Steven J., and Raymond E. Wolfinger. 1980. *Who Votes?* New Haven: Yale University Press.

Schlozman, Kay Lehman, and Sidney Verba. 1979. *Injury to Insult: Unemployment, Class, and Political Response*. Cambridge: Harvard University Press.

Sullivan, Teresa A. 1978. *Marginal Workers, Marginal Jobs*. Austin, Tex.: University of Texas Press.

Sullivan, Teresa A., and Jan E. Mutchler. 1985. "Equal Pay or Equal Work?: The Implications of Underemployment for Comparable Worth Studies." *Research in the Sociology of Work*, 3:175–92.

Tilly, Charles. 1978. *From Mobilization to Revolution*. Reading, Mass.: Addison-Wesley Publishing Co.

Verba, Sidney, Norman Nie, and Jae O. Kim. 1978. *Participation and Political Equality: A Seven-Nation Comparison*. Cambridge: Cambridge University Press.

Wolfinger, Raymond E., Steven J. Rosenstone, and R. A. McIntosh. 1981. "Presidential and Congressional Voters Compared." *American Politics Quarterly*, 9:245–56.

The Politics of Desegregation in Higher Education: Analysis of Adams States Progress

Joseph "Pete" Silver, Sr.
Rodney Dennis

Georgia State Board of Regents
American University

As a rule, traditionally white institutions (TWIs) have overlooked black scholars in selecting who will be a part of their faculty work force. Data show that few black scholars are hired and even fewer are being retained at TWIs. Legislative and judicial intervention have challenged this practice, but the extent to which this intervention has brought about change is open for debate. The Adams *case, one of the most contemporary attempts by the courts to force TWIs to integrate their work forces, gave specific directives relative to strategies, goals, and time-tables. This article examines the progress of nine of the* Adams *states in terms of recruitment, promotion, and retention of black faculty.*

The underrepresentation of black scholars on the faculties of the nation's colleges and universities remains a serious problem in our pluralistic society. In its 1986 *Status Report on Minorities in Higher Education*, the American Council on Education reported black faculty appointments actually declined in the period from 1977 to 1983. During this period, full-time faculty positions held by blacks decreased from 19,675 (4.4 percent) to 18,827 (4 percent), a loss of 4.3 percent (American Council on Education, 1986).

In predominantly white institutions, it is well documented that minorities make up only a tiny portion of the regular teaching faculty. Bok (1982) notes that Asian Americans are represented on university faculties in numbers that equal or exceed their percentage in the population. However, blacks are represented in proportions far lower than their percentage in the total population or in the student bodies of these institutions. Estimates of the number of black faculty in traditionally white institutions (TWIs) are difficult to obtain with any high degree of accuracy, and the data that are available tend not to be very current. Scott-Jones and Harvey (1985) cite a *Wall Street Journal* estimate that blacks constitute only 1 percent of the faculty at TWIs. The American Council on Education (1986) reported more recently that overall representation of black faculty at TWIs is 2.3 percent. Pruitt's (1982) research indicated that black faculty made up 2.9 percent of the faculty of TWIs in eight of the *Adams* states in 1975.[1]

The factors that contribute to the tiny proportion of black faculty in TWIs are multilayered and long-standing. Historical, political, legal, psychosocial, and socioeconomic factors all contribute to the current dearth of black scholars in higher education. The degree to which the small numbers of black professors is symptomatic of a scarce supply or of bias in hiring practices is not clear, and subject to debate. Bok (1982) argues that qualified minority candidates are not ignored or overlooked. Rather, only 3 percent of the nation's Ph.D.'s are black, thus limiting the supply of potential candidates. Bok further contends that black Ph.D.'s were commanding higher average salaries than their white counterparts with comparable experience and publication records. A different view is presented in the report of the U.S. Equal Employment Opportunity Commission (1981). This report found that black faculty had a lower median salary than white faculty. This finding could be an artifact of the concentration of minority faculty in lower ranks, an inequity reported by Fleming, Gill, and Swinton (1978) and the U.S. Department of Health, Education, and Welfare (1978).

The result of this pattern of hiring is that black scholars are forced to seek employment opportunities at predominantly black colleges and universities or elsewhere, effectively causing a dual system of education. Historically, a dual system of education had been the rule rather than the exception. For many years, Jim Crow laws and judicial decisions such as the *Civil Rights Cases of 1883* and *Plessy v. Ferguson* have perpetuated the segregation of public facilities, including education institutions.

The *Brown v. Board of Education* decision, which made racial segregation in public schools unconstitutional, contributed significantly to increasing access for minorities. However, the *Brown* decision did not settle the question concerning segregated facilities. The major issue in that case was the provision of access to public primary and secondary education for all, regardless of race or national origin. Realistically, the decision had little immediate impact on the integration of public schools. Nor did the *Brown* decision address the issue of who would teach students. Accordingly, the racial composition of school and college faculties underwent little or no change. Legislation following the *Brown* decision did, however, begin to address this issue. One such piece of legislation was the Civil Rights Act of 1964, specifically Title VI. This act provided a potent weapon to combat discrimination in hiring practices. It has been used in attempts to eliminate barriers that have prevented black scholars from joining faculties at TWIs.

One of the most contemporary legal developments in the ongoing efforts to integrate faculties at TWIs is the *Adams v. Richardson* case. In 1970, the National Association for the Advancement of Colored People (NAACP) Legal Defense and Educational Fund sued the then Department of Health, Education, and Welfare (HEW) to force ten states to desegregate their dual systems of higher education. These states were Arkansas, Florida, Georgia, Louisiana, Maryland, Mississippi, North Carolina, Oklahoma, Pennsylvania, and Virginia. Black faculty percentages increased in TWIs in the early part of the 1970s. However, the extent to which the *Adams* case caused this increase is debatable. In the mid-1970s there was a noticeable decrease in the percentage of black faculty at TWIs. The American Council on Education (1986) reports that black participation in faculty positions between 1977 and 1983 declined in all but seven *Adams* states. On the other hand, white student and faculty participation in traditionally black public institutions increased during that period.

After the initial suit was filed in 1970, Judge John Pratt ruled in 1973 that HEW should begin enforcement proceedings against states that did not submit acceptable plans for their systems of higher education. In 1978, since many of the states were not making progress on their own, Judge Pratt ordered HEW to develop the criteria for the new desegregation plans. A year later, when HEW was reorganized, the newly created Department of Education was given responsibility for overseeing the case. In 1980, Judge Pratt ordered the Department of Education to incude eight additional states as a party to the suit. They were Alabama, Delaware, Kentucky, Missouri, Ohio, South Carolina, Texas, and West Virginia. In all, a total of eighteen states were required to submit acceptable plans or face the cutoff of all federal funds for higher education.

In 1983 the courts renewed efforts aimed at increasing the number of black faculty at TWIs. Specifically, TWIs were required to set goals for black student enrollment and graduation rates and specific goals relative to attracting black faculty. These institutions were also required to set timetables and develop strategies to achieve these goals. Additionally, in an effort to monitor the progress or lack of progress being made by the TWIs, the court imposed a reporting requirement.

Many of the plans that were submitted by the states involved in the case expired in 1985, and four years later the court ruled that the majority of these states were in compliance with Title VI of the Civil Rights Act of 1964. Yet, the astute observer should question whether or not blacks have really gained access to faculty positions at TWIs. At any rate, Judge Pratt dismissed the *Adams* case in 1987. His rationale was that under the 1984 Supreme Court ruling in the *Allen v. Wright* case, the NAACP Legal Defense Fund no longer had a legal standing to continue the *Adams* case. Judge Pratt further stated that two of his past orders concerning timetables and the process of resolving bias complaints violated the doctrine of separation of powers and intruded on the functions of the executive branch.

After all has been said and done relative to the *Adams* case, we do know that during the period of the litigation, some blacks were hired at TWIs. The questions which resulted are: Who are the black faculty at TWIs in the *Adams* states? How did they get there? Have their numbers increased, decreased, or remained constant as a result of the *Adams* litigation? The intent of this article is to provide answers to these questions. Specifically, there are three objectives of this article: (1) to determine the extent of the presence of black faculty in TWIs in selected *Adams* states, (2) to probe significant factors that appear to be related to their entry into the academy, and (3) to construct an accurate profile of the current black professoriate in these TWIs in the selected *Adams* states. This research has special importance at this time because the employment gains that were made in the 1970s appear to be eroding in the 1980s.

Research Problem

The continued difficulty in substantially increasing minority faculty representation is illustrated in the following excerpt from the *Chronicle of Higher Education* discussing the effectiveness of the *Adams* ruling:

> In hiring, predominantly white colleges and universities have generally done better at recruiting black administrators than at recruiting black faculty members. They have also fared better at recruiting blacks for positions requiring master's degrees, rather than those requiring a doctoral degree. In the 1985–86 academic years, at Virginia's predominantly white colleges and universities, blacks occupied 6.7 percent of the administrative positions for which a Ph.D. was required and 10.8 percent of those requiring the master's, but only 2.15 percent of Ph.D. faculty positions and 5.1 percent of those requiring the master's.
>
> In some states, several public colleges have only one or two black faculty members. (Jaschik, 1987:22)

While most state leaders point to the scarcity of qualified black scholars as the source of the problem, civil rights leaders reject the argument that demographic trends have made it impossible for states to meet the goals mandated by the *Adams* decree (Jaschik, 1987).

Exum (1983), using an extensive review of the literature as his basis, posits that continued underrepresentation of minority faculty in higher education is not only due to a limited supply, but is exacerbated by a limited demand for such faculty and by characteristics of the institution of higher education itself. These characteristics include a fierce resistance to coercion (as opposed to the customary normative consensus) and a rejection of any interference from the outside. Furthermore, academic institutions are dominated by professionals, who stress the importance of merit, autonomy, and neutrality. These institutional characteristics identified by Exum are seemingly threatened by affirmative action efforts that challenge the status quo. This is especially true for court-mandated affirmative action, as in the *Adams* case.

Fernandez (1981) uncovered difficulties that affirmative action met in the business sector. He writes that there was strong resistance from sectors bent upon maintaining the status quo. Additionally, minorities were adversely affected by the perpetuation of myths concerning their "inferior" qualifications. Fernandez notes that even though blacks are hired, they are not fully integrated into the formal network.

Exum et al. (1984) interpret the problems of inequity in higher education as resulting from the nature of academia as an "internal market," where jobs are filled by those already within the system. Affirmative action is resisted because it introduces costly features that are inimical to the customary procedures: for example, different, expanded search-and-recruitment activities; additional or alternative appeals and grievance criteria; and learning new or different ways of evaluation and measuring merit.

Many of the studies that have examined the characteristics, experiences, and perceptions of black faculty in TWIs have been limited in focus.[2] Much of the research has been demographic or has only examined faculty in specific disciplines. A difficulty with some of the studies has been low response rates or small samples. A study by Elmore and Blackburn (1983) dealt with demographic data, as well as important experiences and perceptions that appear to be related to salary, promotion, and tenure. However, the generalizability of their findings remains in question because of the uncharacteristically skewed proportion of associate (40 percent) and full (30 percent) professors in their sample and the Midwest locations of the institutions they sampled. In respect to location, Andrulis et al. (1975) found a higher percentage of black faculty and administrators employed in Central and Midwestern states than other areas of the country. Contrary to Elmore and Blackburn's (1983) speculation, there may not be "more liberal leanings in the East and Far West" in the arena of higher education. For example, in 1985, the percentages of black faculty at MIT was 2; at Cornell, 1.6; at the University of Pennsylvania, 1.2; and at Stanford, 1.6 (Scott-Jones and Harvey, 1985).

In view of conflicting claims and much speculation, an assessment of the black faculty at TWIs is now required. The study is specifically concerned with black faculty in nine *Adams* states: Maryland, Virginia, North Carolina, South Carolina, Georgia, Florida, Alabama, Tennessee, and Kentucky.

One of the significant outcomes of the *Adams* decision was the imposition of nontraditional methods of recruitment and hiring. These methods may involve costly advertising and paperwork, but may be justified if more minorities are hired than under the traditional influence networks that favor white males (Exum et al., 1984). It has not been clear to what degree nontraditional methods have been used to identify and recruit black faculty in the *Adams* states.

The impact of the *Adams* rulings was vigorously debated by all parties involved in the issue. This debate was intensified by the December 1987 decision of U.S. District Court Judge John H. Pratt to terminate the *Adams* case. In July of 1989, the U.S. Court of Appeals for the District of Columbia Circuit reversed Judge Pratt's decision ruling that the NAACP Legal Defense Fund still had legal standing to pursue the case. The decision of the court of appeals was written by Judge Ruth B. Ginsburg. Judge Ginsburg wrote that it was appropriate for the courts to supervise antibias enforcement if federal agencies were not carrying out their responsibilities. She further wrote that "judicial review would serve to promote rather than undermine the separation of powers doctrine, for it helps to prevent the executive branch from ignoring congressional directives." In view of the ongoing controversy over the outcome of this legal intervention in the hiring practices of public TWIs, the present study takes on added significance. Fully 95 percent of the black faculty who participated in this research were hired during the period of the *Adams* decision.

Given the contemporary nature of the mandate from the judicial system and given the political and social ramifications of a black presence on traditionally white campuses, the phenomenon merits scholarly analysis.

Methods and Procedures

There was a clear objective in this study to learn as much as reasonably possible about recruitment and employment patterns of black faculty in the target institutions. In effect, the more comprehensive the data base on this population, the greater the usefulness of the research for planning future actions. A survey was administered by mail to nearly all full-time regular black faculty members in the public four-year colleges and universities of the nine states in this study. The design of the survey instrument in this study was influenced by the research of Anderson, Frierson, and Lewis (1979), Elmore and Blackburn (1983), and Scott (1981).[3]

The number of black faculty members reported by the institutions in this study totalled 1,268. After screening for administrators and other nonregular or part-time faculty members, 1,232 questionnaires were mailed. A second purging of the black faculty list occurred as questionnaires were returned by individuals indicating they were not faculty, or envelopes were returned as undeliverable. Other names were deleted from the lists provided by the states when it was discovered that they were actually staff members. The resulting total of eligible black faculty members in our sample was 948, which represents nearly the entire population of regular full-time black faculty members in the public four-year institutions and universities in the nine states. A total of 523 completed questionnaires were returned, representing a response rate of 55.2 percent. Of these 523 respondents, 474 actually identified their ethnic background as "black." The analyses in this report are based on the responses of this group of 474 respondents.

Questionnaires were mailed in a large envelope containing a cover letter and an addressed, stamped return envelope. Upon receipt of the completed questionnaires, two researchers coded and entered data into computer files. Coding reliability was obtained between the two researchers. Approximately two weeks afer the last series of questionnaires had been mailed, a reminder postcard was mailed to all faculty who had not returned their survey forms.

On-site interviews were conducted at the flagship institutions in four states. These interviews involved small group discussions and individual administration of open-ended questions to black faculty and administrators. Preliminary data from each state were used to guide the focus of the interviews. The on-site research process was designed to provide a meaningful context for interpreting the survey results and to identify important issues that may not have been addressed in the questionnaire. Additionally, these interviews were seen as a method for collecting more candid responses than might be provided through an impersonal survey instrument.

Distribution of Faculty among States and within Departments

As stated earlier, nine states were involved in this study. In these nine states, ninety-six colleges and universities were identified as traditionally white institutions. There were approximately 1,268 black teaching faculty reported to be in these states. However, upon contacting these reported black teaching faculty via the questionnaire, approximately 320 were determined to be visiting professors, teaching assistants, librarians with faculty rank, administrators with faculty rank, or part-time faculty. The approximate total of teaching faculty in the institutions in the target states is 52,095, which means that the reported black teaching faculty represents about 2.4 percent of the total (Table 1). When those who were reported but who were not actually regular teaching faculty were deleted, the number of blacks was 1.8 percent.

The ninety-six institutions in this study ranged in type from small colleges to large universities. For the purpose of this study, small senior colleges were characterized as having a student body of six thousand or less and large senior colleges as having more than six thousand. Small universities were characterized as having a student body of fifteen thousand or less and large universities as having more than fifteen thousand. Other than these qualifiers, normal definitions of colleges and universities were used.

Respondents were asked to give the total initial number of faculty in their departments and the present number. It was determined that most respondents are in small and medium-sized departments. The respondents were also asked to give the total number of faculty in their department who were of the same race. Of the respondents, 43 percent

Table 1. Reported Black Teaching Faculty in Targeted
Adams **States (Senior Colleges and Universities)**

State	Number of Teaching Faculty[a]	Reported Black Teaching Faculty	Blacks as a %
Alabama	6,176	88	1.4%
Florida	6,252	226	3.6
Georgia	6,080	195	3.2
Kentucky	4,562	93	2.0
Maryland	3,203	70	2.2
North Carolina	6,710	186	2.8
South Carolina	4,834	97	2.0
Tennessee	5,453	156	2.9
Virginia	8,825	157	1.8
Totals:	52,095	1,268	2.4%[b]

Source: Chief Academic Officers (CAOs) and System Officers. Correspondences were sent directly to CAO of each state institution, requesting the names and numbers of black teaching faculty. Two of the state System Offices were contacted for the same information).

[a] These data are from American Universities and Colleges 13th ed., (New York: American Council on Education Walter de Gruyter, 1987).

[b] This figure drops to about 1.8 percent when administrators and librarians with faculty rank are screened out.

indicated that they were the only black faculty person in their respective departments initially. Currently, 30.7 percent report that they are the only black faculty person in their department, and there were increases in the percentages of respondents indicating that one to four black faculty members other than themselves were in their departments.

In order to determine the extent to which departments actually increased or decreased the number of black faculty, a cross-tabulation was made of initial number of black faculty within departments by present number of black faculty within departments. This process revealed few overall gains, even though some movement is evident. Of the respondents who reported that they were the only black faculty member initially in their department, 38.7 percent remain the only one. Of the respondents who reported one other black faculty in the department, 65.5 percent still report the same situation.

From the data of the Equal Employment Opportunity Commission (EEOC) reports, it is apparent that there were more black faculty hired at TWIs after the passage of the 1964 Civil Rights Act than before its passage. In order to analyze the length of service the respondents had at their present institution, years of service was grouped in the following manner: zero to five years, five to ten years, ten to fifteen years, and over fifteen years. The data collected in part of this study indicate that in the category of "ten to fifteen years" (roughly the period of the first *Adams* litigation) there is a slight increase in black faculty members over the category of "fifteen or more years," which would be the period accompanying the passage of the Civil Rights Act of 1964. There is a noticeable decline in the number of blacks in the "five to ten years" category; yet, there is a significant increase in the number of blacks in the "up to five years" category. This "up to five years" category is the same period in which the courts renewed the push to get TWIs to hire more black faculty. In 1983, TWIs in the *Adams* states were required to reexamine their plans with the intent to develop new strategies to increase minority presence.

Data on the initial date of hire provide a clearer illustration of the previously mentioned trend. Only 2 percent of the respondents in this study were hired prior to 1964. However, between 1972 to 1977, 25.5 per cent of the population was hired. Even more revealing is the fact that between 1983 and 1986, 42.2 percent of the population was hired. Figures 1 and 2 provide a year-by-year analysis from 1968 to 1986. It is clear that more hiring took place between 1973 and 1976 and between 1984 and 1986 than in any other periods. This increase in hiring coincides with the proactive stance the courts took during these years, requiring institutions to hire more blacks in faculty and administrative ranks.

Further analysis of the data indicates a fairly even distribution of black males and black females in the category of "up to five years" of service. There is a noticeable difference in the category of "fifteen or more years" of service, and a slight difference in the "five to ten years" and "ten to fifteen years" categories. These data suggest that while the total number of blacks teaching in TWIs in the *Adams* states is still low, in the last five years black females are being hired at a greater rate than they were prior to 1974 (Figure 2).

Recent hiring patterns reveal that at TWIs, there has been a shift in focus from the black male to the black female. Black females could pos-

Figure 1. Male and Female Hires 1968–1986

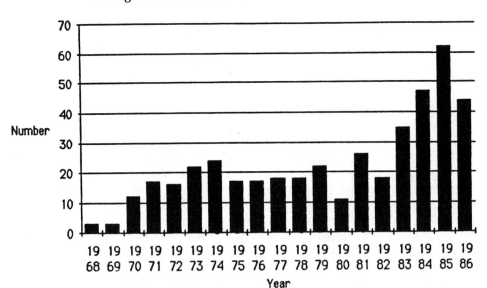

Figure 2. Year-by-Year Analysis of Male and Female Hires

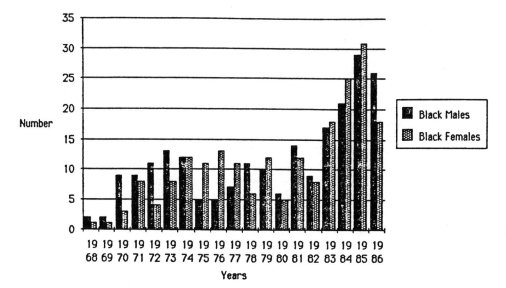

sibly be seen by TWIs as solving two affirmative action problems by simultaneously increasing numbers of both females and blacks, or there
might also be systemic factors that hinder the hiring of black males. Recent reports indicate that black males are not entering the prerequisite
pipelines of education in the same numbers as they have in the past.
Recent data published by the National Research Council show that the
overall number of blacks awarded Ph.D.'s has decreased 26.5 percent
over the last ten years. Further, the number of black males awarded
Ph.D.'s has decreased 47 percent over the last ten years, and the number
of black females awarded Ph.D.'s has increased 15 percent during this
same period.

Recruitment, Degree Selection and Employment Variables

   The first step in attracting black faculty to TWIs is a successful recruitment program. Normally, institutions engage in a diversified approach
when recruiting faculty, whether black or white. A major tool in the process is placement of ads in the *Chronicle of Higher Education,* journals, and
appropriate newsletters. These ads usually give a description of the position (e.g., associate professor of English), a specific date the applications must be submitted, starting date, and a statement concerning the
institution being an equal opportunity employer. Placing ads in the previously mentioned media of advertisement several times for each vacancy can be very expensive and still may not achieve the desired
results. Yet, this is the procedure that is, for the most part, followed by
institutions in their attempt to recruit black faculty. This approach does
not provide the potential black faculty member with a sense of the cam-

pus environment, the institutional commitment to affirmative action, the kind of experiences black faculty may expect, the prior success levels of other black faculty members, and other concerns of this nature.

In an attempt to address this issue in this study, respondents were specifically asked to identify the most important factors in assisting them in finding their present positions. Also, during on-site interviews, a question was posed to each interviewee concerning the same matter. The options listed on the questionnaire were mentor; college placement office; faculty member at present institution; professional journals, newsletters, etc.; advertisement; friends; networking; other personal contact; and "other." Each respondent was asked to indicate the three most important factors instrumental in locating his or her present position. Additionally, the respondents were asked to rank the three choices.

The data indicated that among the first-ranked factors, the most frequently listed was a faculty member at the present institution. This was followed by mentor, friends, advertisement, and journals/newsletters (Table 2). When looking at factors faculty considered most important in locating their positions, the commonality of the three most frequently identified factors is a person-to-person approach.

It is questionable whether some TWIs are serious about recruiting black faculty. However, those institutions that have good intentions in recruiting black faculty may also be victims of a faulty strategy. These institutions may put a great deal of sincere energy into a process that is encumbered by an inadequate approach or procedure, yet they follow this approach year after year, documenting that the process has been followed, even though it may not have yielded the desired results. The findings show that the nontraditional recruitment methods, such as ads and journals, have provided an increasingly significant portal for black

Table 2. Most Useful Factors in Locating Present Position

Factors Ranked First	Percent of Respondents Selecting
Faculty at present institution	24.6
Mentor	18.0
Friends	11.0
Advertisement	9.7
Journals, newsletters, etc.	7.4
Other personal contacts	6.6
Networking	5.5
Institutional placement office	.4
Others (composite)	16.7

faculty candidates entering academia. These methods could be studied and improved, and as a core of black faculty develops at TWIs, the traditional recruitment methods (e.g., friends and mentors) should also be evaluated.

The data show that 53.6 percent of the respondents indicated that the most useful factors in locating their present positions was either a faculty member at the present institution, a mentor, or a friend. These factors suggest a person-to-person approach has a great deal of appeal to black faculty candidates. Furthermore, they suggest a need for TWIs to take a look at how present faculty, particularly black faculty, view the institution and the kinds of experiences they are encountering. Black faculty candidates often place a great deal of weight on the racial and professional climate of the campus, and will ask black faculty at the institution for their perceptions. Faculty members, in turn, tend to describe an institution based upon their own perceptions. Their perceptions are usually influenced by personal experiences. Black faculty members who do not feel that they are treated fairly, in most cases, will not be an ambassador for the institution.

If black faculty members are used in the recruiting process, not only must they portray the institution in a positive manner, but they are also putting their own integrity on the line. If the institution does not live up to this portrayal, the recruit may sometimes vent frustration not only at the institution, but at the individual who persuaded them to come. Silver argues that:

> The trademark of success in the hiring of minority (Black) faculty on a predominantly white campus centers around an environment that is inviting, attitudes that are positive, search committees that are committed, and a recruitment theory that is intrinsically linked to retention. (1987:7)

Another finding that needs attention is the pattern of degree selection—blacks are getting degrees in areas where demand and salary are lower, and the possibility for mobility is limited. They are not receiving degrees in the natural sciences, engineering, computer science, and the languages in any large numbers.

This fact complicates the recruitment of black faculty in these high-demand areas. The irony of this pattern, however, is that even though blacks are represented in greater numbers in the areas of education, English, nursing, business, and social work, their presence in the various departments at TWIs representing these fields of study is not representative of their numbers. This reality puts the black faculty at a double disadvantage in the hiring process. On the one hand, they are not being hired at TWIs in disciplines where they hold degrees, and, on the other hand, not enough blacks are getting degrees in the high-demand disciplines. The consequence of this phenomenon is that, by and large, black faculty represent a tiny pecentage of the employment ranks at TWIs.

Those black faculty who are able to obtain jobs at TWIs, however few, have not been employed for any great length of time. This study has documented that 49.3 percent of the respondents had less than five years of service. It follows that significant numbers of black faculty in the TWIs are not secure in their jobs. This conclusion can be reached because they have not been employed at their present institution of employment long enough to obtain tenure. Additionally, not being initially hired at the higher ranks (see Figures 3 and 4), they would not have been employed long enough to be considered for promotion.

Other issues impacting upon job security and black faculty-employment experience at TWIs revolve around the questions of academic rank and tenure. Departments or institutions that are adverse to cultivating a black faculty presence by sincere recruitment efforts may have the same adverseness to promoting and awarding tenure to black faculty. The large majority of black faculty are initially hired at the lower ranks (approximately 85 percent of the sample in this study). The scrutiny one must endure to advance up the professorial ranks may be just as rigorous as the initial hiring process. Usually the same people are involved in the initial hiring of new faculty and in determining who is promoted (i.e., department chairs, selected members of the department, and deans and other administrators). Black faculty members who are brought in at the lower ranks, such as lecturers, instructors, and assistant professors, must face this process at least two or three times should they decide to stay at a given institution. The faculty members in the present study have shown some facility in negotiating the steps to promotion, if not tenure. Figure 3 shows the relative proportions of the black faculty sample at each rank at their initial hiring. Figure 4, depict-

**Figure 3. Proportion of Black Faculty at Each Rank at Initial Hire
Initial Rank**

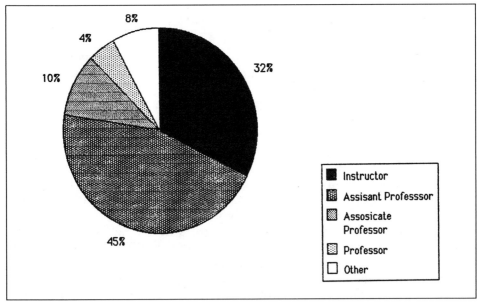

**Figure 4. Proportion of Black Faculty at Each Rank
Present Rank**

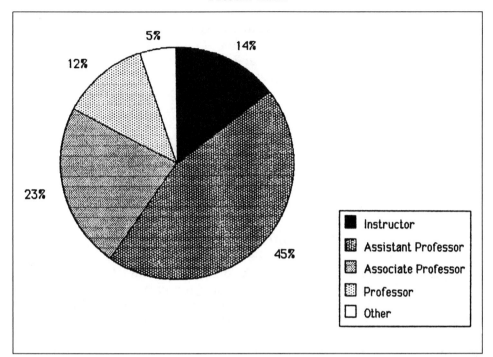

ing present rank, shows how the instructor ranks have decreased from 32 percent to 14 percent, associate and full professor ranks having increased. These data, of course, do not document the attrition rate of black faculty.

If, as the data suggest, the bulk of black faculty has only been employed at their present institution for less than five years, then large percentages of black faculty members will be eligible for promotion (and tenure) at about the same time. On the surface this should not be of any great concern, but, given the realities at many TWIs, it more than likely will cause some stress to decision makers. Hopefully, the campus will prepare itself to act in an affirmative and appropriate manner before this decision has to be made.

If institutions are consciously or unconsciously following a recruitment pattern that lends itself to recruiting inexperienced black faculty candidates in the lower ranks, they face the responsibility of cultivating the success skills that will result in the ultimate retention of these black faculty members. Part of the reason that black faculty are hired at the lower ranks is because TWIs focus their recruitment efforts mainly on recent graduates who have not had prior experience. These young faculty members may be less experienced in assimilating into the professional mainstream, and may be naive about campus politics and the unwritten rules for advancement.

Another issue in the recruitment process is the sentiment among some academic departments that "we have a black faculty in a given department, therefore our job is completed." About 77.1 percent of the respondents indicated that they had at least twenty total faculty members in their respective departments. Yet, 43.5 percent asserted that they were the only black faculty member in their department and 32.6 percent said there was one black faculty member other than themselves. These realities have consequences for comfortable cultural and social interactions and recruitment. In the wake of the *Adams* case, many experts thought that traditionally black institutions (TBIs) would be raided of their faculty in an attempt to increase the number of black faculty at TWIs. Yet, the data indicate that 71 percent of the respondents had no prior experience at a TBI (see Table 3).

Summary and Conclusion

Despite the efforts of the courts, racial diversity at TWIs has not been achieved to any substantial degree. On the other hand, some blacks have gained access to the TWI work force as a result of legal intervention (apparently because of the *Adams* case mandates). The numbers of black faculty teaching at TWIs are not as large as some institutions and states have previously reported, according to the findings of this study. None of the states that are a part of the study has a black faculty presence at TWIs that is proportional to the black population within the

Table 3. Years of Service at TBIs

Number of Years	n = 462	% Total Respondents	Female as a %	Male as a %
0	330	71.4%	46.7%	53.3%
1	27	5.8	48.1	51.9
2	15	3.2	66.7	33.3
3	11	2.4	36.4	63.6
4	9	1.9	77.8	22.2
5	10	2.2	40.0	60.0
6	7	1.5	57.1	42.9
7	6	1.3	16.7	83.3
8	9	1.9	44.4	55.6
9	5	1.1	60.0	40.0
10	10	2.2	40.0	60.0
11	3	.6	33.3	66.7
12	2	.4	0	100.0
13	4	.9	75.0	25.0
14	2	.4	50.0	50.0
15	0	0	0	0
16	0	0	0	0
17	3	.6	100.0	0
18	1	.2	100.0	0
19	1	.2	0	100.0
20	0	0	0	0
Over 20	7	1.5	86.6	13.3

states. Blacks as a percent of the total faculty range from a low of 1.4 in Alabama to a high of 3.6 in Florida. This fact alone speaks volumes as to the job that still needs to be done.

Seemingly, TWIs are still satisfied with the "token" approach to hiring black faculty. This is to say that when one or two black professors are hired, the TWIs consider their commitment to be complete. Of the respondents in this study, 43 percent indicated that they were the only black faculty person in their respective departments initially, while nearly 33 percent indicated that one other black faculty member was in their department. Of the respondents, 24 percent indicated that at the time of hire the size of their department ranged from eleven to twenty-five, and 10 percent reported that the size of their department was over thirty individuals. Certainly one or two black faculty is not an appropriate representaton. The external pressure of the closed-market employment system of higher education has created changes in the entrenched methods for recruiting faculty, as evidenced by the increase over the years in the proportion of black faculty candidates who found out about their positions through methods other than personal networks. Recruitment of black faculty is clearly influenced by professional contacts and relationships, but non-networking pathways into academia (ads, journals, newsletters) play an important role.

Data collected as a part of this study suggest that respondents with ten to fifteen years of service and over fifteen years of service at their present institution felt that responding to advertisements in journals, newsletters, and ads had little or no impact on their being hired. Black faculty who had up to five years of service felt that responding to advertisements was helpful in securing their positions. However, respondents in each category felt that contact with persons already at the institution where a vacancy was being advertised was more useful in helping them secure the jobs than was responding to advertisements or other methods normally associated with job hunting. TWIs should pay close attention to how black faculty presently on their campus are treated. This cadre of faculty is extremely important to the recruitment process. If they are not having a good experience, their portrayal of the institution may not be positive.

The black faculty at TWIs tend to be relative newcomers to TWIs, with over 49 percent having less than five years of service. Further, 77 percent of the black faculty in this study were initially hired at either the rank of instructor or assistant professor. This certainly has an impact on the clout these faculty members have in campus decision making and governance.

The proportion of females in the black professoriate has increased dramatically, resulting in slightly more black females than black males being hired in the past few years. This could result from the black females solving two affirmative action concerns, the pipeline issue, or larger systemic factors.

Evidence has been presented that suggests that TWIs made greater efforts to hire black faculty only when an outside stimulus, such as Congress or the courts, intervened. When the courts were most active in their deliberations and more pointed in their directions, strategies, goals, and timetables, the *Adams* states responded with better results. Given this reality, and given the 1987 ruling by Judge Pratt effectively removing the courts from their previous role of enforcer, we might expect little or no activity from TWIs relative to the hiring and retention of black faculty. This contention could be supported by arguing that even with mandates from the courts, the TWIs have not in any significant manner diversified their work force relative to race. Additionally, when one views the recent actions by the Supreme Court concerning affirmative action (such as *Allen v. Wright, Lawrence v. AT&T, Wards Cove Packing Company v. Antonio, Martin v. Wilkes* and *Patterson v. McLeon Credit Union*), there is really no cause for a great deal of optimism.

The last hope for positive change rests with the fact that Judge Pratt's 1987 decision was reversed by the federal court of appeals in July 1989. The question is whether or not it will be business as usual.

Notes

1. The term *Adams* states refers to the several states directly affected by the *Adams v. Richardson* litigation.
2. For an in-depth analysis of this issue, see Silver, Dennis, and Spikes, 1988.
3. The instrument, "Questionnaire for Faculty of Public Higher Education Institutions," consists of 104 items that focus on educational experiences, prior and present; opinions and perceptions of institutional policies and the equity with which such policies are implemented; and satisfaction with advancement and promotion. The survey required fifteen to twenty minutes to complete. Background data were requested on gender, race, colleges attended, and institutions from which degrees were conferred. Racial attitudes and race relations, recruiting and hiring, and mentoring-relationship implications are also measured. Global items in the instrument are age, gender, tenure, rank, citizenship, levels of academic degree, discipline, and years of higher education experience. Global variables range in scale: for example, 2-point scale for gender; 6-point scale for citizenship. Some of the outcome measures (salary, promotion, rank, class load, etc.) are scaled according to defined breaks or left open-ended. Most of the questions are of the 4-point-scale type, with 1 being the lowest rating and 4 being the highest.

   The survey instrument was designed to fit on a single page that folded into a four-sided 8½ x 11-inch brochure. This format presumably enhanced the response rate because of the ease of administration and the apparent brevity of a single sheet. Obviously, the questionnaire was designed for a larger study and generated a great deal of data. However, for the purpose of this article, those data relating to recruitment and hiring patterns are the focus of the present analysis.

   In developing the sampling frame, the first major decision was to include only faculty from state universities and four-year state colleges. The decision was partly due to the practical imperative to limit the boundaries of the study and partly due to the small numbers of black faculty members reported to be employed in two-year institutions. The institutions included in the study were identified from a listing in *American Universities and Colleges,*

13th edition (American Council on Education, 1987). Because of the focus of the study, only predominantly white institutions were included. The criterion for identifying an institution as predominantly white was a black student population of 33 percent or less. Faculty members considered to be in this study's population were full-time regular appointments. Visiting professors, research assistants, teaching assistants, part-time faculty, and administrators were excluded from the sampling frame.

While a variety of methods, alternatives, and contingency plans for sample-frame construction were developed, the principle method proved to be most effective. This method involved personal contact by letter, telephone calls, or both with officials in the state higher-education boards or with chief academic officers at individual state institutions. Most of these persons were able to directly or indirectly supply the names and mailing addresses of the black faculty members in their systems or institutions. In two cases, where names were not supplied directly, a contact person at the institution agreed to distribute the questionnaire to the black faculty members. To a large degree, the identification of those contact persons—either directly or indirectly—was the result of the professional network of the investigators. Of the ninety-six institutions included in the sampling frame, responses were received from all but one of them.

References

American Council on Education. 1984. *American Universities and Colleges*. 13th ed. Hawthorne, N.Y.: Walter de Gruyter.

———. 1986. *Status Report on Minorities in Higher Education*. Washington, D.C.: American Council on Education.

Anderson, W., H. Frierson, and T. Lewis. 1979. "Black Survival in White Academe." *Journal of Negro Education*, 48:92–102.

Andrulis, D. P., I. Iscoe, M. P. Sikes, and T. Friedman. 1975. "Black Professors in Predominantly White Institutions: An Examination of Some Demographic and Mobility Characteristics." *Journal of Negro Education*, 44:6–11.

Banks, W. 1984. "Afro-American Scholars in the University." *American Behavioral Scientist*, 27(3):325–38.

———. 1982. "Networks, Linkages and the Socialization of Black Educators." In *Blacks on White Campus: Proceedings of a Special NAFEO Seminar*. Washington, D.C.: The National Association for Equal Opportunity in Higher Education.

Bok, Derek. 1982. *Beyond the Ivory Tower: Social Responsibilities of the Modern University*. Cambridge, Mass.: Harvard University Press.

Caplow, T. and R. J. McGee. 1958. *The Academic Marketplace*. New York: Basic Books.

Clark, G. F. 1987. "National Conference on the Role of Faculty in Meeting the National Need for Minority Scholars." *Black Issues in Higher Education*, 19(4):14–15.

Elmore, C. J., and R. T. Blackburn. 1983. "Black and White Faculty in White Research Universities." *Journal of Higher Education*, 54:1–15.

Exum, William H. 1983. "Climbing the Crystal Stair: Values, Affirmative Action, and Minority Faculty." *Social Problems*, 30:389–99.

Exum, W., R. Menges, B. Watkins, and P. Berglund. 1984. Making It At The Top. *American Behavioral Scientist*, 27(3), 301–24.

Fernandez, P. 1981. *Racism and Sexism in Corporate Life*. Lexington, Mass.: Lexington Books.

Fitzpatrick, E. D. 1987. *Salary Report 1956–1987*. East Lansing, Mich.: Michigan State University.

Fleming, E., R. Gill, and H. Swinton. 1978. *The Case for Affirmative Action for Blacks in Higher Education*. Washington, D.C.: Howard University Press.

Jaschik, S. 1987. "U.S. Review of Efforts to Integrate Colleges Likely to Spur Fight." *The Chronicle of Higher Education*, 23 (25 March):1 ff.

Lewis, Lionel. 1975. *Scaling the Ivory Tower*. Baltimore: Johns Hopkins University Press.

Moore, W. J., and L. H. Wagstaff. 1974. *Black Education in White Colleges*. San Francisco: Jossey-Bass.

Pruitt, Anne S. 1982. "Black Employees in Traditionally White Institutions in the Adams States." Paper presented at the American Educational Research Association, New York.

Scott-Jones, Diane, and William B. Harvey. 1985. "Hiring and Promoting Black Faculty." *Academe*, 71:37.

Scott, Richard R. 1981. "Black Faculty Productivity and Interpersonal Academic Contacts." *Journal of Negro Education*, 50:224–34.

Shingleton, J. D., and L. P. Scheetz. 1987. "Recruiting Trends 1987–1988." East Lansing, Mich.: Michigan State University Placement Office.

Silver, Joseph H. 1987. *Minority Faculty Recruitment in Kennesaw College: 1976–1986*. Athens, Ga.: Institute of Higher Education, University of Georgia.

Silver, Joseph H., Rodney Dennis and Curtis Spikes. 1988. *Black Faculty in Traditionally White Institutions in Selected Adams States: Characteristics, Experiences and Perceptions*. Atlanta, Georgia: Southern Education Foundation.

Smelser, N. J., and R. Content. 1980. *The Changing Academic Market*. Berkeley: University of California Press.

Steele, C. M., and S. G. Greene. 1976. "Affirmative Action and Academic Hiring." *Journal of Higher Education*. 47.

U.S. Department of Health, Education and Welfare. 1988. *Higher Education Equity*. Washington, D.C.: U.S. Government Printing Office.

U.S. Equal Employment Opportunity Commission. 1981. *Equal Employment Opportunity Report; Minorities and Women in Higher Education*. Washington, D.C.: U.S. Government Printing Office.

Brown v. Board, 347 US483 (1954)

Civil Rights Cases, 109 US3 (1883)

Plessy v. Ferguson, 163 US537 (1896)

Symposium: Big-City Black Mayors: Have They Made a Difference?

Introduction

Michael B. Preston
(Symposium Editor)

University of Southern California

One of the most striking political developments in American politics over the last twenty years has been the increase in the numbers of black elected officials. Of this group, the election of black mayors, especially big-city black mayors, has received widespread attention. These mayors have received special attention because, like black congresspersons, they tend to speak for blacks "at large." Their legitimacy as spokespersons at large is derived from the fact that they all represent cities with large black populations, many of whom are poor and most of whom have suffered and/or still suffer from some form of discrimination, lack of employment, poor education, and other problems endemic to urban areas. The election of big-city black mayors, then, raised the expectations among blacks that the ills of urban society could be met in a more progressive and humane manner. Thus, the quest by blacks in urban areas for a more egalitarian society came to rest squarely on the shoulders of these mayors.

Today, the election of big-city black mayors has become almost routine. However, the questions people are asking now differ from those of the past. Earlier questions concerning black mayors focused on obstacles to electing them and upon the problems of governance. After two decades of black mayors, the new questions focus on whether *promise* has been met by *performance*.

The basic purpose of this symposium, then, is to provide the kind of dispassionate analysis that will allow us to examine this new set of questions. The cities used for this analysis are significant because they include some of the largest cities in America and are located in both the northern and southern regions of the country.

The first article attempts to provide a systematic way of analyzing black mayors in a historical context. It is followed by a discussion of black mayoral leadership in Atlanta. Starting with Atlanta is appropriate because it is a city with a reputation for a thriving and sophisticated black middle class, and a source of strong black leadership. And, given its large black majority, it provides a good test of how effective electoral politics has been in the black search for equality in American cities. The study of black mayoral leadership in Washington, D.C., provides a vivid example of what happens to a popular leader when he allows his public perception to be tainted by personal scandal.

In both New Orleans and Birmingham, we are able to examine the linkage between electoral success and increased public employment of blacks at all levels of city government. As we move north to Chicago, Philadelphia, and Detroit, we see how different political styles and personalities lead to differences in political vision, and what the outcomes are under these circumstances. And in Los Angeles, we discuss how Mayor Bradley has been able to be elected to a fifth term in a city that is only 17 percent black, and also whether his past popularity will enable him to survive the current scandal that has engulfed him. We conclude with an excellent article giving us a twenty-year perspective on black mayoral leadership in America.

Big-City Black Mayors: An Overview

Michael B. Preston

University of Southern California

One of the fundamental elements of political leadership is obtaining the support of the people one hopes to lead. From the election of the first black mayors in 1967 through the early 1980s, black mayors have enjoyed the enthusiastic support of black voters. They were looked upon as the new leaders who would help blacks achieve political power in urban areas. The belief, by most, was that political power would also open the door to more economic power, as well as increase the probability of social justice. Thus, black mayors came to be seen as the "new cutting edge" of the old civil rights movement and were expected to seek redress for the wrongs that had been perpetuated on blacks for so long (Preston, 1984:65). As they took on the task of governing, black mayors were praised not only for winning elections but for every achievement, however small. Any attack on them was seen as an attack on all blacks in the city. Black mayors were defended with such vigor that they became deified in most of these cities (Nelson, 1982:190; Preston, 1987:158–61).

Indeed, so strong was the early sentiment that not only were whites castigated for any attack on black mayors, but so were black critics, no matter how valid the criticism might have been. For example, when a black alderman voted against a proposal put forth by the late Mayor Washington during his first term, he received such hostile letters and threatening phone calls that he was forced to apologize; he later returned to the City Council for a second vote, in which he then supported the mayor's proposal. Such adoration was based on a deep-seated belief that whites did not want a black mayor, did not support him, and would take any and every opportunity to embarrass him. Even if they (whites) were correct, the defense was that black mayors were only doing what white mayors had done for years—and that black mayors should be given the chance to prove that they could lead as well or as poorly as whites had done. Thus, under this proposition, criticism by blacks was to be kept private because most blacks felt whites would provide more than their share of criticism without black help (Starks and Preston, 1989).

Such adulation by blacks for their new leaders should come as no surprise. Blacks, like other racial and ethnic groups, take pride in having one of their own elected. And, while some blacks had high expectations of black mayors, most realized that these mayors could not solve all of the problems found in the black community.

Thus, it seems that black voters sought two important things from their chosen leaders. First, they sought strong leaders who would seek changes, not just adherence to the status quo. Any such *changes* included addressing the key concerns of the black community. More important, blacks wanted a person who would give them pride, and who would not embarrass them in the eyes of others. After all, black mayors represented the aspirations of all blacks, and if one understands this, one is in a better position to understand why blacks took any attack on these mayors very personally.

Second, blacks have come to understand that politics is more than just symbols or pride. Politics is about the allocation or reallocation of valuable resources. On the one hand, blacks want symbolic representation; on the other hand, they want a reallocation of resources and more equitable policies that protect their interests. Black voters expected black mayors to end police brutality in the black community, to fight for fair housing and better schools, and to provide more equitable and better city services to their communities. In addition, they also wanted their share of the city jobs and the development of new policies that would open up, where possible, more private jobs to qualified blacks. Few blacks assumed that jobs would be provided to all who wanted them, or indeed to all who were qualified for them. What they did expect was that there would be a more equitable redistribution of these resources. After all, while one needs to feel good about oneself, it is rather difficult to survive on pride alone.

Anyone who has studied or seriously thought about the problems of black mayors knows that most inherited declining cities in poor fiscal conditions. They have also had to contend with large groups of poor people whose needs go beyond the ordinary. Not only did they have to halt the decline, but they had to do it in the face of hostile white resistance, institutional barriers endemic to city government, hostile suburban interest—to say nothing of unfriendly state legislators and often less-than-enthusiastic Republican presidents. If that was not enough, there was frequently not enough blacks available with the requisite technical skills to run the key bureaucratic agencies to ensure that the mayor's new policies would be implemented. In short, for black mayors, "Life ain't been no crystal stair."

All of this was yesterday. Today, if one were to give a speech on black mayors to certain black audiences, they might be greeted with hostile stares, snide remarks, and some outright boos. *What has happened in the intervening years to the adulation of yesterday?* Have blacks reached a stage of political maturation where substance is more important than symbols? Or are people saying that, while symbols are still important, they must include substance if black mayors are to maintain their support? Is it possible that blacks have, like most others, become a part of the "instant society" where we adore the "novel" but discard the "old" because it lacks the drama and flair that it once had? Answers to these questions are not as simple as they may seem and vary depending upon the mayor and the circumstances found in each city. One thing is certain, however: the process of political maturation is taking place among blacks at a very rapid rate, and this development will have profound consequences for future black mayors.

Let me suggest four ways by which we may begin to think about these questions analytically. There are four categories that I find useful for helping us understand the present situation of black mayors. They are (1) the politics of personality, (2) the politics of incumbency, (3) the politics of patronage, and (4) the politics of vision. No claim is made here that these are analytically distinct categories, only that, for my purpose, they provide considerable insights into the black mayoral experience in American cities.

The Politics of Personality

Black mayors tend to govern by virtue of their personality, not by the use of political organizations. Most have won elections because of their personal popularity and have shunned "the machine" as organizations of the past even when elected. There are several good reasons why this is so. First, most black mayors have not had the support or control of the party apparatus. And even if they could get control, most lack the resources necessary to sustain it. Second, most are elected as independents (even though almost all are Democrats) and must depend on blacks as well as whites. White supporters of black mayors are normally middle-class voters who would not be likely to support a machine politician. Third, the establishment and perpetuation of a machine take money and time, which are scarce commodities as far as black mayors are concerned. In addition, political machines can also lead to factions and corruption, neither of which a black mayor needs. The list of problems is likely to be long, and factions and corruption cut into his or her major resource—time. Fourth, there is also the possibility that black mayors are more "reformist" than "machinist." That is, they know that when the machine developed, a patron-client relationship existed. Government and voters were dependent upon each other: jobs for votes. Today, welfare is given in most cities by county or state governments, patronage jobs are limited by Shakman I and II, and federal money is no longer available to fuel the patronage armies of the past. In short, black mayors may be reformers because they have little choice (Preston 1987:*viii–ix*).

One of the major flaws of this type of politics is that it does not institutionalize black political power. Political power is dependent upon one leader, and if the leader either dies or is defeated, there is limited organization to develop strategies for the future. Political power is likely to dissipate as factions arise to snap up its strength. In addition, the popularity of a mayor may prevent healthy dissent in the black community and retard the development of future leaders. Finally, leaders who rely too heavily on their personality are likely targets for defeat should a major scandal erupt (Persons and Henderson, 1989).

Black mayoral styles are shaped by their personality and the culture of the cities they govern. One cannot help but notice the aggressive styles of certain early mayors: Stokes of Cleveland, Hatcher of Gary, Morial of New Orleans, Jackson of Atlanta, and more recently, the late Harold Washington of Chicago. Some mayors have been less aggressive and more accommodating because they rely heavily on coalitions to get elected. Mayor Bradley of Los Angeles and Mayor Barthelemy of New Orleans fit into this category. Other mayors may be classified as organizers (Arrington), technocrats (Goode), and risk takers (Coleman Young). Styles depend heavily on a mayor's personality and the political culture of each city. The effectiveness of each mayor can be judged by reading the symposium that follows.

The Politics of Incumbency

One of the major political successes of black mayors has been their ability to get reelected. For almost all of them, their toughest election has been their first one. White resistance during their first election, the lack of party support, poor organization, and the lack of money have been some of the key problems that have confronted them at this stage. The power of incumbency seems to make the second election somewhat easier. In those cities where blacks are a majority, black mayors have seldom faced serious competition in their second election. In cities where black mayors need white support, resistance, while still present, is not as hostile, and support from whites may actually rise a few percentage points. And in those cities where blacks are not a majority (Chicago and Philadelphia), black mayors have been able to win by putting together coalitions consisting of liberal whites, Hispanics, and blacks to form a winning coalition (Starks and Preston, 1989). Incumbency also provides black mayors, like other mayors, with additional resources. Money from big developers, business interests, and various black groups provide the funds to run a city-wide campaign.

For black mayors, then, incumbency, when backed by political skill and popularity, has made them almost unbeatable in certain cities. In Los Angeles, Mayor Bradley won a fifth term in April 1989, although his winning percentage was down substantially from prior elections. In Detroit, Mayor Coleman Young is also expected to win his fifth term in November, although he has a bit more competition this time. Mayor

Barry of Washington, D.C., is expected to run for his fourth term. And while his popularity is at an all-time low, Barry, at least to date, has no real competition. The only long-term, big-city, black mayors to be defeated recently have been Gibson of Newark and Hatcher of Gary—both seeking fifth terms. Sawyer of Chicago was recently defeated, but he was appointed, not elected, to fill out Harold Washington's second term.

We may have arrived at a stage, according to Neil R. Pierce (1989), where we have "almost-for-life mayors." This may well be, in some cases, a very unhealthy development. The problem, simply put, is that while these mayors still have the will to fight and the resources to fight with, many have lost the *vision* they started with or may simply be unable or unwilling to attack the new problems that confront them with the vigor that propelled them to action in the past. Stated differently, as times have changed, so have the problems. Today, black citizens are less concerned with the successes of the past and are more concerned with a mayor's ability to handle the problems of the future.

The Politics of Patronage

All politicians seek ways to reward their supporters; black mayors are no exception. One big difference, however, is that, given the decline of federal funds, fiscal stress in state and local enconomies, and large poor black and Hispanic communities, the amounts of patronage black mayors have had at their disposal has been limited. There have also been court rulings that prohibit the hiring and firing of employees for patronage purposes (Preston, 1982; Starks and Preston, 1989). Yet, if Eisinger, Perry, and other scholars are correct, and I think they are, black mayors have been relatively successful in dispensing some patronage to their supporters (Eisinger, 1984; Perry, 1989; Nelson, 1989; Starks and Preston, 1989); this seems to have been true in all cities discussed in this symposium. Not only have black mayors actively recruited blacks, Hispanics, and women, they have hired large numbers of them. In most of these cities, these mayors made it possible for some blacks to get city contracts for the first time and implemented policies that encouraged private industry to hire qualified blacks. Indeed, one of the problems black mayors face is a lack of black individuals and businesses that qualify for city contracts. In other cities, however, black mayors have taken an inordinate amount of time to develop programs to help black businesses (Perry, 1989).

The Politics of Vision

If there is one major fault that we can attribute to most black mayors and their supporters, it may be found in the lack of vision. By this, I mean the process of diminishing returns. There is a limit to the enthusiasm and vigor with which most mayors are able to attack problems. At what point this limit is reached, I'm not sure. That judgement should be made by the politician—and, where he or she refuses, by the people. In many cases, black mayors remain because they have nowhere else to go. They have the flair for the fight but may have lost the vision. They either refuse to acknowledge their shortcomings or are not made to do so by their supporters.

Let me state the case more succinctly. In Washington, D.C., Los Angeles, and Detroit, Mayors Barry, Bradley, and Young all started out as either community activists, reformers, or both. They helped to define the new agenda for their cities and sought to rethink the role that city government ought to play as far as minorities and women were concerned. They fought for inclusion of the out-groups rather than the old city policies of exclusion. In brief, they led the city in more progressive directions and instilled in city government a new set of values.

Today, these same mayors are not attacking the new problems with the same vigor as in the past. Clearly, the new problems of gangs, drug warfare, homeless, and the need for low-income housing, to name only a few, are difficult problems with regional, state, and national implications. They also call for the expenditure of funds that may not be readily available. Yet, if these mayors seek election and promise results, they must be made to deliver.

It takes political vision to see where intervention is possible, and where incumbent mayors can have the most impact. That vision is lacking today and calls into question whether unlimited mayoral terms are a blessing or a curse. In addition, the political scandals that have engulfed both Mayors Barry and Bradley may have reduced their power and ability to initiate new programs to solve these problems. In the final analysis, the politics of vision calls for leaders who have a vision of the future, and who also have a plan on how to get there.

In this symposium, we hope to provide the reader with a brief but informative overview of the political accomplishments and failures of the mayors represented. Clearly, this brief overview cannot and does not attempt to provide an in-depth study of each mayor; that has been done elsewhere (Preston, 1984, 1987; Nelson, 1977). We do hope, however, that as the reader travels through each city he or she can get a kaleidoscopic view of the political arena in which each of these mayors operates. Above all, we hope the journey is rewarding.

References

Eisinger, Peter. 1984. "Black Mayors and the Politics of Racial Economic Advancement." In Harlan Hahn and Charles Levine, eds., *Readings in Urban Politics, Past, Present, and Future.* New York, London: Longman.

Nelson, William. 1977. *Electing Black Mayors: Political Action in the Black Community.* Columbus, OH: Ohio State University Press.

Nelson, William. 1982. "Cleveland: The Rise and Fall of the New Black Politics." In Michael B. Preston, Lenneal J. Henderson, Jr., and Paul Puryear, eds., *The New Black Politics: The Search for Political Power.* New York, London: Longman.

Nelson, William, 1989. "Black Mayoral Leadership: A Twenty Year Perspective." *National Political Science Review 2.* (forthcoming).

Perry, Huey. 1989. "Black Politics and Mayoral Leadership in Birmingham and New Orleans." *National Political Science Review 2.* (forthcoming).

Persons, Georgia, and Lenneal Henderson. 1989. "Mayor of the Colony: Mayoral Leadership as a Matter of Public Perception." *National Political Science Review 2.* (forthcoming).

Pierce, Neil R. 1989. "Almost-for-Life Mayors." *L.A. Times.* 28 March.

Preston, Michael B., Lenneal J. Henderson, and Paul Puryear. 1987. *The New Black Politics: The Search for Political Power.* 2d ed. New York, London: Longman.

———. 1982. *The New Black Politics: The Search for Political Power,* 1st ed. New York, London: Longman.

Starks, Robert T. and Michael B. Preston. 1989. "Harold Washington and the Politics of Reform in Chicago: 1983–1987." In Rufus P. Browning, Dale Rogers Marshall, and David H. Tabb, eds., *Racial Politics in American Cities.* New York: Longman.

Black Mayoral Leadership in Atlanta:
A Comment

Mack H. Jones

Prairie View A. & M. University

Following the century-long struggle for electoral access, which culminated with the passage of the 1965 Voting Rights Act, there was considerable speculation that the stage had been set for the material transformation of black communities through political participation. The steady rise in the number of black registered voters and the attendant increase in the number of black elected officials, including and especially big-city black mayors, reinforced this disposition. Indeed, a sense of euphoria permeated the political atmosphere as the major cities of the Old Confederacy, such as Birmingham, Alabama, and Atlanta, Georgia, joined the ranks of municipalities headed by black mayors.

However, we are now a full two decades into the period of routine black political access, and the euphoria has been tempered considerably by the chronic stagnation of the cities, particularly of the inner core. Two of the first big-city black mayors, Hatcher of Gary, Indiana, and Gibson of Newark, New Jersey, have been voted out of office by their black constituents amid charges that they were unable to stop the decline of their cities. Few would dispute the claim that central-city residents of other cities with black mayors may share similar deteriorating conditions with their counterparts of Gary and Newark.

Thus, this symposium on cities with black mayors is quite timely. It is time to go beyond celebrating electoral success. We must make a dispassionate analysis of this phenomenon, with a view to placing it in the appropriate historical and theoretical context.[1] This will enable us to understand more clearly the implications of the rise of black mayors for the struggle for black liberation. My task is to comment specifically on black mayors in Atlanta, Georgia.

The Atlanta case is especially important for at least two reasons. First of all, black political strength, as measured by the ratio of the black to white population, ratio of black to white registered voters, and blacks as a percent of elected officials in both the City of Atlanta and Fulton County in which it is located, are all more favorable for blacks than in most other metropolitan areas. Second, Atlanta has long had a national reputation as a city with a thriving, sophisticated black middle class and a source of strong black leadership. Thus, the Atlanta experience may be indicative of both the possibilities and the limitations of electoral politics as a vehicle for black community advancement.

The city of Atlanta has been under black mayoral leadership since 1973. Blacks have majority control in both the Atlanta City Council and the Atlanta School Board, as well as on the Fulton County Board of Commissioners.

Maynard Jackson, the first black mayor, and his successor, Andrew Young, were each elected to two four-year terms, and it is widely assumed that Atlanta will elect its fifth consecutive black mayor in 1989. This is ample evidence that black mayors have become a routine part of the political landscape. As such, other political forces and interests have been forced to either adapt to this new phenomenon or to try to mold it to serve their objectives. In Atlanta, these sources have been able to mold the black mayoralty in line with their interests, and, as a consequence, the presence of black mayors has not changed substantially the function, orientation, or outcome of municipal government in Atlanta. Instead, the black mayoralty has been shaped by the priorities of the dominant commercial interest.

In an article on Atlanta politics published in 1978 (Jones, 1978) after the first term of Mayor Jackson, I argued that the lack of ideological clarity, the absence of organizational discipline, and the limited economic strength of the black community, coupled with the personal interests of black officeholders, made the latter ineffective, if not counterproductive, change agents.

I concluded with the assertion that

> The elected Black political leadership which emerges from these circumstances would be one which, even though propelled into office by Black votes, has no organizationally based support. There are no regular structures for political debate and deliberations between Black officials and Black rank and file. Political discussions of consequence continue to be monopolized by the white commercial and business elite and elected officials. Under these circumstances political empowerment . . . remains a goal to be obtained rather than a milestone already realized. (Jones, 1978:117)

Nothing has happened in Atlanta politics in the decade since that was written that would lead me to reassess my position. Today, I would add that, even though black office holding is a necessary step in the struggle for black empowerment, it has become something of a fetter on the masses of black people. Institutionally black office holding in many instances serves as a conduit for cultural and political domination of the black community, and it becomes part of the apparatus that manages the oppressed masses in the interest of the dominant economic elite.

A brief review of developments that led to the selection of Andrew Young to succeed Jackson and an analysis of the posture and initiatives undertaken by Mayor Young will suffice to support my argument.

After two terms in office, Mayor Maynard Jackson was barred by the city charter from seeking a third term. The lack of any real community-based organization meant that there was no process or structure through which a successor to Mayor Jackson could be annointed. As a consequence, several aspirants for the office struggled in typical American fashion to build their own base. In doing so, they all appealed to the black community for electoral support, while deferring to the material interest of the dominant white economic elite.

One aspirant, a former police chief and one-time confidant and chief aide to Mayor Jackson, Reginald Eaves, had worked to develop an image as a champion and spokesperson of inner-city blacks. Even though his political philosophy and articulated policy choices were well within the political mainstream, his image as a workers' candidate made Eaves unacceptable to both the dominant white and black political leaders. The spectre of Eaves as mayor motivated the black leadership, especially Mayor Maynard Jackson, to recruit Andrew Young to run for mayor. Young became available when he resigned under pressure from the Carter administration. Once in office, Young became both the darling and captive of the dominant economic elite.

Unlike his predecessor, Young was more accommodationist than confrontational, a posture that the white ruling forces found to be attractive and soothing. The business community and its organ, the *Atlanta Constitution*, began to compare the Young administration with that of Maynard Jackson. The latter was said to have been arrogant and antibusiness, but Young, as the litany went, had restored the confidence of the business community in city hall. City government and business were once again partners in progress, or so they claimed.

Perhaps seduced by the flattering, albeit condescending, assessment of the business community and driven by his own neoconservative ideology, Mayor Young became the aggressive champion of business interests. He proclaimed an identity of interest for the wealthy and the black poor.

Within his first six months in office, he led the fight of the Chamber of Commerce to have the city adopt a sales tax, the proceeds from which would be used to reduce property taxes. Invariably he sided with business and commercial interest in conflicts with neighborhood groups involving land-use decisions. He aggressively sought the building of middle- to upper-income housing near the downtown business district, while showing little concern for the housing problems of low-income residents.

As mayor, Young has become a leading spokesman for the capitalist ideology. The key to everything, according to his philosophy, is making money. He was quoted in the local paper as saying "I've made my peace with capitalism. . . . There's nothing better for coping with sin. It rewards people for working hard" (*Atlanta Constitution*, 1983:80). One observer alleged that "Andy Young is doing for Atlanta what Reagan has done for America: He is making rich people feel good again" (*Atlanta Constitution*, 1983:117).

Young has departed from the practice of castigating whites for past and present transgressions. He shocked a group of black lawyers by publicly declaring that one of the barriers to progress was the fact that white males over the past twenty years (presumably as a result of the civil rights movement) had been made to feel guilty. According to Young, "You make people change by making them feel more secure" (*Atlanta Constitution*, 1983:117).

The Young gospel, as it was dubbed by the *Atlanta Constitution*, generated little opposition within the black leadership class or the black population in general. He was reelected to a second term with only token opposition.

Initiatives undertaken by Mayor Young during his second term have been consistent with his general philosophy that the role of city government is to create a supportive environment for the growth and development of the business sector. His State-of-the-City addresses are invariably crafted around glowing recitations of business development stimulated by city government.

In his 1988 address, Mayor Young reported that the city was "at the top, or near the top, on most lists of superlatives of American cities" (Young, 1988:1). The eight-item list of superlatives cited included: first in single-family housing starts; second in number of jobs created; first in attractiveness to business; fourth in success at economic development; second in number of air passengers; first in the amount of air traffic; third in the number of convention visitors; and first in major trade shows (Young, 1988:1).

Additionally, the mayor took credit for bringing in $52 billion in new investments and creating 346,000 jobs in the Atlanta metropolitan area in the 1982–87 period (Young, 1988:3). He also reported that his "approach to the business of government" had led to a reduction of city government positions from 11,806 in 1981 to 8,394 in 1987 (Young, 1988:8), a 29 percent reduction.

On initiatives specifically targeted toward blacks, the goal of 35 percent participation of black firms on major construction projects was realized (Young, 1988:9). The city continued to hold an annual "Dream Jamboree," which brought some eight thousand public-school students in touch with representatives of two hundred colleges, universities, and technical and vocational schools (Young, 1988:10). In 1987 the city funded eleven day-care centers, which served nine hundred preschoolers. Through its job training initiatives in the same year, 1,719 "economically disadvantaged citizens" were trained and 67 percent of them were placed in new jobs. The summer job program placed 1,611 youths (Young, 1988:10).

In spite of the positive results as reported by the city, the overall conditions of black Atlantans, especially those in the inner city, have continued to decline during the incumbency of both black mayors. A 1988 study of the economic status of black Atlantans concluded that

> Regardless of which data one looks at the conclusion is clear. The economic conditions of Blacks living in Atlanta is pitiful and appears to be getting worse.

> Blacks in Atlanta are losing ground relative to whites and to residents of suburbs, both Black and white. Blacks in Atlanta are also losing ground absolutely. Increases have not kept pace with inflation and the rate of poverty is increasing despite the strong regional economy. (Sjoquist, 1988:9)

At first blush the positive assessment emanating from city hall and the dire commentary from the Sjoquist study might appear to be contradictory, but that is not in fact the case. Rather, they simply report on different aspects of an interconnected and inseparable reality. For us, then, the important question is how these two can be brought together in such a way that they help us understand and assess the significance of the rise of black mayors for the struggle for black liberation.

To do so, we must begin by acknowledging the class character of American urban politics. Black mayors, like their nonblack counterparts, are disciplined by that reality. Moreover, the peculiar position of black mayors as a weak and almost supplicatory party in the ruling coalition makes them even more vulnerable to the class prerogatives of dominant interests.

Municipal politics has always been in the service of the dominant commercial interests. The problems of the inner-city poor—joblessness, inadequate housing, under-funded education, etc.—are the consequence, intended or unintended, of the pursuit of such interests. As the economic and social systems change, so too does the role of the city and city governments, but the fundamental interests that it serves remain the same.

Black mayors came to power at the historical moment when cities began to decline as industrial centers. Their sizeable unskilled black populations not only became superfluous but were defined as the major urban problem. As cities began their new life as the location of corporate headquarters, tourist attractions, and convention and service centers, the primary concerns and initiatives of city governments evolved accordingly. The inner-city poor black population that was being created by these changing dynamics of the American economy became an impediment in the city's growth scheme.

The new city needed a more skilled work force. It also required that the "new" downtown central district be insulated from the presence and problems of the teeming masses of inner-city blacks who lived on its periphery. Black mayors and black leadership in general are responsible for ensuring that the appearance of the city as a glittering showcase of success is not sullied by the reality of urban oppression.

This responsibility leads black officials to (1) support class-based growth initiatives justified by the assumption that benefits will ultimately trickle down to the poor, (2) endorse schemes designed to disperse, hide, or manage inner-city residents so that they do not invade the sensibilities of the city's preferred workers and residents, and (3) adopt programs that assume that the problems of the inner-city poor are individual or group based and therefore not systemic, and that attempt to "solve" the problems of the poor by transforming the individual.

The Atlanta black leadership has accepted this role with seeming alacrity. It has supported land-use decisions that displaced inner-city residents for the benefit of corporate interest, and it has supported both taxing and spending policies that favor the dominant economic class. Even more poignant evidence of the willingness of Atlanta's black leadership to accept this role is to be found in their support of certain initiatives designed to hide or cosmetize the problems of the inner city. These include things such as (1) adopting a special admission fee for unaccompanied youth at the city zoo to rid that facility of neighborhood kids, whose presence was thought to frighten tourists and middle-class patrons; (2) agreeing to relocate the interstate bus station out of the central business district so that the sensibilities of conventioneers and privileged Atlantans would not be violated by the presence of the disheveled who frequent the bus terminal; and (3) developing a dress code for cab drivers and cosmetic codes for their vehicles in keeping with the city's contrived image.

What are we to make of all of this? How can we explain the willingness of black leadership to accept such a role? One key to understanding this development may be the asymmetrical relationship between the black leadership class and its coalition partner cum benefactor, the dominant commercial elite. The dominant white political elite represents established wealth and privilege. For them, influence in city government is a means through which they sustain class domination and the attendant privileges that it affords. It is not a vehicle for primary capital accumulation, social standing, or personal prestige. For black officeholders the opposite is often the case. In Atlanta, an alarming proportion of black officeholders have no visible means of support other than politics. Many have only scant histories of gainful employment unrelated to politics or the civil rights struggle. Indeed, when a successful black lawyer filed to run for one position, a local columnist wrote, perhaps tongue in check, that it was refreshing to have a candidate who "didn't need a job" (Shipp, 1986:10A). Under these circumstances, politics becomes a major personal economic resource for many officeholders, and their ability to convert this resource to their personal advantage is dependent upon the nature of their relationship with the dominant commercial elite. Thus, personal economic interest and the interest of that segment of the black community with whom they identify would predispose black leaders to defer to the interest of their more powerful benefactors. In the process, they become functionally integrated into the process and apparatus that create and sustain the problems of the urban poor. As one sage has reminded us, instruments made for sowing cannot be used for reaping.

Note

1. For two examples of such efforts see Reed, 1984, 1987; and Barnes, 1987.

References

Atlanta Constitution. 1983. "The Capitalistic Gospel According to Rev. Young." 22 September.

Barnes, Claude. 1987. "Urban Political Economy and the Study of Afro-American Politics." Unpublished paper presented to NCOBPS.

Jones, Mack H. 1978. "Black Political Empowerment in Atlanta." *Annals, American Academy of Political and Social Science,* 439 (September).

Reed, Adolph, Jr. 1984. "Black Political Management." Unpublished manuscript.

———— . 1987. "The Black Urban Regime: Structural Origins and Constraints." Unpublished paper presented to NCOBPS.

Shipp, Bill. 1986. "A Candidate Who Doesn't Need a Job," *Atlanta Constitution,* (4 January).

Sjoquist, David. 1988. *The Economic Status of Black Atlantans.* Atlanta: Atlanta Urban League.

Young, Andrew. 1988. "State of the City, January 1988." Atlanta: Atlanta City Government.

Mayor of the Colony: Effective Mayoral Leadership as a Matter of Public Perception

Georgia A. Persons
Lenneal J. Henderson

Georgia Institute of Technology
The University of Baltimore

The literature on mayoral leadership is replete with postulations of models (Lawrence and Kotter, 1974), arguments that ensue from group conflict about the sources of constraints on leadership (George, 1968; Levine, 1974; Persons, 1985), delineations of the varied preconditions for effective leadership (Pressman, 1972), and characterizations of varied leadership styles (Levine, 1974). Leadership gets defined as agenda setting coalition building, the exercise of influence so as to ensure desired outcomes, and the setting of a tone within which issues get resolved (Edinger, 1967, Paige, 1972). Leadership as management gets defined as goal attainment in affecting the activities and output of administrative bureaucracies in service provision, and policy output in regard to addressing problems and needs of the community. Among the preconditions for effective leadership are popularity, adequate support staff, less-than-rancorous levels of conflict, and an authoritative base for effective decisionmaking and the exercise of power in regard to issues that impact upon the city and its citizens. Another critical factor that gets little attention in analyses of mayoral leadership is public perceptions of the mayor's effectiveness. Favorable perceptions of mayoral leadership are arguably the most valuable political capital available to a mayor.

Washington, D.C., presents an interesting case of a mayor who enjoyed immense popularity during two terms in office despite a host of shortcomings in the management of the city in areas over which the mayor had reasonable levels of control. However, into his third term in office, Mayor Marion Barry experienced a leadership crisis that stemmed in part from objective conditions over which he had little control, but that nonetheless created a crisis mainly of negative public perceptions.

The Political Context

The District of Columbia exists as something of an anomaly in the American federal system. It is the capital of the nation, originally designated as such so as to ensure a neutral site for a fledgling Union. Washington, D.C., has evolved into a kind of accidental city with a social and political culture significantly separate from the presence of the relatively spatially discrete and highly visible federal district within its midst. The District of Columbia is at once constitutionally a federal district; by congressional statute a legalized unit of city government with substantial but limited autonomy, via what is erroneously characterized as a home-rule charter; and, by virtue of the nature of intergovernmental relations, it is the functional equivalent of a state with all of the responsibilities of a state within the federal system. This unique status and complex political character significantly defines some major parameters and dynamics of politics in the city. Succinctly put, a major facet of politics in the District of Columbia pivots around the issue of the political and legal status of the city within the federal system.

The issue of political status is closely related to the second major facet of politics in the city, the issue of race. The District is more than 70 percent black, and heavily Democratic. Table 1 shows the population and racial and income distribution of D.C. wards. Its surrounding political

Table 1. Population and Racial and Median Income Distribution of D.C. Wards

Ward	Population[a]	Race Distribution			Median Household Income
		Black	White	Other	
1	78,400	57%	30%	13%	$18,900
2	82,500	46	43	11	$23,000
3	76,400	7	86	7	$37,700
4	80,500	87	9	4	$24,000
5	81,500	93	6	2	$20,300
6	74,200	68	30	2	$21,700
7	79,900	95	5	0	$18,200
8	75,100	90	9	1	$17,000
D.C. Total	628,500	67%	28%	5%	$22,400

Source: District of Columbia Government, INDICES: A Statistical Index to District of Columbia Services (Washington, D.C.: Office of Policy, July 1988).

[a]1986 population estimates rounded off.

jurisdictions, with the exception of Prince Georges County, Maryland, are predominantly white. The elected representatives from surrounding jurisdictions frequently join with other members of Congress in restricting the exercise of autonomy by the District in managing its internal affairs (examples include opposition to the residency requirement for employment in city government and opposition to specific expenditures in the city's budget) and in accusing the city of not being capable (read incompetent) of handling the responsibilities of full home rule. Proposals for statehood or full voting representation in Congress for the District have encountered strident opposition in Congress. To the majority black population in the city, such opposition to full-fledged legal and political status is largely seen as a racial affront.

Although this racial dynamic generally gets directed towards elements external to the city, the racial dynamic internal to the city is also very strong. It is a truism in the city that "the plan" is for a white political takeover. "The plan" is offered as explanation for a range of incidents and developments, especially real estate transactions and criticisms of the city's black elected officials. Like all truisms, this one embodies some kernel of validity as well as much myth and paranoia. The result, nonetheless, is that many issues get evaluated in regard to the racial implications of their possible implementation, and/or in regard to whether the originators of the ideas are black or white. Given the lopsided racial demographics of the city, there appears to be a tacit tolerance of white elected officials in the city's politics rather than a genuine acceptance of their legitimate role and presence.

The maturation of politics in the District came with the granting of limited home rule in 1973. Previously, residents had elected school boards starting in 1968, but all other local officials, including the mayor and the city council, had previously been appointed by the president of the United States. This appointment of local officials had reinforced a then–very strong class bias within the black community. Home rule converged with the new black politics movement as a national black strategy for seeking political and social justice. Marion Barry had emerged as an activist during the earlier civil rights movement and parlayed his activist grass-roots politics into the mainstream position of mayor in a three-way race in 1978. Barry's election represented the triumph of a new democracy of inclusion for low-income blacks in the governance of the city.

Despite a reasonable diversity of political party labels, competition for political office in the District tends to be more between individuals and their followers than between parties as organized interests. For example, the D.C. Statehood party has a relatively small official membership and holds no exclusive or special claim to advocating statehood, despite its suggestive name. Its most highly visible presence is attributable to a single member of the city council. The local Republican party is small as well, very weak in relationship to the local Democratic party, and while "Republican" is a useful label in at-large council races, it is generally a distinct disadvantage in ward-based races and in mayoral races. The political label "Independent" is generally used by Democrats who seek to circumvent legal requirements for a distribution of council seats by party affiliations and who wish to avoid confrontations with incumbent Democrats. The Democratic party enjoys a lot of internal competition and, in the 1982 mayoral primary, fielded some eleven candidates. This reflects the fact that the real hotbed of political competition in the District is at the community and ward level, with a focus on individuals. This pattern of competition is reinforced by ward-based elections for the school board, and the further division of wards into numerous Advisory Neighborhood Commissions, which, too, are elective posts.

The Rise of Marion Barry

Within the context of individual-oriented politics, the incumbent mayor, Marion Barry, has emerged triumphant. In mayoral politics, Barry got his start with support from low-income blacks and a critical component of young white liberals. He quickly expanded his base among the city's black middle class during his first term, and in 1982 had successfully transcended class divisions to defeat the late Patricia Roberts Harris, a grande dame of the city's black elite. More than anything else, Barry has built support the old-fashioned way: with patronage in the form of jobs and contracts for city services. In fact, patronage is the name of the game of politics in the District, with city council members exercising considerable influence over hiring in city agencies under their committee jurisdictions and similarly sharing patronage control with school-board members from their wards in regard to school-system jobs and contracts.

Barry has been by far the undisputed broker in the patronage game, sustained in this role by his great popularity among the voters, and by an unrivaled citywide political organization effective enough to influence most of the races for all elective offices within the city. As a result, Barry emerged as a machine-style boss, dominating the local political arena, and reigning as undisputed and unrivaled master politician. For a long time, the city belonged to Marion Barry.

Issues in D.C. Politics

Issues have generally been the side-orders in District politics. Issues get talked about in political races, but largely at the rhetorical level. There is one level of issues that have been politically significant, mainly to the local press and to Congress, members of the extended local political configuration. These include issues of prison overcrowding, corruption in city government, and the mayor's rather public personal life. These issues have never been effectively used against the mayor by local opponents. Issues significant to competition for local elective offices are mainly more secondary in nature, primarily of importance when affecting different neighborhood groups rather than real constituent groups. Such issues include zoning issues, debates over who will get development rights and associated concessions to community groups, and debates over the location of objectionable projects such as halfway houses and a proposed prison and drug-rehabilitation center. Such issues have generally been resolved by the mayor in a way that satisfied the key representatives of community groups and business interests where business interests are involved. In this way, the mayor tended to act to protect his primary support base at the community level.

The mayor has satisifed business interests by streamlining processing of permits and regulations requisite to new construction and big development projects. The city has also offered very favorable terms to developers seeking to acquire development rights to city-owned properties. In turn, some of the most notable business leaders have been identified as close advisors to the mayor, and the local business community has been among his most loyal supporters.

Questions of Effective Leadership

How then does the question of leadership effectiveness get defined in a political context (1) with clearly defined external enemies, that is, Congress and surrounding political jurisdictions; (2) with an exaggerated concern about a white takeover conspiracy that serves to obfuscate many critical issues and to deflect frequently legitimate criticism; (3) with mobilization of voters more around individuals than party organization; and (4) wherein would-be constituent interests are subordinated to the symbolic significance of black political dominance and a well-established machine-style patronage system?

In the District of Columbia the question of mayoral effectiveness has traditionally been upstaged by the mayor's formidable popularity. Barry's strong support in the black community has been bolstered by the ready willingness of business leaders to provide him with a campaign fund that in the elections of 1982 and 1986 was so abundant as to sorely discourage much of the potential opposition. The real money was on Barry. Moreover, the mayor has been immensely successful in brokering between business interests and community groups and is widely credited with balancing the city's budget, establishing a sound financial-accounting reporting system and the city's bond rating, and in improving service delivery and the overall service function of city agencies. Primarily, formidable popularity has shielded the mayor from the consequences of questions of effective leadership. This has been the case despite a long series of scandals involving corruption in city government, gross inefficiency in management of the city's public housing program, and scandals involving the mayor's alleged womanizing and associations with known drug dealers. (Table 2 illustrates voter participation in D.C. wards.)

However, into his third term in office, the mayor's "Teflon shield" started to disintegrate. For the first time, polls taken showed an unusually high level of dissatisfaction with the mayor, and indicated that if an

**Table 2. Voter Participation by Ward in the November 1987
General Elections in the District of Columbia**

Total Registered Vote 1987: 253,830
Total Votes Cast 1987: 79,126 (31%)

Ward	Percentage Voting Turnout
1	28.3%
2	28.1
3	39.7
4	34.5
5	32.3
6	30.3
7	31.1
8	17.5
City Average	31.0%

Source: District of Columbia Government, INDICES: A
Statistical Index to District of Columbia Services
(Washington, D.C.: Office of Policy, July 1988), p. 55.

immediate election were to be held, it would lead to the mayor's defeat. The primary factors behind Barry's sudden vulnerability have evolved from issues that the city government has not been equipped to handle: a growing social-services crisis stemming from a large and growing homeless population and a frightening escalation in the number of drug-related homicides and shootings. These two issues became major weapons used by the media in an unrelenting questioning of the mayor's leadership ability and contributed to a significant and precipitous erosion in his popularity. Both issues have contributed as well to a growing budget deficit for the city. (Table 3 illustrates appropriated spending, 1985–1988.) The city's expenditures for the homeless increased from $9.2 million in fiscal year (FY) 1985 to $27 million in FY 1986 (*Washington Post*, 28 February 1989), largely driven by an initiative passed in 1984 (against the mayor's opposition) that requires the city to guarantee adequate overnight shelter to anyone who needs it. Homelessness is a cumbersome and untidy social problem, and the city's responses have been predictably inefficient, inadequate given the scope of the problem, and highly vulnerable to dramatic and piercing criticism. For example, one plan had homeless families (mainly women and children) sheltered at night in a hotel, cleared out in the mornings with all of their belongings, bussed to another city-funded site for meals, and returned to the hotel for the night.

**Table 3. Appropriated Spending in the District of
Columbia by Appropriation Title, 1985–1988**

Appropriation Title	Fiscal 1985	1986	Year 1987	Percent Change 1985 - 87	1988
Governmental direction & support	$90,772	$101,598	$110,906	22.2	$112,971
Economic dev. & regulation	$79,670	$96,570	$111,597	40.1	$129,331
Human support services	$564,932	$594,312	$660,631	16.9	$688,775
Public educ. system	$490,379	$515,070	$544,929	11.1	$579,480
Public safety & justice	$535,023	$613,330	$657,865	23.0	$679,780
Public works	$191,108	$196,319	$198,757	3.6	$207,361
Finance and other uses	$193,120	$198,317	$211,308	12.4	$271,627
Total Expenditures	$2,145,705	$2,315,516	$2,495,992	16.3%	$2,669,325

Source: District of Columbia Office of the Budget
Note: Totals may not add due to rounding

However, the greatest crisis for the mayor has been the extremely high homicide rate, which reached a total of 372 deaths for calendar year 1988. Predictions for 1989 project that the homicide rate will be even higher, at more than 600 deaths.[1] Understandably, the homicide rate undermined the sense of safety and security all District residents felt about the city streets and its neighborhoods. While all citizens suddenly felt vulnerable, some neighborhoods were literally under siege from drug dealings and associated violence. As citizens expressed outrage, their ward-based leaders in turn pressed the mayor to respond. As each day brought news of more shootings, the shifting of responsibility to the mayor increased. The mayor's credibility on the drug issue was seriously undermined by national news reports of his visitations with a suspected drug dealer in a local hotel, a suspect who was later arrested in an FBI sting in the U.S. Virgin Islands.

The homelessness crisis and special police operations in response to the drug war contributed to and converged with a budget deficit of $14.3 million in FY 1988 (of a total $3.5 billion budget), a projected deficit of $175 million for FY 1989, and the prospects of layoffs of city workers and severe cutbacks in programs and services (*Washington Post*, 8 January 1988). The result was that the mayor's effectiveness in leadership was seriously questioned, as was his general fitness for office.

Issue Types and Leadership Crises

Why is it that the issues of homelessness and drug-related violence generated a crisis of leadership effectiveness for Mayor Barry when numerous other problems did not? On the one hand, the standards against which the mayor's actions get evaluated in regard to both issues are considerably less than definitive. For example, what constitutes *adequate* shelter for the homeless, a temporary hotel room or a fully furnished apartment or home? How long should shelter be provided at city expense for individual families? Do homeless families have a right to subsidized housing in one of the nation's most expensive cities? How will the city pay for such an open-ended responsibility? How many police officers on the street are enough to stop drug violence? How can a mayor justify arresting more and more suspects when the prisons are already under court penalty for serious overcrowding? Can the police actually deter crime? On the other hand, both issues are driven by strong requirements for definitive actions by the mayor, and definitive results as well. By law, adequate shelter must be provided, and by public demand the drug trafficking and related violence must be stopped. In both cases, the city's budget gets held hostage.

Administratively, the magnitude of the homeless problem and the legal requirement for city-provided shelter make homelessness essentially a new problem, for which the city must develop and fund programmatic responses. Because the scope of the problem cannot be contained, all programmatic responses are inadequate. Thus, the issue of sheltering the homeless is a classic example of expectations of effective leadership in the absence of the resources necessary for effective responses.

Public-safety issues are unique among the set of issues with which a mayor must deal (Persons, 1987). While many aspects of public safety may be considered routine administrative matters, these activities constitute a critical background of decisions and actions that support the daily functioning of urban life. Among the issues likely to confront a mayor in the course of a day's governance, none are likely to escalate to a crisis level with the rapidity, potential proportions, and possible consequences of public-safety issues. Similarly, none are likely to require such concentrated decision making or involve possibly starkly zero-sum outcomes. Nonroutine public-safety activities are more likely to involve the mayor in the kind of crisis management in which decisions must be made quickly, under intense pressure, and with a high level of uncertainty about the potential dynamics of a situation, and to involve circumstances likely to yield unpredictable outcomes. Although the public demands an effective response to daily multiple homicides and other shootings, this type of unorganized, randomly dispersed, drug-related crime does not readily respond to tough gun-control laws, increased police presence, or community anticrime efforts. Again, the mayor is faced with a problem for which he is held accountable, but for which he cannot devise solutions.

Ineffective Leadership as a Crisis of Perception

The crisis confronting Mayor Barry in early 1989 stemmed from a set of actual problems that could not be resolved by the dispensation of pro grammatic goods, the brokering of deals, or the manipulation of racial symbols. This was not altogether something new, in that mayors have always been faced with problems for which they do not have resources or solutions, such as unemployment, low-income housing, and crime. Generally such problems have been met by tapping funding and other resources from federal sources or by resorting to manipulating symbols of obfuscation. Substantial federal resources are not presently available to mayors in dealing with such problems. In the case of the District of Columbia, Mayor Barry had accumulated an enormous pool of personal liabilities as a leader, some attributable to the natural and steady erosion of resources available to him due to longevity in office, and some attributable to the cumulative drain of resources due to scandals involving many of his appointees and other city employees over the years, as well as to a series of scandals involving the mayor's personal life.

In sum, Mayor Barry's ideas and approaches to solving problems were no longer new, his credibility as a leader had been severely diminished, and he was no longer viewed by the public as an effective leader. It was not so much that the mayor's abilities as a leader had changed in the objective sense, but rather that the public's perception of him as a leader had changed.

Notes

1. Projections of the homicide rate for 1989 were developed by a team of researchers at the University of the District of Columbia and presented in media reports from yet-unpublished papers.

References

Edinger, Lewis. 1967. Editor's Introduction. In Lewis Edinger, ed., *Political Leadership in Industrialized Societies*. New York: John Wiley & Sons.

George, Alexander. 1968. "Political Leadership and Social Change in American Cities." *Daedalus*, 97 (Fall): 1,194–1,217.

Lawrence, Paul L., and John P. Kotter. 1974. *Mayors in Action*. New York: John Wiley & Sons.

Levine, Charles. 1974. *Racial Conflict and the American Mayor*. Lexington, Mass.: D. C. Heath.

McFarland, Andrew S. 1969. *Power and Leadership in Pluralist Systems*. Stanford: Stanford University Press.

Paige, Glenn, ed. 1972. *Political Leadership: Readings for an Emerging Field*. New York: The Free Press.

Persons, Georgia A. 1985. "Reflections on Mayoral Leadership: The Impact of Changing Issues and Changing Times." *Phylon*, 46 (September): 205–18.

——— . 1987. "The Philadelphia MOVE Incident as an Anomaly in Models of Mayoral Leadership." *Phylon*, 48: (Winter) 249–60.

Pressman, Jeffrey. 1972. "Preconditions for Mayoral Leadership." *American Political Science Review*, 66 (June): 511–24.

Black Political and Mayoral Leadership in Birmingham and New Orleans

Huey Perry

Southern University

The black-politics literature is increasingly characterized by an examination of the impact of black political participation. This is especially
true of the urban-black-politics literature. This article describes and analyzes the impact of increased black political participation and mayoral
leadership on selected policies and actions of local government in Birmingham, Alabama, and New Orleans, Louisiana. In both cities the
number of black voters increased appreciably during the early 1960s (see
Table 1), and, as their numbers increased, blacks, in coalition with
middle-class whites, began to exert a greater impact on electoral outcomes. The growing black vote played an increasingly important role
within the structure of a biracial coalition in electing seriatim in both
cities the first racially moderate white mayor, the first racially liberal
white mayor, and the first black mayor. The growing black vote in both

Table 1. Black Voter Registration in Birmingham and New Orleans

Year	Birmingham Percent Black of Total Voter Registration	Year	New Orleans Percent Black of Total Voter Registration
1960	10%	1960	17%
1967	36	1969	30
1975	40	1977	42
1979	45	1982	46
1983	51	1986	51

154

cities also played an important role in electing, over the several city elections since the early 1960s, a more racially progressive city council, a process which eventually resulted in the election of a black majority to the council.

This article analyzes governmental policies and actions in four categories of public-sector activities: (1) executive appointments, (2) appointments to boards and commissions, (3) municipal employment, and (4) minority-business participation. These are important categories of local governmental authority that provide heuristically important opportunities for assessing the impact of black political participation and mayoral leadership. While the impact of black politics on blacks' representation in municipal employment has been widely studied (Nelson and Meranto, 1977; Eisinger, 1980, 1982; Dye and Renick, 1981; Perry, 1983; Perry and Stokes, 1987; Browning, Marshall, and Tabb, 1984; Mladenka, 1989), the impact of black politics in the other three categories under examination in this article has not been as widely studied. Thus, this article contributes to the literature by examining the impact of black politics in the three other categories of public-sector activities.

Additionally, the four categories of public-sector activities examined in this article allow an examination of the conclusion reached by previous studies that black political participation is capable of producing significant public-sector benefits, but that it is incapable of producing significant private-sector benefits. Benefits produced in the first three categories would be public-sector benefits; benefits in the last category, private-sector benefits. Thus, this article also contributes to the literature by its focus on the impact of black political participation and mayoral leadership on multiple categories of public-sector activities that produce both public-sector benefits and private-sector benefits.

Executive Appointments

This category includes appointments by the mayor to his top personal executive staff and heads of departments of city government. In Birmingham, black representation in key executive positions increased from 0 percent in 1975 prior to the election of David Vann, the city's first racially liberal white mayor, to 44 percent of the mayor's top personal executive staff positions (four out of nine positions) and one department head during Vann's administration (Perry, 1983:212). Throughout his first two terms, the current mayor, Richard Arrington, maintained a 50 percent black representation in his fourteen-member top personal executive staff.

In New Orleans, black representation in department-head positions increased from 0 percent in 1969 prior to the election of Moon Landrieu, the city's first racially liberal white mayor, to 42 percent of the department-head positions (five out of thirteen) during Landrieu's mayoralty. During Morial's mayoralty, the number of black department heads increased to seven out of twelve, or 58 percent (Perry and Stokes,

1987:244–45). Under the present mayor of New Orleans, Sidney Barthelemy, blacks comprise 58 percent of the executive positions. In terms
of unclassified and appointed staff with incomes equal to or over
$19,500, blacks in 1988 comprised 51 percent of persons holding such
positions.[1]

Appointments to Boards and Commissions

As late as 1970 there was no black representation on Birmingham's
boards and commissions. The first black to serve on a board or commission in Birmingham was not appointed until 1972. By 1978, 26 percent of
all the seats on municipal boards and commissions were held by blacks
(Perry, 1983:213). In 1987, the proportion of blacks on the city's boards
and commissions was just under what it was in 1978—25 percent.[2] In
1960, no blacks served on New Orleans boards and commissions. By
January 1988, blacks had come to comprise 25 percent of all appointments to the city's boards and commissions. Thus, increased black political participation in both cities has been successful in increasing black
representation on municipal boards and commissions to one-fourth of
the total membership of those bodies.

Municipal Employment

One of the strongest relationships in the black-politics literature is the
relationship between increased black political participation and blacks'
obtaining a more equitable share of municipal employment. The black
proportion of the municipal work force in New Orleans increased from
40 percent when Morial assumed office in 1977 to 53 percent by the end
of the Morial mayoralty in 1985 (Perry and Stokes, 1987:243). Table 2
shows that blacks have achieved substantial representation in all levels
of the municipal work force in New Orleans. Therefore, blacks are not
only well represented in the service/maintenance (66 percent) and office/
clerical (67 percent) categories where they traditionally do well; they are
also well represented in the middle-level categories of skilled craft workers (52 percent), paraprofessionals (39 percent), protective services (54
percent), and technicians (67 percent), and in the professionals (46 percent) and officials/administrators (32 percent) categories, which generally
have been more resistant to black penetration. By March 1988 the proportion of blacks on the city's municipal workforce had increased to 55
percent of the classified workforce and 59 percent of the unclassified
workforce.[3]

In Birmingham, the proportion of the municipal work force comprised
by blacks increased from less than 1 percent in 1960 to 9 percent in 1975
(Perry, 1983:210–11). However, more recent data show that blacks have
achieved much greater progress toward realizing an equitable proportion
of municipal employment. Table 3 shows that blacks not only have

Table 2. Full-Time Employees of the City of New Orleans by Race, 1985

Occupational Classification	Black N	Black %	White N	White %	Other N	Other %
Officials/administrators	35	31.8	75	68.2	0	0.0
Professionals	131	45.8	145	50.7	10	3.5
Technicians	30	66.7	14	31.1	1	2.2
Protective services	13	54.2	10	41.7	1	4.2
Paraprofessionals	7	38.9	10	55.6	1	5.6
Office/clerical	549	67.2	251	30.7	17	2.1
Skilled craft workers	63	52.1	47	38.8	11	9.1
Service maintenance	48	65.8	21	28.8	4	5.5
Totals	876	58.6	573	38.4	45	3.0

achieved a more equitable proportion of total municipal employment in Birmingham, but also, and more important, they have succeeded in integrating the city's work force at all occupational levels. In 1985 blacks comprised 37 percent of the city's total municipal work force, which represents more than a fourfold increase in the black proportion of the city's municipal work force in 1975. In terms of representation in the various occupational classifications, blacks are well represented in the service/maintenance (66 percent) and office/clerical (47 percent) categories, as well as in the middle-level categories of skilled craft workers (29 percent), paraprofessionals (46 percent), protective services (19 percent), and technicians (20 percent). They are also well represented in the professionals (22 percent) and officials/administrators (16 percent) categories.

Comparatively, blacks in New Orleans are faring considerably better than blacks in Birmingham in terms of municipal employment. New Orleans blacks have not only realized a greater proportion of total employment than Birmingham blacks, but they have also significantly surpassed their Birmingham counterparts in all occupational categories, except service/maintenance (where they are equal) and paraprofessionals (where Birmingham exceeds New Orleans by 7 percentage points). Part of the reason why blacks in Birmingham have had difficulty in significantly increasing their representation in the city's municipal work force is that the Jefferson County Personnel Board, which certifies candidates

Table 3. Full-Time Employees of the City of Birmingham by Race, 1985

Occupational Classification	Black N	Black %	White N	White %	Other N	Other %
Officials/administrators	11	15.9	58	84.1	0	0.0
Professionals	97	21.7	346	77.2	5	1.1
Technicians	62	20.2	245	79.8	0	0.0
Protective services	186	19.2	782	80.7	1	0.1
Paraprofessionals	52	46.4	57	50.9	3	2.7
Office/clerical	173	47.3	193	52.7	0	0.0
Skilled craft workers	43	20.8	163	78.7	1	0.5
Service maintenance	651	65.7	339	34.2	1	0.1
Totals	1275	36.8	2183	62.9	11	.3

for vacancies in local governments throughout the county, has been hostile to Birmingham's efforts to hire more blacks in municipal government.

Minority-Business Participation

This category refers to public officials awarding contracts for services and products needed by the city to black companies and perhaps also to providing technical assistance for those companies. Increased black political participation in both cities has not achieved significant results in increasing the dollar amount of municipal contracts awarded to black companies. The minority-business participation program in Birmingham was begun by a city ordinance in 1977. Mayor David Vann initiated a 10 percent minority set-aside program, which stipulated that 10 percent of the city's construction business would go to minority contractors. The Association of General Contractors successfully sued in state court to have the set-aside program overturned. The court ruled that the program was not constitutional because the city council had not approved it. Vann's set-aside program was eventually approved by the city council, thus overcoming the court's objection. The program was finally implemented by Arrington, but it has not substantially improved minority businesses.

Arrington acknowledges in this regard that his major disappointment with regard to the interests of blacks is his failure to advance the black business community. This sentiment is echoed by Arrington's former chief of staff: "The city's minority-assistance program has not helped black businesses much. Blacks have not moved into the mainstream of the business sector. In every other way, blacks in Birmingham have been successful."[4] Arrington had hoped that his minority-business participation program would have been successful in creating a strong black business sector to complement blacks' outstanding success in the public sector. This has not occurred. Thus the political economy of Birmingham is characterized by a duality that is clearly racially identifiable. The public sector in Birmingham is clearly black dominated, whereas the private sector is as strongly white dominated.

The business participation program in New Orleans also has not enjoyed much success in strengthening the black business sector. The city authorized its minority-business participation program in late 1983; however, the implementation of the program did not begin until 1985. By the end of Morial's mayoralty in 1986, the city's minority-business participation program was widely regarded as a failure (Perry and Stokes, 1987). As in Birmingham, the public sector in New Orleans is black dominated, whereas the private sector is as strongly white dominated.

Summary and Conclusions

Increased black political participation in both cities has resulted in blacks receiving a significantly fairer share of the benefits and opportunities provided by city government in three of the four categories of governmental policies and actions examined. Consistent with prior research findings, increased black political participation in Birmingham and New Orleans is strongly associated with blacks receiving a more equitable share of municipal employment opportunities. The category of governmental policies and actions in which increased black political participation has exerted its weakest influence in both cities is minority-business participation programs. The overall findings of this research support the conclusion of prior research that black politics is capable of producing significant public-sector benefits but incapable of producing significant private-sector benefits.

In both cities the principal remaining realm of racial segregation is the private sector. Blacks have not enjoyed much success in penetrating the private sector. Using their control of governmental authority to attempt to advance opportunities for blacks in the private sector in the two localities has not proven to be a very successful strategy. Blacks are limited to this approach because their small degree of representation within the private sector makes a direct assault on the private sector infeasible. Moreover, there is nothing in the locus of decision making in the private sector that is exactly comparable to the vote in the public sector that would allow blacks to influence the private sector from within as they have done in the public sector. The dollar and the vote are not exactly comparable in this regard. The lesson of Birmingham and New Orleans in this regard is that black political participation and mayoral leadership from black mayors committed to use governmental authority to advance blacks' interests in the private sector cannot do much in the way of providing appreciable private-sector benefits to blacks.

The challenge of black politics and mayoral leadership in the 1990s will be to use the resources of governmental authority to increase opportunities for blacks in the private sector. If successful, this would be the most significant breakthrough in black politics since the black political empowerment of the 1960s and 1970s and the increased allocation of public-sector benefits to blacks that it has brought about.

Notes

1. This information was provided by Mayor Sidney Barthelemy's office. The percentage was calculated from the information provided.
2. This information was provided by Mayor Richard Arrington's office. The percentage was calculated from the information provided.
3. These percentages were calculated from information provided by Mayor Barthelemy's office.
4. Personal interview with Dr. Edward LaMonte, former Executive Secretary to Mayor Richard Arrington.

References

Browning, Rufus P., Dale Rogers Marshall, and David H. Tabb. 1984. *Protest Is Not Enough*. Berkeley: University of California Press.

Dye, Thomas R., and James Renick. 1981. "Political Power and City Jobs: Determinants of Minority Employment." *Social Science Quarterly*, 62:475–86.

Eisinger, Peter K. 1980. *Politics of Displacement: Racial and Ethnic Transition in Three American Cities*. New York: Academic.

———. 1982. "Black Employment in Municipal Jobs: The Impact of Black Political Power." *American Political Science Review* 76:380–92.

Mladenka, Kenneth R. 1989. "Blacks and Hispanics in Urban Politics." *American Political Science Review*, 83:165–91.

Nelson, William E., Jr., and Philip J. Meranto. 1977. *Electing Black Mayors: Political Action in the Black Community*. Columbus: Ohio State University Press.

Perry, Huey L. 1983. "The Impact of Black Political Participation on Public Sector Employment and Representation on Municipal Boards and Commissions." *The Review of Black Political Economy*, 12:203–17.

Perry, Huey L., and Alfred Stokes. 1987. "Politics and Power in the Sunbelt: Mayor Morial of New Orleans." In Michael B. Preston, Lenneal J. Henderson, and Paul Puryear, eds., *The New Black Politics: The Search for Political Power*. New York: Longman.

Stein, Lana. 1986. "Representative Local Government: Minorities in the Municipal Workforce." *Journal of Politics*, 48:694–713.

The Political Legacy of Harold Washington: 1983–1987

Robert T. Starks
Michael B. Preston

Northeastern Illinois University
University of Southern California

Harold Washington's popularity as mayor of the city of Chicago was unquestionable. In 1987, on the eve of his reelection, Washington was reported to have an overall citywide job-approval rating of 67 percent according to a poll conducted by the *Chicago Tribune* (24 March 1987). This same poll showed that "when asked what kind of job he would do if reelected, 65 percent of the voters said either excellent or good (*Chicago Tribune*, 24 March 1987). While it is clear that the great majority of his support and job-approval rating came from blacks, to the tune of 94 percent, the *Tribune* further reports that the high approval rating from the white community on the northwest and southwest sides of the city was also unmistakable, and it explains the overall city rating of 67 percent.

On the northwest side, those polled gave him an approval rate of 47 percent, with 11 percent strongly approving of his job performance and 36 percent saying they approve somewhat of the mayor's actions in his first term.

That approval rate drops on the southwest side, where only 9 percent approve strongly of his performance as mayor and 23 percent approve somewhat, giving a total approval of 32 percent in that area (*Chicago Tribune*, 24 March 1987).

The loyalty and respect that Washington enjoyed came as a response to the growing power that he was amassing as a result of his solid black constituent base and his expanding multiethnic coalition. He had a political style that exemplified strength, aggressiveness, fairness, open-

161

ness, and reform. It was from this position of strength and power that he was able to achieve the goals that he had placed on his agenda.

His major accomplishments can be categorized as political, and governmental or administrative. The following is a survey of the most significant ones.

Political Accomplishments

In any political system, a chief executive must command respect and effective political influence within that system in order to govern. Indeed, effective performance and leadership is not possible without some measure of political influence. Richard J. Daley, who served as mayor from 1955 to 1976, understood the importance of this relationship and combined his political role with his governmental role.

Richard J. Daley emerged as both Cook County chairman in 1953 and as mayor in 1955. Having combined the two most powerful offices in the city, Daley spent the next twenty-two years presiding over the strongest urban political organization in America. The Daley machine not only dominated Chicago and Cook County government, but it also had considerable influence in Springfield and a major voice in presidential politics (Gove and Massotti, 1982:x).

It was not possible for Harold Washington to follow this path to the mayor's office because he was never a ward committeeman, the major prerequisite to being a member of the Cook County Democratic Central Committee, and the fact that his mayoral campaign was based upon his pledge to destroy the machine by destroying the patronage system. The patronage system is an elaborate system that distributes the spoils of electoral politics to ward committeemen and the party workers based upon what the party leadership determines to be each worker's contribution to the party victory in the last election (Starks, 1982:54–56).

The Washington route to city hall was one of reform. As a top priority, the Washington reform movement and reform coalition targeted the patronage system for elimination. In an attempt to fulfill this campaign promise Washington began his tenure by signing a federal court agreement to adhere strictly to the limitations on political hiring as defined by the Shakman Decree.

Michael Shakman "filed suit in 1969. He argued that he had lost his campaign for delegate to the 1970 state constitutional convention because city workers had been coerced into hustling votes for his opponent who was backed by the regular Democratic organization" (Joravsky, 1984b:6–8). As a result of the 1969 lawsuit, the city of Chicago agreed to stop forcing employees to engage in political work as a condition of employment for its 42,000 workers in 1972. The decree signed by the mayor in 1983 further restricted his powers by exempting only 790 positions from the total of 42,000 employees.

After striking this masterful blow against the patronage system by signing the Shakman Decree, Washington immediately began instituting the next phase of his reform program, empowering community groups and organizations. These community-based groups were the ones that had come together to form the basis of the coalition that elected him, and now they were being given access to city-controlled federal and state discretionary funds for planning, job training, and development. They were also given appointments to city boards, commissions, and agencies. Most important, the leadership of these groups formed the core of the mayor's inner circle of political advisors. In effect, these groups replaced the Machine's ward organizations by performing many of the functions that were traditionally carried out by the machine.

Washington had effectively dismantled the machine and its control over the black community and established in its place a reform coalition that was community based, but broad enough to make it comfortable for a wide variety of people including reformed or "born again" machine politicians. These seasoned and "born again" elected officials and ward committeemen whom he had grown up with in the party were essential to his electoral success because of their knowledge of the mechanics of the electoral process and their control of the electoral apparatus. Because of the needs of these diverse groups and individuals, he had to construct his reform coalition in the broadest and most inclusive manner possible, while building in checks and balances that would assure maximum accountability, comfort, and loyalty to his leadership and the ideas of reform.

These checks and balances allowed for the coexistence and cooperation of movement people, grass-roots activists, community groups, liberals, reformers, and "born again" machine ward bosses to work together to advance the reform agenda. This arrangement provided political support for the elected officials in the form of an endorsement by Washington at election time, which guaranteed coalition votes and other forms of support. The threat of withholding an endorsement was always used to keep elected officials in line.

Minimal political spoils were doled out to the politicians in the form of jobs and appointments that could be passed out to their workers and constituents. However, even in these instances, Washington was still able to maintain hegemony over the politicians because of his enormous popularity and his practice of appealing over the heads of the politicians directly to the voters through mailings, frequent visits to the neighborhoods, television and radio appearances, and dramatic maneuvering in the city council. Thus, constituents most times attributed any personal benefits received from the system or any individual politician to the benevolence of Harold Washington and the existence of the coalition rather to than the machine, as was the tradition in the pre-Washington era.

After moving forward aggressively to put the reform agenda in place by dismantling the black sector of the machine and replacing it with his reform coalition, Washington proceeded to remove the white Democratic party's resistance to his control of the City Council. The removal of this barrier called upon most of his political skills and resources. The Cook County Democratic party's rejection of his candidacy after he won the

Democratic nomination for mayor was carried over into the City Council. When he moved to reorganize the City Council after winning the general election, he was blocked by Alderman Edward R. Vrdolyak and his group of twenty-nine white aldermen. These white Democratic aldermen blocked his legislative agenda, held up confirmation of his appointments to boards and commissions, and otherwise undermined and frustrated his entire reform agenda. This obstacle was not removed until the special aldermanic election in the spring of 1986.

The election was ordered by the federal court as a result of the settlement of the city reapportionment case. All four of the Washington-sponsored candidates won in their respective wards, and he added four additional allies to his side. With the defection of Alderman Vrdolyak to the Republican party after the mayoral election in 1987 and the subsequent election of the president of the Cook County Board, George Dunne, to the post of Chairman of the Cook County Democratic party with the help of Washington, the mayor was able to count Dunne's alderman (Burton Natarus, Forty-Second Ward) as a Washington ally. Because he could not add Dunne's alderman as an ally until after the mayoral election, the council was split 25 to 25 from the spring of 1986 (after the special election) until the mayoral election, and it was only by the mayor's parliamentary power to break a tie vote that he was able to pass his legislation. Washington received high marks from most of his critics for the manner in which he was able to work throughout this period.

However, Washington's major political accomplishment was the dethroning and subsequent forcing of his political nemesis out of the party. Mr. Vrdolyak, the former alderman of the Tenth Ward, was the chairman of the Cook County Democratic party in 1983 and supported Jane Byrne in the primary and the Republican candidate Bernard Epton in the general election. Vrdolyak led the fights against Washington in the Chicago City Council and worked vigorously to undermine his administration. In 1987, he resigned from the City Council, sponsored his brother for his seat, and ran for mayor on the Solidarity party ballot. After losing the election, he declared himself a Republican and announced his candidacy for the Cook County Clerk of the Circuit Court. Thus, less than two months before his death in November 1987, Washington was proud to declare that he had run Vrdolyak out of the Democratic party to the Republican party (Starks and Preston, 1989).

Harold Washington's considerable political skills combined with his intellectual gifts and enormous popularity enabled him to become very effective as a political leader. His political effectiveness was felt in every sector of city life, primarily because he was able to revolutionize the thinking and broaden the horizons of the black masses and command the respect, if only grudgingly, of the white community. This political legacy was one of the most valuable, beneficial and lasting aspects of the Washington era. It is clear that regardless of what changes may occur from this point on, black voters will never allow themselves to be subjected to political subordination again.

Washington's political effectiveness and accomplishment can be summarized as follows:

- Dismantling the patronage system and, thus, rendering the machine ineffective
- Empowering community groups and grass-roots activists, and shifting clout away from the elected officials to these groups
- Integrating "born again" ward bosses into his electoral and governing coalitions and instituting a checks-and-balance system that held them accountable
- Expanding his governing coalition by sponsoring and electing additional allies in the City Council from the Hispanic community, which broke the back of the white stronghold on his administration
- Dethroning and subsequently forcing Edward Vrdolyak out of the party and the City Council

Overall, Washington was one of the most powerful and effective mayors in the history of the city. His effectiveness is even better appreciated when the full extent of the constraints, both structural and environmental, are understood. When these constraints are placed within the context of only five years as mayor, it is clear that he was a skillful politician and administrator.

In spite of all of his talents and the accelerated pace of his agenda after his reelection, he died before completing some major aspects of it.

Unfinished Agenda Items

While the Washington 1987 election platform was a more sophisticated and seasoned version of the 1983 reform agenda, reform, fairness, and openness were still the major themes. Within this ambitious platform were promises of major central-city and neighborhood redevelopment projects, job development, affordable housing, education reform, and an even more streamlined and efficient service-delivery system.

Washington was himself highly disappointed at his inability to bring about as much change as he wanted. He was especially disappointed by the consistently poor administration and high debt at the Chicago Housing Authority (CHA), where some 145,000 predominantly black and poor people resided. The poor performance of Washington appointees at the CHA was punctuated by the fact that CHA residents voted consistently strongly in each election for Washington and for those candidates that he endorsed. At his death, he was working hard to put together a more coherent and comprehensive development strategy for the neighborhoods, which had been neglected for decades. The Washington development philosophy was one in which neighborhood development and reform were closely tied together. However, despite some brilliant efforts in this regard, he was unable to affect the growing unemployment and homelessness, because he did not have the time to put into

action his comprehensive neighborhood development strategy. The fact
that he did not designate a successor to continue his reforms facilitated
the power struggle that ensued after his death. This power struggle has
severely fractured the Washington coalition and threatened the completion of the Washington agenda.

Conclusion

Chicago was brought into a new awareness of itself during the tenure
of Harold Washington. He vastly increased the political confidence and
efficacy of black citizens, while laying the foundation for the first real
multiethnic progressive coalition in the city's history. At the heart of this
coalition was the black voter. He combined the black vote with that of
liberal whites and Hispanics. One of his greatest accomplishments was
bringing the *outs* into his administration and giving them responsible
positions of leadership. Second, blacks became leaders of the progressive multiethnic coalition—not just followers. Third, he set up parallel
structures to reduce the power of "born again" machine politicians by
giving more influence to community organizations in black, Hispanic,
and some white communities. Fourth, he gained gradual control of the
Democratic party by using his political skill, the courts, and his popularity in the black and Hispanic communities. He was, in brief, the right
man at the right time; his untimely death was a blow to all of Chicago's
citizens—especially blacks—but before his death, he left a legacy that
would be hard for other black politicians to follow.

The crisis of black leadership in Chicago became readily apparent after
Washington's death. Eugene Sawyer's appointment to office split the
black community down the middle. Here was a black being supported
by the same people Washington fought so hard to defeat. Tim Evans,
the other black politician, hoping to succeed Washington, lost out to
Sawyer in the 1987 succession fight.

In the special mayoral primary election held in February of 1989 to
choose a successor to complete the remaining two years of the late
Harold Washington's term, Richard M. Daley, the son of the former
mayor Richard J. Daley, handily defeated Eugene Sawyer to win the
Democratic primary. Tim Evans, the other black mayoral candidate, did
not run in the primary but instead chose to run in the general election.
The Evans people, however, did not support Sawyer in the primary and
neither did the Hispanics nor the liberal whites. Thus, the Washington
coalition fell apart, and it all but assured Evans defeat in the general
election.

In the general election for mayor on 4 April 1989, Alderman Timothy
C. Evans ran on the Harold Washington party ballot (Independent).
Former Democratic alderman and Washington nemesis, Edward Vrdol-
yak, ran on the Republican ballot, while Richard M. Daley ran on the
Democratic party ballot. Daley beat Evans and Vrdolyak rather easily by
getting most of the white ethnic, liberal white lakefront, and Hispanic

vote. And while Evans received some 428,000 black votes, almost 300,000 black voters stayed at home in the general election. About the same number stayed home during the 28 February primary. The Sawyer people were among the groups not supporting Evans for mayor.

More important for the future of black politics in Chicago is the fact that an NBC television exit poll on election day, 4 April, found that 14 percent of black voters gave Daley a favorable rating and 24 percent reported "not sure." These polling data, combined with the low black turnout, make the job of black political leadership all the more difficult if the goal is to recapture the mayor's office in 1991. Indeed, 1991 is the next regularly scheduled election for mayor, since the 1989 election was a special one necessitated by the death of Harold Washington and the subsequent unexpired term.

Daley, then, has less than two years to destroy the last remnant of the Washington coalition and build a new coalition that is loyal to him. This new Daley coalition must have a majority of whites, a majority of Hispanics, and 20 to 25 percent of the black vote in order to win. While Daley only received 6 percent of the black vote in the general election, he can still win if he can keep the majority of the Hispanic vote that he received in the 1989 election along with his white vote and succeed in building the black vote to the 20 percent level. His political strategy has been directed towards that end. He has made significant Hispanic appointments and has promised to keep an open-door policy toward blacks. In addition, he has made some significant black appointments to his cabinet, although not as significant as those of the Washington and Sawyer administrations.

Clearly, the Washington movement must rebuild and rehabilitate itself and move significantly in a relatively short period of time in order to regain the mayor's office. Three significant things must happen in sequence: (1) complete and clear analysis of the causes and effects of political action that has occurred over the last ten years, with emphasis on the composition and decomposition of the Washington movement; (2) the development of a rebuilding strategy based upon the findings of that analysis; and (3) the choosing of a candidate based upon the principles that underlie the goals and objectives of the coalition formation that will allow for black cohesion and interethnic coalition building. Whether or not black political leaders, along with black organizations, can do this may well determine the future of black politics in Chicago for many years to come.

> Well, son, I'll Tell you
> Life for me ain't been no crystal stair.
> It's had tacks in it,
> And splinters.
> And boards torn up,
> And places with no carpets on the floor—
> Bare.
>
> But all the time

I's been climing on
And reachin' landin's,
And turnin' corners,
And sometimes goin' in the dark
Where there ain't been no light.
So, boy, don't turn your back.

Don't you set down on the steps
'Cause you finds it's kinder hard.
Don't you fall now—
For I's still going honey,
I's still climbin',
And life for me ain't been no crystal stair.

—Langston Hughes

References

Davis, Robert. 1987. "Mayor is Cruising Job-Rating Poll." *Chicago Tribune*, (24 March).

Gove, Samuel K., and Louis H. Massotti, eds. 1982. *After Daley: Chicago Politics in Transition*. Urbana, Ill.: University of Illinois Press.

Joravsky, Ben. 1984a. "Mayor Slow to Fill Top City Jobs: Blames Shakman Decree." *Chicago Reporter*, 13(8):4–10.

———— 1984b. "Midterm Report: Washington Reform Progress Burdened by Errors, Politics." *Chicago Reporter*, Vol. 14(4):1–5.

Starks, Robert T. 1982. "Reapportionment and Black Politics: The Case of Chicago." In Anna J. Merritt, ed., *Redistricting: An Exercise in Prophecy*. Urbana, Ill.: University of Illinois Press.

Starks, Robert T., and Preston, Michael B. 1989. "Harold Washington and the Politics of Reform in Chicago: 1983–1987." In Rufus P. Browning, Dale Rogers Marshall, and David H. Tabb, eds., *Racial Politics in American Cities*. New York, N.Y.: Longman Publishing.

Black Political Power in the City of Angels: An Analysis of Mayor Tom Bradley's Electoral Success

Byran Jackson

California State University (Los Angeles)

Tom Bradley has been reelected to an unprecedented fifth term as mayor of Los Angeles, our nation's second-largest city. Bradley's career in Los Angeles local politics spans over twenty-six years, beginning with his 1963 election to the Los Angeles city council. After a bitter but successful 1973 campaign for mayor against Sam Yorty, the flamboyant white incumbent, Bradley became not only the first black to head the Los Angeles city government but also one of the first black men in the United States to preside over a major city. His electoral success, by many accounts, has reshaped the political landscape of Los Angeles (Sonenshein, 1984).

While the city of Los Angeles has had its share of problems receiving national attention (e.g., race riots, smog, traffic congestion, exorbitant housing prices, etc.), it has been able to boast of peace and tranquility in the political arena over the past sixteen years under the leadership of Mayor Bradley. Unlike Midwestern and Northeastern cities experiencing severe economic and population losses over the past two decades, the city of Los Angeles has witnessed sustained economic and population growth. This growth, until now, has boosted the popularity ratings of the mayor, who takes a large share of the credit for building the Los Angeles economy. The images of Los Angeles and Mayor Bradley were also enhanced when the city hosted the 1984 Olympics, where 140 nations were represented. Indeed, under the mayor's leadership, the city of Los Angeles has become known as an international city of trade on the Pacific rim.

Nevertheless, despite Bradley's accomplishments over the years, critics of the contemporary Los Angeles political scene ponder the basis of the mayor's high approval rating in a city where problems such as crime, transportation, uneven economic development, gang warfare, and inner-city decay are left waiting for serious attention. When voters were asked in a *Los Angeles Times* poll, conducted prior to the election, "Who do you think can best solve the problems of traffic, crime, growth, and the environment for Los Angeles, Mayor Bradley or someone else?" the majority felt that someone other than Bradley would be better suited for the job in each issue area.

Moreover, even though Bradley remains popular in the Los Angeles black community, critics argue that the quality of life for black Angelenos has worsened over the past sixteen years under his leadership. For example, south-central Los Angeles, a predominately black community, has benefited least from Bradley's growth initiatives. While other communities (particularly on the city's Jewish west side) complain of overgrowth, the problem in the black community is no growth. Black-owned small businesses in these areas (e.g., liquor stores, grocery stores, and gas stations) have in large numbers sold out to foreign interests, such as the Japanese and Koreans, or have gone bankrupt (Levine, 1988).

How do we reconcile these massive problems facing the city of Los Angeles with the mayor's popularity with the Los Angeles electorate? In this essay I will argue that Bradley's popularity and political success can be attributed to two major factors: (1) his political style and (2) the structure of the political environment in Los Angeles within which he operates.

Political Symbolism and the Bradley Success Story

Mayor Richard Daley's quote "Don't make no waves and don't back no losers" (Rakove, 1975) characterizes the political style of Mayor Bradley. Described as a quiet, dispassionate man in both private and public life, Mayor Bradley is known more for resolving conflict as an arbitrator than he is for creating conflict or becoming controversial. As a high-school and college student in predominantly white environments, as a policeman, as a city council member, and as mayor of the city, Mayor Bradley has been portrayed as a man strongly believing that problems of racism, racial discrimination, and general social injustice can be solved by working within the confines of the political system. His personal political accomplishments not only exemplify his success with this approach but have become symbolic of the black struggle for social justice in Los Angeles (Payne and Ratzan, 1986).

One could argue that in the aftermath of the Watts riots, Mayor Bradley over the years has shaped black politics in Los Angeles in his own image and has amassed a loyal black following. This following remains despite the lack of a substantive policy agenda coming from the mayor's office addressing issues within the Los Angeles black community. Moreover, on controversial issues regarding race relations in the city or involving the black community, the mayor has taken either a low profile or a conservative profile. For example, on the controversial bussing issue, which polarized the city of Los Angeles, the mayor steered clear of the issue rather than serve as a community leader as requested by the judge handling the case.

More recently, the mayor advocated, along with black councilman Robert Farrell, that the black community (south central Los Angeles) be taxed for extra police services. It was only after an outcry from the community that the mayor reversed his position. Even more critical is the growth issue. While Bradley takes part of the credit for the Baldwin Hills Crenshaw shopping mall located in the black community, there are few other development projects in the area to be claimed. Black economic and community development have not been on his priority list. Perhaps it would be unfair to the mayor to point out that he endorsed George McGovern's failed candidacy for the presidency in 1972 but chose not to endorse anyone in 1988 during Jesse Jackson's bid for the office.

In light of this behavior, how does one explain his loyal following in the black community? As Murray Edelman points out, "emotional commitment to a symbol is often associated with contentment and quiescence regarding problems that would otherwise arouse concern" (Edelman, 1964:32). Bradley's election as the first black mayor of the city of Los Angeles made him a symbol among black Angelenos.

I argue that the symbolic Bradley has overshadowed the substantive Bradley and thus aids us in understanding the insignificance of race in a city where race is very significant. By employing the strategy of placing low priority on issues such as gang violence, drive-by shootings, drug-abuse problems, and other problems plaguing the predominantly poor black communities of Los Angeles but at the same time providing political access and making high-level political appointments to members of the black middle class, the mayor has skillfully defused the issue of race.

In addition to cultivating a following in the black community, Mayor Bradley has developed a citywide network of supporters reaching from the Jewish west side of the city to the Hispanic east side. He also has very strong ties with the downtown business establishment. This network again can be attributed largely to Bradley's style. A thorough investigation of local newspaper articles and an inspection of the mayor's appointment log demonstrate that over the last sixteen years the mayor has studiously pursued the activities necessary for reelection. He is known for spending countless hours attending special events held in the city for all groups, as well as birthday parties, bar mitzvahs, and other social functions for private citizens. These pieces of evidence, along with Bradley's high popularity rating, strongly suggest that the mayor has achieved his goal of being mayor "symbolically" for all of the people of Los Angeles.

Using theoretical work on the symbolic uses of politics, we attempt to provide a general explanation for why citizens divorce their general policy concerns from their evaluations of Mayor Bradley. However, before doing so, the following competing explanations have been offered as explanations for the mayor's popularity and deserve exploration: (1) citizens view the mayor's office as ceremonial and void of powers to make policy, (2) citizens are generally apathetic when it comes to local politics and fail to become involved, or (3) citizens feel that the mayor is doing all that he can do given the size and number of problems confronting the city.

Although the Los Angeles City Charter does not provide the mayor with formal powers to control the city bureaucracy or other similar powers granted other big-city mayors, it by no means renders the office of the mayor powerless. In terms of formal power, the City Charter gives the mayor the power to appoint commissioners and general managers to run departments. He has veto power over council legislation and has the responsibility for developing the city's budget (League of Women Voters, 1986). While indeed the ceremonial activities of the mayor are highly publicized and constitute a large share of the image projected by the mayor, one has to also consider other powers of the mayor and, more important, his use of those powers.

As Richard Neustadt points out in the case of presidential power, powers are those duties and responsibilities of executives laid out in constitutions and charters, whereas executive "power" comes from the personal ability of executives to persuade and bargain in order to have their will felt among those they choose to influence (Neustadt, 1960). I argue that, while formal powers do not alone constitute power by chief executives, neither does the lack of formal powers constitute powerlessness. Again, using Neustadt's argument, it is the ability of the chief executive to persuade and bargain that measures an executive's power.

In the case of Bradley, we find the mayor being well known for his powers of persuasion and bargaining. The economic growth and development of Los Angeles over the past sixteen years can be attributed in large part to Mayor Bradley's bargaining ability. Through skillful uses of appointment powers and veto powers, the mayor's will is felt in areas such as housing, community development, and the environment. Thus, the power argument lacks merit, particularly around those who are highly involved in Los Angeles politics and realize the formal and informal political influence of Mayor Bradley. The mayor recently has been attacked through the local media coverage for alleged incidents involving the mayor's use of his power to influence the city's banking activities, as well as for special appointments for his longtime friends.

The second argument concerning political apathy also appears weak. While voter turnout in city elections is very low, and other forms of mass involvement are rare, the label "apathetic" seems more convenient than genuinely descriptive of citizen attitudes. If apathy were the case, how could we explain citizen concerns for policy issues concerning the city and their ability to assess the mayor's performance? It appears that the masses can be described more as "unorganized" than as "apathetic." Also, their choices of leadership may appear very constrained and thus minimize their enthusiasm.

The third argument, portraying the mayor as operating under constraints and doing all that he can to serve all of the people follows closely the argument we will make concerning the symbolic uses of politics. However, when one examines closely the Bradley administration activities, one can see the great disparities that exist in the attention given to problems across the city. For example, during a campaign visit to Los Angeles during the 1988 Democratic party primary, the Reverend Jesse Jackson called Bradley's attention to the social problem in Watts and asked the mayor to renew his commitment to this portion of the city. Nevertheless, in the case of downtown business development, the mayor is well known for his promotion activities. Thus, while the mayor has successfully created the image of doing all that he can, such an image is, in reality, questionable.

Theoretically the question is, How can we explain the behavior of the mayor and his beneficiaries? According to Elder and Cobb (1983), the political system offers a wide range of political communications that are symbolically reassuring to the public. They point out that this reassurance promotes acquiescence and sustains a low level of involvement by reinforcing perceptions that the normal order of things is being maintained (Elder and Cobb, 1983:16). Furthermore, they suggest that substantive transactions by a few politically well-organized segments of society proceed largely unattended by the public at large. Thus, in their view the status quo is sustained and existing patterns of privilege and biases in the system preserved.

In the case of Los Angeles we can argue that, by offering the masses or the unorganized a feeling that efforts are being made to address their problems in the city (symbolic reassurance) and by acting in good faith when major crises arise (quiescence), organized groups in the city under the mayor's leadership have been able to maintain their claims on tangible resources and power. While the general public is made to feel that the system is working for them, they are in reality powerless.

The Political Environment and Political Power in Los Angeles

The city of Los Angeles is unique in its structure and operation compared with other cities of comparable size. Unlike New York, Chicago, and Philadelphia—all cities with histories of partisan politics and political machines—Los Angeles is known for its reform-oriented political structure. The City Charter calls for nonpartisan elections, a weak mayor, strong City Council, and the use of the referendum, recall, and initiative as major features of city government. While the city does not have at-large elections for City Council, a common feature of reform governments, power is concentrated in fifteen large council districts serving a population of over three million people.

Another distinguishing feature of Los Angeles is the decentralized nature of its politics. Lacking in terms of strong party rule, politics in the city is dispersed among political factions and power brokers, who in turn form ruling coalitions of varying compositions. For example, much of Tom Bradley's early electoral success has been attributed to a coalition consisting of blacks and Jews in the city. Since that time the mayor has extended his power base to include the downtown business and commercial community, oil companies such as Occidental Petroleum, and major developers in the city.

Political power depends largely on a group's ability to organize and its resources to organize; thus, group mobilization in the city is sporadic and often focused on a single issue (e.g., the environment, the homeless, the location of prisons, etc.). Broad-based coalition politics characteristic of political machines do not exist. It is the absence of party organization or some other form of mass organization that suppresses mass political involvement. Furthermore, large council districts often place together very heterogeneous groups in the environment. Group members with power and resources dominate the political process. Therefore, politics in the city becomes a battle over resources instead of ideas or ideology.

Given the structure of Los Angeles city government, power brokers such as mayor Bradley are able to unite the assortment of factions and rule for long periods of time without serious opposition. The question of whether or not the "reform structures" advocated by political reformers at the turn of the century have brought about "mass democracy" is a debatable one here in the case of Los Angeles. While citizens have power to control government in terms of their votes, the vehicles for access to power (money, organization) are unavailable.

The recent scandal involving Mayor Bradley points to some important similarities as well as differences between the political behavior in machine-run cities such as New York and Chicago and in reform cities like Los Angeles. In terms of similarities we find that machine politics is commonplace in both type cities. The city of Los Angeles is not immune to patronage politics. For example, special-interest groups, primarily from the business community, contributed heavily to the mayor's campaign fund. All evidence points to the mayor offering substantive rewards to such contributors. Furthermore, we find contracts awarded without bids to contractors performing work for the city's public-housing authority. It has been further revealed that these contractors were acquainted with the mayor. Whether the mayor is charged with impropriety or not, the fact suggests that his office is not beyond patronage politics. Strategically, it places the mayor at the focal point in the electoral arena and gives him a large edge over any would be competitors.

On the other hand, Los Angeles is quite different from machine cities in terms of voter mobilization. In the city's most racially polarized election, involving Bradley and Yorty in 1969, 76 percent of the electorate turned out. In the most recent election, only 23 percent of the voters turned out to vote for mayor. City Council races are won with less than four thousand voters in districts where well over one hundred thousand voters reside. Unlike in machine cities, where mass voter turnout is emphasized, the opposite occurs here. Consequently, the unorganized and low voter activity in Los Angeles may explain in part why the use of symbolic politics by the mayor has been so successful.

Conclusions

The focus of this analysis has been on the sources of Mayor Tom Bradley's success, the beneficiaries of his power, and the effect his term in office has had on black Americans. It is clear from the analysis that the mayor's skillful low-key organizing tactics and his high-profile use of symbolic politics accounts largely for his success in office. This behavior causes the mass public to divorce their general policy concerns about the operation of the city from the mayor's performance. However, we find that the strategy of symbolic politics also allows well-organized groups an opportunity to maintain control of city government without question, making the mayor a pawn for the power elite.

In the case of black Americans, the quality of life has decreased under the Bradley administration. Black communities are plagued by gang warfare, drug abuse, poor housing conditions, lack of jobs, and poor schools. However, there are few if any substantive policy statements stemming from the mayor's office to address these issues. Many would argue that a few black political appointments are not enough for the black vote in Los Angeles. However, lacking an alternative to Bradley, black voters have given their support to the regime out of symbolic pride. Currently, while there are many black organizations engaged in politics in Los Angeles, the larger black community has not been able to organize in such a way to exact substantive policy concessions from the Bradley regime. However, symbols do erode, and the future may bring violent outbursts in the city similar to the Watts riots.

References

Edelman, Murray. 1964. *Symbolic Uses of Politics*. Urbana: University of Illinois Press.

Elder, Charles, and Richard Cobb. 1983. *The Political Uses of Symbols*. New York: Longman Press.

Levine, Jay. 1988. "Malign Neglect: The Killing of South Central." *L.A. Weekly*, 11(4):8–60.

League of Women Voters. 1986. *Los Angeles: Structure of A City*. Los Angeles: League of Women Voters.

Neustadt, Richard E. 1960. *Presidential Power: The Politics of Leadership*. New York: John Wiley & Sons.

Payne, Gregory J., and Scott C. Ratzan. 1986. *Tom Bradley: The Impossible Dream*. Santa Monica: Roundtable Publishing Company.

Rakove, Milton. 1975. *Don't Make No Waves . . . Don't Back No Losers*. Bloomington: Indiana University Press.

Sonenshein, Raphael J. 1984. "Biracial Coalition Politics in Los Angeles." *PS*, 19:582–90.

The Politics of Detroit: A Look Ahead

Wilbur C. Rich

Wayne State University

Coleman Young has been mayor of Detroit for fifteen years, the second longest of black mayors of a large city and longer than any of his white predecessors. He has won reelections primarily because he has been able to maintain his core constituency (working-class voters) and co-opt all current issues as his own. While Mayor Young has enjoyed the advantages of incumbency, he has not been seriously challenged in either of his last two campaigns. So far, administrative missteps, scandals, and party factionalism have not helped his opponents. In previous elections, Young has been able to turn out a majority of black voters in key inner-city precincts. Nevertheless, the mayor has yet to convince a majority of the remaining white voters (25 percent) that they should vote for him. This group and disaffected black voters make up about 35 percent of the vote. Although Coleman Young won in 1985 by a landslide, he cannot seem to break the cycle of white anti-Young voters. This is true despite the fact that his administration has not been antiwhite in spirit or practice, perception in some circles and suggestions in some of the media to the contrary notwithstanding. White appointees hold higher percentages of cabinet positions than the percentage of white representation in the population. Ironically, the presence of this white anti-Young voting bloc may be a key in contributing to Coleman Young's continued electoral success. His practice of not courting white voters through preferential treatment has enabled him to keep his emotional bond with the black working-class voters and to sustain their support.

The election and reelections of Coleman Young do not imply an unqualified endorsement of the man or his policies by the electorate. The same voters who returned him to office for the fourth term have rejected his proposal for casino gambling three times. They voted in the last municipal special election (1988) to reduce the number of council votes necessary to override mayoral vetos of the budget. In the same election, voters defeated the incumbent school-board members who were endorsed by the mayor. In the past, the mayor has attempted to purge his nemesis James Bradley, the city clerk and election administrator, but he has not been successful. Nor has endorsement of Jesse Jackson's opponents in the last two presidential elections prevented a heavy Jackson voter turnout in Detroit.

There are also other signs of voter uncertainty and discontent. Some critics have raised the Mayor's age (seventy) as a factor, while others believe his staff has lost sight of the mayor's mandate. Still others are dissatisfied with the pace of economic recovery. A recent newspaper poll found that 60 percent believe that Detroit needs a new mayor (McGraw, 1989).[1] The poll also revealed widespread concern in the black community about drug abuse and drug-related crime. A leading black minister has even suggested the reestablishment of a decoy unit in the police department similar to the one (STRESS, Stop Robberies, Enjoy Safe Streets) that Young ran against in his first campaign. As a result of the crime issue and the perception that it is time for a change, several candidates are gearing up for the 1989 mayoral primary. Even the president of the City Council, Erma Henderson, the second-most-popular politician in the city, has announced her intentions to enter the mayoral race. Meanwhile, Mayor Young has been entangled in a paternity suit brought by a former city employee.

In light of the defeat of Harvey Gantt of Charlotte, Richard Hatcher of Gary, Kenneth Gibson of Newark, and Eugene Sawyer of Chicago, some journalists are espousing a domino theory of black mayoral incumbents. Is this characterization justified? Is this willingness by black voters to dump black mayors for untested personalities a sign of political maturity or is it simply another indicator of widespread disillusionment in the black community? Will Detroit be next? This paper will argue that it is unlikely that Mayor Young will be defeated, and that much of the evidence of his alleged vulnerabilities has either been misinterpreted or is wishful thinking by his opponents, or both.

Electoral Politics in Detroit

The 1973 election of Coleman Young marked a profound shift in the city's governing coalitions. Blacks gained registration majority that would not be threatened in the near future. The 1980 census revealed a black majority population (63 percent). The 1990 census will reveal an ever-higher percentage of black residents. Indeed, more white flight has occurred along with the beginning of a black middle-class flight. The city's politics reflects the attitudes of the black working-class voters who work in the automobile plants and the new, emerging service industries. The black community, reassured by Coleman Young's rhetoric, has consistently renewed his license to lead. Yet there is no evidence that he has built a political machine nor that he has attempted to structure the post-Young era by grooming a successor.

The 1988 casino gambling referendum defeat was interpreted by local newspapers as an erosion of support for Young and his projects. It is true that casinos would be a magnet for his convention/tourist strategy to rebuild downtown and create more service jobs. However, I have argued elsewhere that the collapse of the gambling initiative was related to factors other than the mayor's popularity (Rich, 1989). First, newspaper polls reported consistently that over 60 percent of Detroit residents were opposed to the idea of casino gambling. Second, the mayor did not place the issue on the ballot. Indeed, Young's position remained unchanged throughout two previous casino elections: that the city should not dismiss any potential source of revenue without at least studying it. Third, as a reaction to the anticasino efforts, the mayor did establish a citywide blue-ribbon study commission. It recommended that the city proceed with the introduction of a limited number of casinos. The report also analyzed the social aspects of gambling and offered ideas about crime control and revenue distribution. Meanwhile the anticasino forces were conducting a vigorous media campaign against casinos. A pro-casino campaign organization was hastily put together. Consisting mainly of members of the mayor's blue-ribbon casino commission, the group did not have a cogent theme and was unable to mount a coherent campaign strategy. The election was won by a highly motivated but loosely organized antigambling coalition of ministers, neighborhood organizations, and would-be mayoral challengers who were successful in getting people to vote their morality rather than their personal habits. Casino gambling was effectively denounced as sinful and a magnet for crime. This campaign was successful despite the high rate of racetrack, sporting, and lottery betting in the city. Also joining the campaign against the casinos were the Chamber of Commerce and the business community. The group claimed that casinos would further soil the image of the city and undermine their fledgling (but largely unsuccessful) efforts to attract new industry to the city. As a result, Coleman Young had few political allies and financial supporters in this initiative. Indeed, the record shows that most, if not all, pro-casino campaign expenses were paid by the mayor. Ironically, one of the big spenders in the anticasino advertising campaign was the extant legalized gambling enterprise.

The casino defeat was significant but can hardly be viewed as a referendum on the mayor's leadership. The campaign was a very lackluster effort kept alive by media sensationalism. In Detroit, the last election is always a millennium ago. Some of the same ministers who opposed the casino idea have indicated that they plan to support the mayor for reelection. The labor unions, which did not participate in the gambling campaign, planned a full organizational effort in support of the mayor for reelection.

The defeat of the incumbent school-board members was also hailed as yet another defeat for Coleman Young. Actually the defeated candidates were not closely identified with the Young administration. The mayor, along with several other incumbent politicians, did endorse these school-board members, although hardly in glowing terms. However, Detroiters do not take school-board political cues from the mayor. He has had no formal role in school governance. Having been implicated in several questionable issues of policy and ethics, and having presided over a $100 million deficit, and having supported the automatic renewal of the superintendent's contract, these incumbents had little to recommend their reelection. The Young endorsement was a pro forma one, but it is doubtful that even an all-out effort by the mayor could have saved these incumbents. The reform coalition candidates (called the HOPE team) had a better press, were more articulate, and had plenty of ammunition to use against the incumbents.

Finally, some journalists cite the victory of the Reverend Jesse Jackson in the 1988 Michigan primary as more evidence of the mayor's losing touch with the voters. Coleman Young did make headlines by endorsing Michael Dukakis for president, but it was a personal endorsement. He also publicly released his staff to work for the candidate of their choice. Jackson won the primary not in spite of Young, but because his Michigan supporters were better organized, financed, and led than the Dukakis supporters. Journalists who interpreted the election results as a defeat for Young were, in effect, belittling the organizational effort made by the Jackson people.

The Jackson victory in the 1988 Michigan primary is not likely to have much bearing on the 1989 mayoral primary. The mayor has accumulated a multimillion-dollar campaign chest for reelection and plans a major effort to secure endorsements and support. Can Mayor Young be defeated? It depends upon the cast of candidates and the issues. If Council President Henderson remains in the campaign (she withdrew from the 1985 primary), then other candidates may not be able to mount a serious contest for the runoff election. In a runoff election, Young not only has the advantages of incumbency and experience working for his candidacy, he would be freed from the charge that he is getting too old. The mayor is seventy and Henderson is seventy-one. If Mr. Thomas Barrow, the mayor's 1985 opponent, decides to run and survives the primary, then we would have a replay of the 1985 election.* Barrow played an important role in the anticasino campaign but is yet to expand his anti–Coleman Young voting base. In order to do that, Barrow would need a stronger campaign organization and money. Currently, he is relying upon favorable media coverage to advance his candidacy. The strategy may again open him up to charges that he is the suburb's choice for mayor. In any case, the mayor has never been accused of underestimating his opponents, regardless of age, money, or source of support.

---

*Subsequent to writing this article the primary election has been held. Barrow and Young survived the primary. They will contest each other in the November election.

Issues in the 1989 Campaign

The 1989 campaign promises to be a debate over the so-called down
town versus neighborhood rehabilitation strategies. There is a percep
tion, sometimes reinforced by the local media and actively promoted by
several city councilpersons, that the mayor has concentrated on rebuilding the city skyline at the expense of the neighborhoods. The front side
of this issue looks good, but the back side begs for a plan and a revenue
source. There is very little money, federal or otherwise, to repair homes,
streets, and other infrastructures. Nevertheless, candidate Henderson
has already launched her campaign to improve the neighborhoods. She
and others have claimed that the mayor has deliberately neglected the
neighborhoods in his revitalization schemes.

The opposition has also attacked the mayor on the issue of street
crime and his reluctance to endorse a gun-control law for the city. Of
these issues, crime seems to be the mayor's Achilles' heel. Although
Detroit lost its title of Murder Capital of America to Washington, D.C.,
it still has a major crime-control problem. Crime, particularly street
crime, seems to be the top issue for most Detroiters, according to newspaper polls. Crime is a difficult issue for the mayor because of its link to
drug abuse. Many of the drug dealers are black youth and adhere to a
kind of reckless nihilism. They are not afraid of the police, nor is there
any evidence that they fear incarceration. Putting more policemen on
the street may be reassuring to city residents, but it is unlikely to stop
drug use and dealing. Establishing decoy units with authority to violate
the civil liberties of suspects has received a lot of press coverage, but not
one incumbent politician has endorsed the idea. It is unlikely that the
mayor will support the decoy idea because of his views that law and
order apply equally to police and civilians. Mayor Young has repeatedly
stated that he has no intention of unleashing the police on city residents. However, he is aware that some anticrime initiative is in order
before the mayoral primary. In addition to convening a Crime Summit in
which a hundred invited guests discussed the problem, the mayor appointed a deputy mayor to coordinate law-enforcement efforts. Yet fighting crime will remain an issue unless the mayor can effectively
neutralize it.

The plight of the public schools will be an issue in the campaign.
There are problems of mismanagement, safety, and finance. Announced
and unannounced candidates are also blaming the mayor, in part, for
the problems of the schools. This is ironic, since the mayor has no formal role in school governance. The mayor has occasionally ruminated
about a participatory role for City Hall, but has never taken any steps to
play a larger role. This issue is one of the most emotional items on the
city agenda.

The plight of the underclass, single-parent households, and the homeless should get some attention from the candidates. It is unlikely that
these problems will be deciding issues in the campaign, because the

candidates' views are so similar. There is no radical conservative candidate espousing views that would spark a serious debate about the disposition of these individuals. Accordingly, candidates will probably stick to the neighborhood and crime issues.

Because of the mayor's age, the issue of succession is clearly on the minds of Detroiters. In this election, politicians are more speculative than ever about the future leadership. The politics of the 1990s and 2000s are clearly a part of this campaign. There are various candidates maneuvering and queuing up for the expected competitive council race and the mayoral contest of 1993.

Finally, the personality of the mayor should not dominate the election. The city can ill afford a replay of the 1977 and 1985 elections. These were referendums on the mayor's combative political style and his personal life-style. There are many too substantive issues that need to be debated. If they are not, the election will become a personality contest. In such a race, Coleman Young's record speaks for itself.

Conclusions

In *Coleman Young and Detroit Politics* (1989), I suggested that the secret of Young's success as mayor was his eudaemonistic behavior. This risk-taking behavior has resulted in an aggressive affirmative action policy, a rebuilding of the downtown skyline, and the construction of a people mover, a sports arena, and an automobile plant within the city limits. The mayor has quickly embraced the new service economy based on the convention/tourist industry rather than romanticizing about the return of the city's automobile industry to its previous standing in the city's economy. In addition, the mayor's attempt to develop the riverfront property must be considered a bold move, for it contains the seeds of gentrification. The expansion of the city airport, opposed by the residents, is now seen as the anchor for revitalization of the east side.

Despite these accomplishments, the mayor has also been associated with more dubious enterprises. The new municipal incinerator project has been attacked as increasing the air pollution in the city. The mayor's support of the Grand Prix racing for Belle Isle was opposed by many groups in the city. The International Grand Prix authorities saved the mayor on this issue by escalating their demands for a better racecourse to include a permanent grandstand on the Island Park. (The mayor finally backed out of the deal). The mayor's attempt to facilitate Chrysler's new Jefferson Avenue plant has been mired in controversies concerning the amount the city paid for land and waste removal problems at the site. The mayor has also been criticized for his advocacy of a domed stadium for the Detroit Tigers.

It is clear that public criticism of the mayor has modified his original plans in a few instances. Yet none of these criticisms has diminished Young's ability to set the city's agenda, nor have they seriously threatened his prospects for reelection. Candidates for his job have criticized the mayor but have not been able to articulate an alternative to his policies. In their speeches, opposition candidates have stressed that they are pro neighborhood revitalization. None have suggested an economic alternative to Young's service-economy strategy. In addition, an alternative economic development plan cannot completely ignore the automobile industry. Young has included the automobile industry in his plans but has also begun the slow process of changing the economic base of the city. The 1989 election is likely to turn on whether those who seek a license to lead have better ideas than Young's. Individuals currently expressing interest in the mayor's job admit that their campaign is for a more cautious and consultative administration. They vow to return the city to the golden years of its history. Simultaneously they promise a more vigorous revitalization effort. Apparently they believe that the mayor will not be able to do anything about the issues before the election. Candidates who underestimate Young's proactive skills do so at their peril. Primary candidates opposing Young will also have to convince Detroit voters that the city can afford to elect an inexperienced individual who might need four to five years to learn to govern effectively. The issue is whether Detroit's economy can afford to drift, in view of competition from other cities for residents and investors. Finally, if Council President Henderson gives up her seat, it will make the race for the presidency of the City Council more significant. For example, a nonincumbent could put his or her energy into replacing Henderson. Under the City Charter, the council president, who is elected by virtue of receiving the highest number of votes for Council, succeeds to the mayoralty in case of a vacancy. Accordingly, the 1989 election promises to be significant on its own terms, regardless of the outcomes of the mayoral primary.

Note

1. The results were based on a small sample of 250 city residents. The Market Opinion Research (The Pollster) issued a disclaimer on the mayor's tenure question, because it came after the crime questions.

References

McGraw, Bill. 1989. "Poll: Young Gets a Low Mark For Crime Fight." *Detroit Free Press*. (1 March): Sec. A.
Rich, Wilbur C. 1988. "The Politics of Casino Gambling: Detroit Style." Presented at the annual meeting of the American Political Science Association, Washington.
———— 1989. *Coleman Young and Detroit Politics: From Social Activist to Power Broker*. Detroit: Wayne State University.

Mayor W. Wilson Goode of Philadelphia: The Technocrat

Bruce Ransom

Stockton State College

The 1983 mayoral election in Philadelphia heralded a breakthrough for big-city mayors, particularly black mayors. The election of Wilson Goode, a professional manager educated at the Wharton School of the University of Pennsylvania, would permit a public administrator to occupy the mayor's office. That is, professional and technical competence and experience rather than traditional political acumen would shape his tenure (Goode, 1984a). Indeed, Goode's management background, particularly his outstanding tenure as the former city managing director and his chairmanship of the Pennsylvania Public Utility Commission, were unique routes to the mayor's office. Although Wilson Goode had had experience as the director of the Philadelphia Council for Community Advancement and had served as president of the Paschall Betterment League, his experience in Philadelphia politics was limited.

What can be concluded about Mayor Goode's performance? Now in his second four-year term, there is considerable evidence that Wilson Goode, the successful managing director, is a less-successful political leader. The purpose of this essay is to examine Mayor Goode and his administration. Special attention is devoted to Mayor Goode's image, the major focus of his agenda, the Goode record, and an assessment of the Goode administration. Newspaper reports, especially in the *Philadelphia Inquirer* but also in the *Philadelphia Daily News* and the *Philadelphia Tribune*, interviews with city officials and members of the Philadelphia First Corporation, and documents generated by the Goode administration are the basis for this assessment.

The Image

Wilson Goode's 1983 quest for mayor, his first attempt to win an elective office, emphasized his previous record of competence, strong work habits, experience, and a reputation as a "no-nonsense" city managing director in the William Green administration (Ransom, 1987). This emphasis on technical competency and experience in preparing the city budget, managing city employees, delivering municipal services, and day-to-day management, rather than on being nurtured on "politics and partisan activity" defines Wilson Goode. This image propelled Wilson Goode to the 1983 Democratic nomination against former Mayor Frank Rizzo and an easy victory in the general election. Thus, the son of a former sharecropper in North Carolina became Philadelphia's first black mayor and a historic figure.

The tragedy of the bombing of the MOVE house on Osage Avenue by the Philadelphia police in May of 1985 resulted in open criticism from Mayor Goode's supporters and opponents. Indeed, those who had been quietly critical of Mayor Goode now openly voiced their opposition, and many supporters were now critics. The MOVE incident opened the door for attacks on Goode's image and weakened his administration (Ransom, 1987).

Yet, Mayor Goode maintained enough of his black base (along with liberal white support) to win reelection in 1987. Although Mayor Goode was reelected with 51 percent (as opposed to 55 percent in 1983) of the votes in the 1987 general election race, once again against his archfoe, former mayor Frank Rizzo, his personal political revival has not been translated into strong leadership, and consequently, the ambitions and expectations of 1983 have failed to be realized. Because of the MOVE incident, Mayor Goode's political foes became vocal and persistent in their opposition.

Mayor Goode's Agenda

Principles of strategic planning and other management techniques (Bryson, 1988) have been widely used by the Goode administration "to buffer and counter" powerful economic forces so that Philadelphia could regain control of its economic destiny and improve the quality of life for residents across the city. Building a "New Philadelphia" has been this administration's vision. This pronouncement endeared Mayor Goode to the Philadelphia First Corporation and the Greater Philadelphia Economic Development Coalition, both prominent and prestigious business-led organizations. It also contained an implicit pledge to create jobs for city residents and offer opportunities for black entrepreneurs.

Economic development became the Goode administration's top priority. Mayor Goode's economic development strategy, entitled "Philadelphia's Economic Strategy: Seizing Control of our Destiny" (Goode, 1984b), was unveiled before the end of the administration's first year. The mayor's Economic Roundtable, a collection of prominent business leaders, was Mayor Goode's panel for nurturing support for the economic-development agenda.

Contending that strategic planning would permit the city to overcome circumstances it did not control and enable it to seize control of its destiny, the Goode administration intended to foster and enhance Philadelphia's role as the economic hub of the Delaware Valley (Summers and Luce, 1987). The city's assets—location, educational and scientific-research institutions, transportation and port facilities, health-care facilities, telecommunication facilities, and bank and business services—would be the anchors for developing Philadelphia into the international gateway to the Northeast.

The propensity of the Goode administration to generate planning documents and other technical reports was not limited to economic development. Other plans ranged from center-city redevelopment to the revitalization of north Philadelphia, a predominantly black area. The strategic-planning process and the generation of technical documents became the hallmarks of the Goode administration.

The Record

According to newspaper accounts of the Goode administration and interviews with city officials and business leaders, planning paralysis, not leadership and program implementation or service delivery, has become associated with the Goode administration. Perceptions of declining city services, along with the extensive analysis of issues without indications of program implementation, began to draw criticism. More attention was focused on trash-strewn streets and unfilled potholes than strategic-planning processes. The ability to research and study city problems and produce technical reports initially drew praise, but the paucity of follow-up policies and programs was soon viewed more and more with jaundiced glances.

Plans and reports without the political leadership to develop programs and implement them generated questions about the political skills of Mayor Goode. Business and community leaders, the media reported, wondered if nice-looking documents would take the place of meaningful policies and programs. Others (in interviews with the author) were harsh, and wondered whether Mayor Goode, or those advising him, understood the economic and social realities, or whether he was capable of making the hard choices. Still others asked if he was capable of developing a program and moving it through the city council successfully. Observations were made that the black president of the city council, demonstrating political skill, was outmaneuvering the mayor. Mayor Goode's inability to exhibit political astuteness has been costly, but his historic standing in the black community enables him to maintain much of his original electoral base.

Mayor Goode's inability to demonstrate strong political leadership for building a broad consensus for many of his major initiatives has reduced his tenure to a caretaker administration. Strong political opposition and the inability to fulfill Mayor Goode's agenda is noticeable in several issue areas. For example, his proposal to build a trash-to-steam facility in south Philadelphia has been stifled by neighborhood opposition and a lack of support on the city council. The proposal to build a new convention center, which needs additional state aid, has been blocked in Harrisburg, the state capital, by state legislators from surrounding counties in suburban Philadelphia. Residents in the Hunting Park section of north Philadelphia have attacked the Goode administration for inadequate police surveillance of open drug deals in the neighborhood. Philadelphia's continuing budget problems and the mayor's proposal to meet shortfalls by selling municipal buildings and cutting funds for social services, rather than raising taxes, have generated additional opposition. Clearly, governing a big city is difficult, but the MOVE incident removed the mayor's protective shield. He has generally been unable to demonstrate an ability to build political support across the city in key constituencies and in the city council in some significant issue areas. (The lone exception is his strong, unyielding, and successful stand against the sanitation workers' union during their strike.)

An Assessment

The hallmark of the Goode administration has been a reliance on strategic-planning approaches and a style of governing that is devoid of political adroitness. The problems would have been challenging without the MOVE incident, and their solution would have been problematic regardless. Nonetheless, in areas of critical controversy, Mayor Goode has not demonstrated that he possesses the political leadership required to build a consensus for his proposals. The MOVE incident, a major human catastrophe, exposed this weakness. Yet Mayor Goode has been able to maintain the necessary support in the black community, thereby achieving a narrow reelection victory in 1987.

Politically weakened and unable to exert political leadership skills, Mayor Goode made little progress in building a political consensus for some of the most critical issues facing the city after the 1985 incident. Problems such as solving the trash-disposal problem, maintaining quality service, or getting the city's budget and fiscal house in order show little, if any, progress. In addition, revitalization plans ranging from riverfront development in Penn's Landing to construction of a new convention center to plans for predominantly black north Philadelphia have not progressed significantly.

Conclusion

In essentially a crusader/caretaker capacity (Yates, 1977), the Goode administration continues to display weak political and leadership skills. Indeed, a series of neighborhood town meetings across Philadelphia in the winter of 1989, reported by the media, and the more recent reaction to service cuts in Mayor Goode's proposed budget for the 1990 fiscal year have exposed the mayor to hostile residents in predominantly white neighborhoods in northeast Philadelphia, but the relatively more receptive audiences in predominantly black neighborhoods of north Philadelphia have pressed Mayor Goode on his plans to follow through with his pre-reelection plans to revitalize the area.

In addition, Mayor Goode continues to be rebuffed by the city council in a number of his major initiatives. The MOVE tragedy revealed Mayor Goode's limitations in consensus building. The absence of the MOVE incident would not have meant that the unresolved issues facing the Goode administration would have been resolved. However, the incident opened the door for his opponents to attack a historic figure and softened some of his support, resulting in the disclosure that Mayor Goode is a weak and ineffectual political leader. He has yet to demonstrate that he has the leadership to move his agenda (Goode 1988) and get the city council and other key players to be supportive. Unfortunately, Wilson Goode's effectiveness and success as city managing director has not contributed to the persistent display of the political adroitness required of the mayor of Philadelphia.

References

Bryson, John M. 1988. *Strategic Planning for Public and Nonprofit Organizations.* San Francisco: Jossey-Bass Publishers.

Goode, W. Wilson. 1984a. "Mayor's Annual Report." Philadelphia: City of Philadelphia.

——— 1984b. "Philadelphia's Economic Strategy: Seizing of our Destiny." Philadelphia: City of Philadelphia.

——— 1985. "State of the City Speech." Philadelphia: City of Philadelphia.

——— 1988. "The Text of Mayor Goode's Inauguration Address." Philadelphia: City of Philadelphia.

Macdonald, Michael C. D. 1984. *American Cities: A Report on the Myth of Urban Renaissance.* Cambridge, Mass.: The M.I.T. Press.

Office of the Mayor. 1984. "Report of Actions on the 100 Day Agenda." Philadelphia: City of Philadelphia.

Ransom, Bruce. 1987. "Black Independent Electoral Politics in Philadelphia and the Election of Mayor W. Wilson Goode." In Michael B. Preston, Lenneal J. Henderson, Jr., and Paul L. Puryear, eds., *The New Black Politics: The Search for Political Leadership.* 2nd ed. New York: Longman Inc.

Summers, Anita A., and Thomas F. Luce. 1987. *Economic Development within the Philadelphia Metropolitan Area.* Philadelphia: University of Pennsylvania Press.

Yates, Douglas. 1977. *The Ungovernable City: The Politics of Urban Problems and Policy Making.* Cambridge, Mass.: The M.I.T. Press.

Black Mayoral Leadership: A Twenty-Year Perspective

William E. Nelson, Jr.

Ohio State University

The Emergence of Black Mayoral Leadership

The search for power by blacks in the American political system over the past two decades has witnessed the emergence of black mayors as the unrivaled champions of black social, economic, and political aspirations. During this period, the black community became deeply committed to a new political consciousness, ethos, and program, one that stressed the utilization of the electoral process as a mechanism for capturing major public offices and transforming the content and the impact of public policy. The election of blacks to the mayorship of some of America's most important cities—beginning with the historic victories of Carl Stokes in Cleveland and Richard Hatcher in Gary in 1967—symbolized in a profound and poignant way the quest by blacks to enhance their bargaining power in the political process, to control large blocks of strategic economic and political resources, and to engage in self-governance in accordance with the primordial principal of self-determination. Changing social demographics in American cities, characterized by the flight of whites to the suburbs and the concentration of black majorities in the cities, created prospects for a thorough-going and permanent transformation in the structure of local power. Blacks, whose potential for political influence had been negated by the dominant power of white-led urban machines, were now in a position to design and implement their own political revolution. Taking advantage of their superior numbers and high political consciousness, blacks could now use the electoral process to elevate black politicians to the pinnacle of power and authority in local jurisdictions.

As symbolic acts, the election of black big-city mayors represented landmark events in the political history of black America. The luster of black victories in the courts was muted by the reality that judicial policy changes could only be brought to fruition through complicated legal maneuvering and voluntary compliance. Black mayoral victories symbolized defiant acts of self-liberation. They were concrete evidence of a new consciousness, a new determination, a new political sophistication, and a wellspring of courage reminiscent of the heroic slave rebellions and abolitionist campaigns of the eighteenth and nineteenth centuries. Decades of self-doubt by blacks about their capacity to break free from machine control and change the course of public policy under their own momentum was washed away. The skeptics who counseled Richard Hatcher that he could not win—that he could not overthrow Eastern European domination in Gary—were proven wrong. The lessons of Gary and Cleveland were not lost on hundreds of black communities across the country where effective political mobilization by blacks could, possibly radically, alter the process of governance at the local level.

Demands and Expectations

As the political significance of the civil rights movement began to wane and the electoral strength of black voters began to surge—especially in local races—in the decade of the 1970s, black mayors began to ascend to the apex of the leadership hierarchy in the black community. Enormous responsibility was placed on their shoulders to fight and win the ongoing struggle for black social justice and economic security. In the wake of a dramatic recession and rising poverty in the black community, black mayors were expected to be the premier leaders in the search for jobs. This was to be accomplished, in part, by halting the outmigration by old industries from the cities, while attracting new industries into a declining economic environment. Black mayors were also expected to be skillful political brokers. In this role, they were pressured to maintain effective relations with the media, fend off efforts by machines to build new bases of power in city politics, satisfy the continuing demand by whites for preferential treatment, and establish the kind of rapport with other local governments and Congress required to prevent cities from being shortchanged in the allocation of state and local fiscal resources (Nelson, 1978).

Outstanding Accomplishments

To what extent have black mayors been able to live up to these demands and expectations? The list of major accomplishments by black mayors over the past twenty years is extraordinarily impressive. Adopting the posture of activist entrepreneurs, black mayors have been frontline warriors in the struggle to avert the total collapse of the local fiscal economy. They have played prominent roles in organizations like the National League of cities, the Urban Coalition, and the National Conference of Mayors. Their leadership roles were critical in the fight waged by mayors across the country against proposals advanced by the Reagan administration to savagely cut General Revenue Sharing, Community Development, Block Grants, and other important sources of federal fiscal assistance to the cities.

The work of black mayors has been path breaking in the vital arena of fiscal resource mobilization. During their first year in office, Carl Stokes in Cleveland and Richard Hatcher in Gary were extremely successful in bringing federal and private funds into their cities to address a multiplicity of critical problems faced by their black constituents (Nelson and Meranto, 1977). Similarly, Coleman Young of Detroit was able to convert his cordial political relations with the Republican governor, William Milliken, and the Democratic president, Jimmy Carter, into strong support for economic development in Detroit by the state and federal governments (Rich, 1989:150). Under the leadership of black mayors, the priorities of city government began to significantly change. Demonstrating extraordinary sensitivity to the needs of their black constituents, black mayors began to make issues such as increased availability of low- and moderate-income housing, expanded job-training services, and improvement in police-community relations major components of their legislative and administrative agendas. Research on the administrative performance of black mayors clearly shows that black mayors have been more responsive to the needs of low- and moderate-income citizens than their white counterparts. A quantitative study of spending patterns in American cities by Albert Karnig and Susan Welch found that cities with black mayors increased both their total expenditures and their social-welfare expenditures more than other municipalities (Karnig and Welch, 1980). Black mayors have also been more assertive in the pursuit of affirmative action goals through the employment of unprecedented numbers of minorities in significant positions in their administrations. Within two years after his election, Mayor Hatcher of Gary had managed to place fourteen blacks as head of the city's twenty-nine departments. During his four years as Mayor of Cleveland, Carl Stokes promoted 274 minority individuals to supervisory positions in Cleveland city government. The aggressive action taken by black mayors in the area of affirmative action has often produced radical change in some of the most conservative and intractable city bureaucracies. A study by Peter Eisinger of affirmative action practices in cities governed by black mayors reveals that over a ten-year period, black representation in the police force increased sixfold in Detroit, and threefold in Newark and Atlanta (Eisinger, 1984:251). Eisinger underscores the proactive nature of affirmative action programs in black mayoral cities. Personnel departments in these cities do not wait for black candidates to file applications but actively initiate searches for appropriate candidates (Eisinger, 1984:251).

Studies have also shown that black mayors have been instrumental in expanding the participation of minority-owned firms in city contracting and purchasing. In Newark, Detroit, and Atlanta, black participation in public purchasing contracts increased from nothing in the early 1970s to a substantial share by 1980 (Eisinger, 1984:253). Joint-venture policies promoted by the administration of Mayor Maynard Jackson in Atlanta in the construction of the Atlanta airport resulted in the creation of $36 million worth of contracts for minority firms in 1977 (Eisinger, 1984:254).

The outstanding record of legislative and administrative achievements compiled by black mayors over the past twenty years clearly establishes the fact that black mayoral offices are not hollow prizes. Black mayors have established new instructional mechanisms for delivering benefits to less-well-off citizens; in the process they have transformed the lives of individuals who have historically been the intended and unintended victims of non–decision making in the urban-policy process. The late Harold Washington is a shining example of what can be done by a black mayor who is committed to the progress of his people. In a few short years, Washington totally reconstructed Chicago's economic-development model. Washington designed a growth model that emphasized the inclusion of neighborhood groups and small businesses in economic planning and the use of the city's purchasing power to generate business for minority-owned firms (Judd and Ready, 1986.) Clearly, these are the kind of policy initiatives by black mayors that can make a critical difference in the social and economic status of the black community.

The Limits of Leadership

The past twenty years have not only revealed the possibilities of black mayoral leadership, they have also illuminated important limitations on the programs and powers of black mayors. Despite the heroic effort of black mayors, the urban agenda for black America remains unfinished. Twenty years of effort by black mayors has not eliminated the social, economic, and political crisis faced by blacks in America. This should come as no surprise since many of the most critical problems facing the cities are beyond the reach of local officials. Black mayors cannot be blamed for the failure of Congress to halt the piling up of deficits and the construction of supply-side economic policies that transfer funds from the cities to the military. Welfare, poverty, joblessness, and juvenile crime are the results of national and international forces; the solution to these problems cannot be found by focusing exclusively on public-policy practices at the local level. The environmental settings in which black mayors function also deeply constrain their capacity to solve many pressing issues that impact on the lives of their black constituents. Black mayors are not and cannot be dictators; they must share power with a wide variety of individuals, institutions, and associations (Nelson, 1978). It is important to observe that some of the strongest opposition to black mayoral policy initiatives has come from dissatisfied and disenchanted elements of the black community. The high-pitched, emotional campaigns run by black mayors frequently produce unrealistic expectations about what a black mayor can accomplish. Black mayors find it difficult to convince individuals with these kinds of attitudes that they remain unswervingly committed to an agenda of community progress (Nelson, 1972).

A part of the blame for the black community's difficulty in translating its electoral resources into policy benefits can be laid at the feet of black mayors. Black mayoral leadership has not always lived up to the minimum requirements of a new, progressive politics. It is distressing to find recent black mayoral candidates entering into coalitions with conservative white-led political organizations to block the election of race-oriented black candidates. This pattern suggests the possibility that a new generation of black mayors will emerge committed to the agenda of old politics that served to suppress the ascendancy of blacks in the political process in the decades before the 1960s civil rights revolution. Many of these new black leaders were not active in the civil rights movement and were not socialized into activist entrepreneurial roles. In contrast to the first generation of black urban leadership, the new black leaders appear to suffer from a poverty of vision and a poverty of analytical sophistication. They have therefore been less inclined to embrace policies that challenge the system of racial subordination in the political process.

Some black mayors have also embraced too enthusiastically corporate-center strategies for urban development. Coleman Young of Detroit has been one of the chief architects of plans to rescue the cities fiscally by encouraging corporate investment in the cities, especially in declining downtown central business districts (Rich, 1989). The stress on corporate development, while potentially beneficial in terms of the generation of new jobs and taxable revenue, creates the danger of unbalanced urban growth (promoting the interests of the affluent while neglecting the needs of the nonaffluent) and expanding private-sector control over the policy-making process (Hill, 1983; Swanstrom, 1985). The strategy of balanced growth adopted by Mayor Washington in Chicago appears to be more in keeping with the long-term economic and social interests of the black community than the corporate-center models now in place in Detroit, Atlanta, Oakland, and Philadelphia.

The Issue of Political Incorporation

The most serious failing of black mayors has been their unwillingness to play a major leadership role in moving the quest for black political incorporation beyond the narrow confines of elected office. Effective black political incorporation must involve the institutionalization of black influence across broad dimensions of the policy-making process, not merely the election of black politicians to public office. In this regard, it is important that we keep in mind the distinction made by James Jennings and Mel King between "access" and "power." Black office holding is not synonymous with black power; at issue in the final analysis is the extent to which the resources of public offices can be utilized to institutionalize black control in the realms of public and private decision making.

The history of the political emergence of European ethnic groups in American politics suggests that the process of political incorporation has traditionally involved strategic consideration of the transfer of a range of benefits to upwardly mobile, politically significant, demand-making interest groups. In Providence, Rhode Island, the Irish began making demands for representation on Democratic party committees as early as 1876. By 1900, 73 percent of the committee memberships of the Democratic party were in the hands of the Irish (Cornwell, 1960:205–10). Italians began making demands on the Democratic and Republican parties after World War I, in the wake of the growth of Italian electoral strength to a position of commanding influence. By 1957, Italians had gained 35 percent of the memberships in the Republican party and 22 percent of the memberships in the Democratic party (Cornwell, 1960:205–10). In New York City, the Irish began infiltrating the Democratic party via Tammany Hall in the 1850s. By 1880, the Irish had taken complete control of this organization. Building from the ward level, the Irish were successful in establishing an elaborate party bureaucracy extending from block and building captains to top party positions in the county (Glazer and Moynihan, 1963). Thus, long before they developed the clout to elect a member from their ethnic group to high public office, the Irish and Italians began to demand and receive major instrumental benefits. The election of Irish and Italian politicians to high public office did not represent the culmination of the process of political incorporation but was an interim step in that process. The process continued with the institutionalization of ethnic power through the control of the electoral organization, the domination of the city bureaucracy, and the infiltration of Irish and Italians into important private sectors of the economic order (Dahl, 1961).

In contrast to the European ethnic incorporation pattern, the election of black politicians to high public office has not led to effective black penetration of other sectors of the economic and political system. Blacks have not used their control over mayorships to substantially infiltrate existing party structures, or to build permanent independent organizations of their own. The logical focal point for such institutional development would be the mayor's office, where extensive patronage benefits could bring the personnel and the energy of the campaign into the formal arena of governmental administration. Black mayors have tended not to be receptive to the notion of building and maintaining racially cohesive, nonelectoral organizations. There appears to be a visceral fear that such organizations would be difficult to effectively manage and might inappropriately intrude into delicate day-to-day administrative matters (Nelson, 1972). In many respects, this fear is unwarranted. Mayor Carl Stokes of Cleveland demonstrated unequivocally that the advantages of an ongoing black organizational alliance far outweigh its potential liabilities. During his term as mayor, Stokes was able to build one of the most effective political organizations in urban America. In doing so, he greatly increased black political influence over the outcome of elections as well as the stock of concrete social and economic benefits the black community was able to demand (Nelson, 1982).

A look across the black political landscape reveals a paucity of stable, black-led political organizations. It is at once informative and heartbreaking to note that after more than twenty years of black control in Gary, no organization exists to lobby for black goals, and to organize black political resources on a continuous basis. The failure to build such an organization in Chicago meant that when Harold Washington died, black political momentum was lost, and the programmatic agenda of the Washington administration became the shattered victim of the machinations of a multiplicity of warring factions. In the midst of this political chaos, the white machine stepped forward to reassert its dominance over black social, economic, and political decision making in Chicago.

Critical Lessons

The failure of black leadership and organization has prevented the process of black incorporation from translating itself into major gains in the private sector. This is a critical failure, since much of the decision-making authority exercised in urban politics is exercised in the private sector (Judd, 1988). Effective black political incorporation must result in greater black involvement in and control over the politics of corporate decision making. The public-private partnership forged between Coleman Young and the business community in Detroit may be good for General Motors, but its savory benefits for Detroit's black poor (many of whom used to work for General Motors) are questionable. Clearly Mayor Wilson Goode did not have the interests of his black constituents principally in mind when he made the campaign to keep the Eagles in Philadelphia a top priority of his administration. Sky boxes and tax abatements are poor substitutes for health-care centers, family-counseling programs, job training and development programs, and head-start initiatives. Nor will coalitions between blacks and liberal whites of the kind endorsed by Browning et al. in *Protest Is Not Enough* be effective in diluting the hegemonic power of corporate interests if blacks cannot summon sufficient internal strength to design, propose, and ratify Afrocentric approaches to urban policy making (Browning et al., 1984).

The pivotal lesson to be learned from the past experience of black mayors is that black political leaders in the decades ahead must help to define and implement a new programmatic agenda for the black community. This agenda must, at least, seek to achieve a fundamental redistribution of resources, reverse the subordinate position of blacks in the political system, and establish mass-based political formations at every level of the political process that will be actively and effectively involved in setting and implementing the civic agenda.

References

Browning, Rufus P. Dale Rogers, Marshall, Tabb, and David H. Tabb. 1984. *Protest Is Not Enough: The Struggle of Blacks and Hispanics for Equality in Urban Politics*. Berkeley, Los Angeles, London: University of California Press.

Cornwell, Elmer E., Jr. 1960. "Party Absorption of Ethnic Groups" *Social Forces*, 38 (March).

Dahl, Robert. 1961. *Who Governs?: Democracy and Power in an American City*. New Haven and London: Yale University Press.

Eisinger, Peter. 1984. "Black Mayors and the Politics of Racial Economic Advancement." In Harlan Hahn and Charles Levine, eds., *Readings in Urban Politics, Past, Present and Future*. New York, London: Longman Incorporated.

Glazer, Nathan, and Daniel Patrick Moynihan. 1963. *Beyond the Melting Pot*. Cambridge, Mass.: The M.I.T. Press.

Hill, Richard Child. 1983. "Crisis in the Motor City: The Politics of Economic Development in Detroit." In Susan S. Fainstein, Norman I. Fainstein, Richard Child Hill, Dennis Judd, and Michael Peter Smith, eds., *Restructuring the City*. London, New York: Longman Incorporated.

Judd, Dennis L. 1988. *The Politics of American Cities: Private Power and Public Policy*. Glenview, Illinois, Boston, London: Scott, Foresman Incorporated.

Judd, Dennis L., and Randy L. Ready. 1986. "Entrepreneurial Cities and the New Policies of Economic Development." In George E. Peterson and Carol W. Lewis, eds., *Reagan and the Cities*. Washington, D.C.: The Urban Institute Press.

Jennings, James, and Mel King, eds. 1986. *From Access to Power: Black Politics in Boston*. Cambridge Mass: Schenkman Books Incorporated.

Karnig, Albert, and Susan Welch. 1980. *Black Representation and Urban Policy*. Chicago, Ill.: University of Chicago Press.

Nelson, William E., Jr., 1972. *Black Politics in Gary: Problems and Prospects*. Washington, D.C.: Joint Center for Political Studies.

———. 1978. "Black Mayors as Urban Managers." In John R. Howard and Robert C. Smith, eds., *Urban Black Politics. The Annals of the American Academy of Political and Social Science*, 439 (September).

———. 1982. "Cleveland: The Rise and Fall of the New Black Politics." In Michael B. Preston, Lenneal J. Henderson, Jr., and Paul Puryear, eds., *The New Black Politics: The Search for Political Power*. New York, London: Longman Incorporated.

Nelson, William E., Jr., and Philip J. Meranto. 1977. *Electing Black Mayors: Political Action in the Black Community*. Columbus: Ohio State University Press.

Rich, Wilbur C. 1989. *Coleman Young and Detroit Politics: From Social Activist to Power Broker*. Detroit: Wayne State University Press.

Swanstrom, Todd. 1985. *The Crisis of Growth Politics: Cleveland, Kucinich, and the Challenge of Urban Populism*. Philadelphia: Temple University Press.

The Pioneering Books on Black Politics and the Political Science Community, 1903–1965

Hanes Walton, Jr.
Leslie Burl McLemore
C. Vernon Gray

Savannah State College
Jackson State University
Morgan State University

There was a beginning. It commenced almost imperceptibly, without fanfare, commotion, or any attendant publicity. It came during an era when politics and the political process was being foreclosed to people of color. No one knew then that black politics as an academic discipline was being born. In fact, when a black congressman and diplomat published a volume of his political speeches (Langston, 1883) and later put out his political memories (see chapters 23, 28, 29, and 30 of Langston, 1894), few took notice. The same thing happened when a black city judge and U.S. consul produced his memoirs (see chapters 8,10,12,15,20, and 32 of Gibbs, 1902). And when black journalist Timothy Thomas Fortune wrote about black political partisanship, a needed black political realignment, and the U.S. political economy as an oppressive force, the academic world did not stand still (Fortune, 1884). Two years later, in 1886, Fortune issued a pamphlet, *The Negro in Politics* (1886) in which he enlarged upon his views about black partisanship and political realignment. And all of these works are predated by the political reflections of a black female activist, Maria W. Stewart, who wrote and published her remarks (Richardson, 1987).

The intellectual basis of black politics rested in part on the political memoirs and reminiscences of black officeholders and compilations of political speeches and essays, as well as the pamphlets of black political activists like Frederick Douglass in the Reconstruction and post-Reconstruction eras. Yet this entire period is only one epoch that gave birth to black politics.

Prior to the Reconstruction period, there were pamphlets of speeches, biographies, autobiographies, etc., of those who spoke out about human bondage and its crippling impact on America's evolving and fledgling democratic institutions. Outstanding among these works are David Walker's *Appeal to the Colored Citizens of the World*,[1] issued in September, 1829, and Henry Highland Garnet's *The Past and the Present Conditions and the Destiny of the Colored Race: A Discourse*, released in February, 1848. It is here in the slave period, when blacks began to "speak themselves into being," that the earliest roots of black politics exist. This period, like the others, would be rich with seminal ideas. But it was different from the Reconstruction era, because the works of that era produced empirical insights about black political participation in America's maturing democratic institutions. And while these writers about the American political system may have not known that they were laying the very bases and foundations for black politics as an intellectual area, they did know—particularly the former black elected officials—that the black political experience in the government was worthwhile noting and transmitting to the next black political generation and beyond. For them, it was a story valuable enough to tell. And as we can see, these efforts to record the black political journey and effort arose long before the *formal* study of political science began.

In fact, when the American Political Science Association institutionalized itself and the discipline in 1903,[2] the analysis and assessment of black people's political experience was being undertaken by many in and out of the profession. And if we throw our academic net as wide as possible and include as many books as possible, including those written *not only* by political scientists, but by historians, sociologists, former black elected officials, journalists, race-relations think tanks like the Southern Regional Council, laymen, interested observers, and so forth, in the period 1903 to 1965, one can then really see the total body of works that provide the intellectual underpinning for this area in the formative years of the discipline.

The Literature on Black Politics in the Formative Years

In the sixty-two years (1903–1965) under scrutiny, there are some ninety-two books, which comprise some thirteen categories. In Table 1, these thirteen categories have been put in a rank ordering by number of works in each category, because these works do not readily lend themselves to *both* categorization and sequencing as some contemporary assessments have done (Walton, 1985, 1989). These works are much more scattered in their perspectives and conceptualization and far less holistic because of our effort to be comprehensive. Yet despite their diffusion

and divergences, they do provide a vision of black politics that clearly
relates to the ongoing black political experience in these years. The appendix lists the title and author of each work; it is arranged by category
in rank order.

During these years, 1903–1965, books on black protest politics and
black electoral politics dominate. In fact, they account for almost half
(44.5 percent) of everything that was written. And this dominance is
clearly in line with the black experience, which worked hard for civil
rights and the right to vote. People who were barred from political participation (except in the North and West on a limited basis) had to resort
to pressure politics. Hence, observers of the black political scene paid
close attention to this fact, as well as to the demand from black pressure
politics for the right to vote and basic civil and political rights.

Next came black protest and political leadership studies. Here, some
eleven books account for 11.9 percent of the works. Writers in this category endeavored to give the reading public some insights into who the

Table 1. The Categories of Pioneering Books on Black Politics: 1903–1965

Category	N	%
Electoral studies	21	22.8%
Pressure and protest politics	20	21.7
Political leadership	11	11.9
Judicial studies	10	10.9
State politics	7	7.6
Party politics	6	6.5
Congressional studies	5	5.4
Presidential studies	3	3.3
Bureaucratic (regulatory) studies	3	3.3
Urban politics	2	2.2
Ideology	2	2.2
International politics	2	2.2
Federalism	1	1.1
Total	92	100.0%

Source: Adapted from various bibliographies on black
history and politics.

black leaders were, where they came from, and what factors helped to move the black community forward.

Leadership studies were followed by some ten works (10.9 percent) that looked at how judicial politics impacted and/or reflected on questions of racial discrimination, the Constitution, and the Supreme Court's role in the matter. Yet the judicial branch of government was not the only one to attract attention. Beyond the judicial studies are seven books on blacks in various state political systems. Essentially, these were studies on several states of the Old Confederacy and how they have fared since the removal of blacks from state politics.

Nearly equal to the number of studies on state politics is the number of studies on black party politics. The six books (6.5 percent) analyze not only the major parties, the Republicans and the Democrats, but half of the works look at blacks in the Communist party. This exclusive focus on one particular third party again emerges out of the black political experiences of this period, because in this era the Communist party was making a major effort to attract black voters. Moreover, one must remember that this was the Cold War period.

Black congressmen and black presidential politics, with some five (5.4 percent) and three (3.3 percent) books, respectively, garnered nearly the same attention. The congressional books looked at blacks in that body, while the presidential works explored the relationship between certain presidents and the black community, and commented on a black on the White House Staff.

Surprisingly, following books on these major decision-making institutions are three books (3.3 percent) on the federal bureaucracy. Each of these works is devoted to analyzing early efforts to create and operationalize civil rights regulatory bodies. Two of the books look at the Fair Employment Practices Commission, and one covers from the establishment of the civil rights sections in the Justice Department in 1939 to the rise of the U.S. Civil Rights Commission. These books are unique because they look at civil rights machinery in government rather than the usual glance at the civil rights struggle itself.

Two categories, black urban politics and black political ideology, each had two books, for a total of 4.4 percent. Surprisingly, both of the urban politics works look at Chicago, while the two books on ideology look at the Reconstruction and post-Reconstruction period.

The last two categories had three books, for a total of 3.3 percent. Two works explored international relations and the third looked at civil rights in terms of the federal structure in America.

Moving now from books to authors, black political scientists account for six of the ninety-two authors, while white political scientists account for eleven of the ninety-two. However, the six blacks were more than 7 percent of the total number of black political scientists at this time.[3] Black elected officials, black political candidates, and black appointed officials (i.e., Powell, Lynch, Ford, Du Bois, and Morrow) account for five of the authors, while black protest leaders (Burns, Holt, Young, King, and Clark) account for five.[4] (King, M. Price, Ten Broek, and Record

account for two books each.) All total, these three categories of black
authors account for nearly one-fourth of all the works. When taken collectively, when the authors could be identified by race, black authors
account for nearly half (thirty-nine) of the total. Essentially, the books
produced on black politics in the formative years were produced by
black individuals.

Electoral Studies

A perusal of the works in black electoral politics will reveal that there
are four basic subsections. Ten of the electoral studies look at black suffrage rights and voting in the South. The dominance of the concern with
the South is because in the South, blacks had had their right to vote
stripped away. It should come as no surprise then that three of the
seven studies were released by the Southern Regional Council (Price,
Price, and Jackson). Besides this regional perspective, five of the books
attempted a broad overview of the black voters' efforts in the political
system (Moon, Olbrich, Aiken, Jarrette, and Ford). In the earliest work
in this formative period, Olbrich attempted a chronological overview
from Colonial to pre–Civil War America, while Moon covers the period
from Reconstruction to the late 1940s. Aiken's edited volume is a compi-
lation of articles. Ford—the vice presidential candidate on the Communist party ticket for 1932, 1936, and 1940—expressed a need for a
particular type of black partisanship.

Two of these works look at poll taxes (Odgen and Lloyd) and, particularly the Lloyd volume, at the impact of those taxes on voting behavior.
Two works look at black voting in specific locales. Fleming looks at the
first effort in Baltimore's fourth district to break away from machine and
boss control, while Wardlaw reviews black voting in Athens, Georgia,
from Reconstruction to the beginning of the New Deal.

Finally, Taper looks at racial gerrymandering in Tuskegee, Alabama,
in the 1960s and how the Supreme Court ruling in *Gomillion v. Lightfoot*
changed that reality. In fact, this book should be read with Charles V.
Hamilton's volume for broader insights. The Charles V. Hamilton volume is a case study of black efforts in Tuskegee to get the vote. It details
the obstacles and tactics devised to keep whites in power, while it reveals black efforts to overcome these barriers. Charles V. Hamilton was a
member of the Tuskegee civic organization that sponsored the black
efforts.

The James Hamilton volume and the W. R. Smith volume are little
more than apologies for the white South's denial of black voting rights.
The Hamilton volume is especially racist.

Methodologically, the vast majority of these books use aggregate election data to make their case about black voting behavior. The sole exception is the Lewinson book, which uses the results of a survey
questionnaire sent out to tap black political attitudes. Along with aggregate election data, Lewinson adds a historical perspective. One of the

works that stands out in this category is by black journalist and NAACP- publicist Henry Lee Moon. Moon's volume came out when the other empirical voting studies were emerging (i.e., *The People's Choice, The Voter Decides*); it creates a new and unique model of the black voter, but one from which only the "balance-of-power" component was taken.

Pressure and Protest Politics

In this category of studies, eight are works that look at the collective black struggle (Powell, Burns, Clark, McCord, Belfrage, Sutherland, Jackson, and Westin) and of the eight, three (Clark, Westin, and Sutherland) are edited volumes. The 1963 Clark volume is an edited volume of three interviews with black leaders (James Baldwin, Malcolm X, and Martin Luther King, Jr.), the Sutherland volume is an edited version of the letters of the volunteers that participated in the 1964 Mississippi Summer Project, and the Westin volume brings together documents, speeches, laws, etc.

Four of the volumes are works on the NAACP—the premier protest organization of this era (St. James, Jack, Hughes, and Saddler). Young's book looks at the National Urban league, Peck's at CORE and the Freedom Riders, Zinn's at Student Non-Violent Coordinating Committee (SNCC), Garfinkel's at the March on Washington Movement, and the Holt, McCord, Belfrage, and Sutherland books are on the Mississippi Freedom Summer Project. In fact, of these nine books, one can see in action some five black civil rights organizations and a cooperative effort in the Freedom Summer.

Of the other books, only Sindler's book looks at protest politics in one city; Knovitz's is an overview of federal civil rights laws and King's work is a request and justification for specific public policies from the government.[5]

Political Leadership

The black political leadership studies tended to concentrate on a single individual, a collection of individuals, or black politicos. In the first sub-category, six of the books (Bennett, Reddick, King, Kugelmass, Broderick, and Rudwick) probed Martin Luther King, Jr., Ralph Bunche, and W. E. B. Du Bois. Three of the works singled out King, the dominant figure during the period. Two of the books look at W. E. B. Du Bois, also a major black leader in this period. Three of the books probed black leadership collectively (Burgess, Thompson, and Larkin) and offered typologies as a tool for categorization and analysis. The last book, by Clayton, is a journalistic account of several black elected officials currently inpower. Basically, these works are either biographical or autobiographical descriptive studies of black leaders in action.[6]

Judicial Studies

The judicial works examine the Supreme Court (Tussman), the Fourteenth Amendment (Nelson and Ten Broek), the question of restricted covenants (Vose, Clark, and Perlman), equality (Ten Broek), and a variety of legal issues in regard to the civil rights movement (King and Quick). Lastly, there is a look at the *Dred Scott* case (Hopkins). Here, the works are truly scattered and defused and they show no concentration or focus. Moreover, two of the volumes are edited versions, which adds to the general diffusion of focus in this area. This category demonstrates the least unity of all of them.[7]

State Politics

The next category is that of black state politics. Two books look at black politics in Virginia and North Carolina, while one book each looks at black politics in Florida, Tennessee, and Texas. In short, five states of the Old Confederacy come under review. One of the books, Brewer's, analyzes black legislators in Texas during Reconstruction, while Jackson's work is a review of Virginia's black officeholders during the same period. The two works on North Carolina look at the Reconstruction period. Here the emphasis is primarily upon black elected officials in another era. Only Price's work reflects on the current postwar world situation; Mungo's work also covers the current situation.[8]

Party Politics

In terms of black party politics, three of the books look at black third-party politics *only* in terms of the Communist party. Two of the works are by Wilson Record and one is by Nolan. One book looks at black Republicans (Hirshon), while Nowlin reviews black efforts in the Republican and Democratic parties from Reconstruction to the early 1930s.

Tatum's book, on the other hand, is a work on black political realignment during the period 1915–1940. It is a qualitative assessment using little election data, but surprisingly it is fairly correct and somewhat insightful. In fact, many of the works dealing with political realignment have basically overlooked this pioneering work.

Collectively, what one sees here are works on black Communists, black Republicans, black partisanship, and black political realignment. Conceptually, factually, and methodically, the works on the black Communists are by far the weakest. They can scarcely by called books. At best, they either decry, denounce, or reject black Communist affiliation. This is propaganda, particularly apparent in the Nolan book. The other works lack solid factual data, including the historical work by Hirshon.[9]

Congressional Studies

While the judicial area lacks focus and unity, the congressional studies are significantly marred by factual error. The Smith and Mosley volumes are badly marred. The Smith volume, a work by a trained historian, demonstrates sloppy data gathering; there is no excuse for its faulty historiography. Mosley's work is that of an interested amateur and the flaws can, in part, be understood. Former Congressman Lynch's book, on the other hand, is a personal memoir combined with useful recollectionsto refute and set the historical record straight. That record was being distorted and reinterpreted by the white historians of the Dunning-Rhodes school, who had in one way or another denigrated black Reconstruction and black elected officials of that era. Later, Lynch wrote his political autobiography which was published posthumously (Lynch, 1970).

Finally, the Hickey and Edwin volume is a popular account of everybody's whipping boy—Congressman Adam Clayton Powell. Especially during the 1950s and 1960s, academics, scholars, laymen, and journalists could not get enough of describing, analyzing, and evaluating Congressman Powell. In fact, to date, there is more written about this black congressman than any other. Unfortunately, what is written, like the Hickey and Edwin volume, gives little insight into the man, his politics, or his troubles. Another volume to appear in this time frame on the congressman was a skewed journalistic account of Tammany Hall's attempt in 1958 to "deny the Democratic nomination to the Harlem Congressman." In 1956, Powell urges his voters to support Republican Dwight Eisenhower for president, although Powell himself stayed on the Democratic ticket. Then on 8 May 1958, the congressman was indicted for income-tax evasion. On 15 May, a week later, Tammany announced that they would not back the congressman. That effort failed, and Powell beat the machine candidate by a margin of three-to-one. This journalistic account, while quite descriptive, tries to portray Powell as a true political scoundrel. Thus, of this collection, the most useful and obvious choice is the Lynch work.

Presidential Politics

At the presidential level, the book by E. Frederic Morrow, a former White House staffer, is an invaluable insider's view, never before seen and rarely used in analysis, of the Eisenhower presidency.[10] Besides this insider's account, there are two non-insider's accounts of two different presidents. The Golden book is a liberal journalistic account of the Kennedy years and Kennedy's civil rights efforts. The Quarles volume is a black historian's look at Lincoln and the role he played in the black freedom struggle and its aftermath in early black Reconstruction. The emphasis in these books is on policy formulation, with the Golden and-

Quarles volumes being rather balanced assessments (See also Southern Regional Council, 1960).

Bureaucratic (Regulatory Studies)

On several occasions between Reconstruction and the passage of the 1964 Civil Rights Act, various segments of the national government sought to extend to the black community some portion of their request for civil rights and the protection of these rights.

The Carr volume assesses Attorney General Frank Murphy's efforts to establish a civil rights section in the Justice Department in 1939 and to give it regulatory powers. Following the Attorney General's efforts, and because of pressure from the black leader A. Philip Randolph, President Franklin Roosevelt established an executive agency, the Fair Employment Practices Commission, to handle job discrimination. The Kesselman and Ruchmanes volumes explore the attempt to create this new regulatory agency via an executive order in the employment area. Yet, despite the fact that these new regulatory bodies have different sources (one a bureaucratic creation and the other an executive creation), both used prosecutorial regulatory procedures to halt and limit racial discrimination in America. Each agency had very marginal success.

Urban Politics

Chicago, both historically and currently, has captured the attention of vast segments of the American populace in general and the academic community in particular when it comes to black politics in the big cities. Thus, it should not come as a surprise that Chicago was the first place to capture the attention of political scientists who studied black urban politics. It provided the setting for the first pioneering work on black urban politics. Even today, the number of books that use Chicago as an empirical base continues to increase. Part of this fascination probably emerges out of the fact that the first black congressman of the twentieth century was elected in 1928 in Chicago, long before New York (1944), Detroit (1956), Philadelphia (1958), and Los Angeles (1962).

Therefore, it is not surprising that both books in this category use Chicago. The Gosnell and Wilson books are the two pioneering works on black urban politics, and they present two different paradigms. But while focused on the same city, the Gosnell and Wilson works are quite different and, for all practical purposes, light years apart; yet both were written by political scientists on the faculty of the University of Chicago.

Gosnell's pioneering work appeared in 1935 after five years of work and analysis. Gosnell is, to date, the *only* one of the "Great Men" in the discipline to have devoted his talents to the study of black politics (Somit and Tananhaus, 1964:66). His work appeared just as black politics in the city was beginning to emerge. Wilson's work appeared in 1960, twenty-five years later, and the research was conducted during "1958–1959" (Wilson, 1960:17, footnote), just as the black politics of the formative years that Gosnell had written about had reached maturity and was beginning to decline. But, despite the fact that Wilson's book follows Gosnell's, there is little connection or continuity. In fact, a perusal of the Wilson volume will quickly reveal that Gosnell is not listed in the index, and in the 155 notes for the twelve chapters, Gosnell's name is mentioned only twice: his *Negro Politicians* volume is mentioned once, and his *Machine Politics: Chicago Model* is mentioned once (Wilson, 1960). But both times, Gosnell's works are simply listed as part of a footnote cluster of books and not as the primary source.

Furthermore, of the ten pages of notes that are included in the body of the book, Gosnell's 1935 study is cited on page 79. In fact, of the ten pages of notes and the 155 footnotes, Gosnell's 1935 study accounts for 1 percent of the sources. Thus, as planned and conceptualized by Wilson, Gosnell's study was of little value and use, not even in his historical overview section. Wilson, in the final analysis, showed little regard for Gosnell's book. Moreover, when Gosnell's work was reissued in 1966, Wilson wrote the introduction, albeit in a critical and less than favorable vein, for a work that was now considered a classic.

Bearing in mind that Wilson distanced his book from Gosnell's and was less than enthusiastic about Gosnell's work, when the two works are examined collectively the differences between the two are even more telling. Gosnell's book was well conceived, meticulously executed, and offered a balanced interpretation.[11] In the final analysis, Gosnell's work shows an appreciation for his subject matter that resulted in producing the finest analysis possible. Wilson cares little for his subject matter except that it supports a particular line of reasoning and viewpoint.

Gosnell's book is about black politics, Wilson's book is little more than conservative propaganda. Gosnell's book is an empirical assessment carried out with historical data and twenty-one tables, two figures, and five illustrations; Wilson's book is essentially a sermon to black people. Gosnell's book is now a classic[12] and rightfully so; Wilson's book is barely worth reading and is useful only to conservatives and neoconservatives who want to pass off their ideas and biases as scholarship.[13]

Ideology

The two books in the ideological category focus on the Reconstruction and post-Reconstruction eras. Du Bois uses a Marxist analysis to explain the failure of the first period of significant black political activity, and he includes the issue of the political economy into his analysis of black politics. If Du Bois was analyzing the external and systemic forces that were operative, Meier looked only at the Negro himself—internal groups and individuals within the black community. It is not surprising that when Meier finished, the problem as seen and suggested, is with black leaders and their ideas. There are too many leaders, too many means, and too many ends. Hence, the outcome is and can be easily foretold. Meier's book ends with the passing of B. T. Washington. One wonders why.[14]

The King volume of *Strike Toward Freedom* could be easily added to this section because it clearly deals with the concepts of nonviolence. But in addition, it discusses a black civil rights organization, the MIA (Montgomery Improvement Association), and therefore it is summarized under protest politics instead.[15]

International Affairs and Federalism

In these categories, there are two books in international affairs and one in the area of federalism. The two books on blackness as a force in international affairs show a uniqueness and similarity even though they were written some twenty-five years apart. One is written by a black political scientist, while the other is written by a black U.S. soldier.

The Bunche volume, *A World View of Race*, is a carefully reasoned analysis and discussion of the impact of racial beliefs and stereotypes on the international and domestic affairs of nation-states. Bunche reveals that these racial theories and beliefs have no basis in scientific fact, but have led to racial domination and imperialism on the international plane because of their emotional content and the motive of human greed. In fact, Bunche argues that the use of race on the international scene is a mere *cover*. He writes: "That is to say that differences in 'race', . . . are employed as devices by the privileged, ruling classes of the society to rationalize and promote their continued domination over and exploitation of the great numbers of the population" (Bunche, 1936:89).[16] Simply put, the international and domestic race problem is "merely one aspect of the class struggle" (Bunche, 1936:89). Hence, as Bunche sees it, the coming world struggle will not be a race struggle, but a class struggle (Bunche, 1936).

Robert Browne, a black soldier who had traveled extensively abroad—in more than forty countries—uses the contacts that he made and the insights that he developed to tell American policymakers and academics how important race will be in international and foreign affairs as Third World nations gain their independence. Browne sees a race war looming on the horizon.

As Browne argued it, this war will evolve because of the humiliation—social, not economic—that Third World people have suffered at the hands of whites. On this point, he and Bunche agree. Bunche wrote: "Cultural conflict goes on, however, and there is much smoldering resentment among the native masses which may some day break out in violent conflict" (1936:44). Bunche and Browne disagree, however, on the class dimension. In fact, Browne doesn't see such an economic dimension. To avoid this coming race war, Browne develops a concept and theory called "Neutraracialism," which posits a foreign policy that can help the United States to avoid this coming race war. This is the centerpiece of the book, but when it was reviewed in the *Western Political Quarterly* it was simply overlooked or not discussed.

The importance of these two works in terms of international politics cannot be overstated. Here are two theories about race in international politics that scholars of the area never bother to incorporate in their models of international affairs.[17]

Now to the matter of federalism. Burke Marshall, who wrote the volume on federalism and served as head of the Civil Rights Division and who never really believed in strong federal enforcement of civil rights, wrote this book in part to express the reasons why the federal government—particularly during the Kennedy administration—would not strongly support and protect the rights of the civil rights workers. He concluded that it was the structure of the American system, which inhibited strong actions. The book is little more than an excuse, and it shows why the civil rights workers decided to take stronger measures against the federal government (see Holt, 1965; Walton, 1982; McAdam, 1988).

African Politics

Table 1 and the appendix do not list any works in this category; however, there are several works that deserve special mention and consideration. Rayford Logan penned two books that not only looked at the mandate system under the League of Nations but examined how the black African colonies fared under this system. In his *The Senate and the Versailles Mandate System* (1945b,) he analyzed the U.S. Senate's view towards the League's proposed mandate system, particularly Southwest Africa as a "C" mandate (Walton, 1972b). This work was preceded by his *Operation of the Mandate System in Africa, 1919–1927* (1952), which is a comprehensive look at how South Africa moved to annex its "C" mandate, Southwest Africa, or Namibia. Finally, Logan wrote about the role that U.S. blacks could play in the post–World War II era with other darker people (Logan, 1945a). This group of books offers a rare look at the Third World by a black historian.

Beyond these works on African politics, there are two notable works by W. E. B. Du Bois. In his *Color and Democracy: Colonies and Peace* (1945), he reflected on colonialism and Third World people. Moreover, in his *The World and Africa* (1965), he specifically addressed the question of African politics within a global and international context.

Overall, these works have gotten lost in the current appraisal of and reflections on blacks and African politics, but they are still useful and valuable because they raise and reveal issues rarely discussed in current commentary.[18]

Reflections: The Pioneering Books and Black Political Events

All in all, from these works it was difficult to see black politics as a field and area of genuine concern. After 1965, several books emerged (Walton, McLemore, and Gray, 1973). Prior to 1965, the literature was heavily skewed toward electoral and protest matters (Walton, 1972a: 2–11). Beyond the matter of scope and concentration, most of the works suffered from conceptual, methodological, factual, and interpretative problems in the formative years. In addition, several works, like the Wilson volume, promulgated an overt and covert specific racial ideology.

But there are still some other interesting things about the literature if one arranges the books by years to see not only how the works clustered over time and in specific years, but how they related to specific historical political "first" events occurring in the black community, for instance, the dates of the rise and fall of the white primaries (1923–32, 1944), key Supreme Court decisions (1954), passage of key civil rights bills (1957, 1960, 1964, and 1965), and the rise of new black congresspersons (1928, 1942, 1944, 1956, and 1958). Analyzing the books in this way, very useful insights arise. First of all, forty-nine books (55.1 percent) appeared between 1956 and 1965, a single decade. Furthermore, if one adds the years 1951–65, fifty-eight books (65 percent) appeared. Put another way, it took about half a century—fifty-two years—to produce forty of the books and less than a single decade to produce the majority. The next question, then, is what motivated these works. Using our key-events approach, it becomes readily apparent that there was no clustering of works around any of the key black political first events. In fact, not only is there no clustering, but many of these events are yet to be written about by political scientists, black or white.[19]

Hence, the majority of the works seems to have arisen not in relationship to any one single event, but more in relation to an entire era—the rise of the contemporary black civil rights or black freedom rights movement. With the majority of the books emerging from 1956–65, this period fits neatly into the period framed by Martin Luther King's movement in Montgomery and the passage of the 1965 Voting Rights Act.

This is quite interesting, because in the first four decades (1903–43), after the creation of the American Political Science Association, only eighteen books (20.2 percent) appeared on black politics. Hence, it took a major social movement for black freedom to stimulate more interest and concern into and with the black political experience. Recently, the Jesse Jackson efforts have likewise stimulated further interest. These realities truly reveal much about epistemology and the growth of knowledge and facts in a society where racism is a fact of life. It impacts not only political, social, economic, and cultural aspects of society, but the intellectual realm also. But let us take the next step. How did the political science community receive these works?

The Literature on Black Politics and the Political Science Community

One way to empirically address this question is to look at the book reviews of these works in the major political science journals (e.g., *American Political Science Review, Journal of Politics, Political Science Quar-*

terly, and *Western Political Quarterly).* In order to control for political scientists, as well as to minimize interdisciplinary bias, our analysis will look only at the books written by black political scientists.

Of the five books written by black political scientists before 1965 (Nowlin, Bunche, Tatum, St. James, Charles Hamilton, and Fleming), only the 1931 book by Nowlin—it is also the first work by a black political scientist—was reviewed in a major journal of the time, the *American Political Science Review.* Although the *Political Science Quarterly* was in existence (since 1885), it either through disinterest or oversight did not receive a copy. The former seems more likely, however.

The review in the *American Political Science Review* was very brief, only eighty words in length, and unsigned. This is the entire review:

> *The Negro in American National Politics* (The Stratford Company, pp. 148), by William F. Nowlin, deals briefly with the activities and position of the negro in Congress, in national party conventions, and in presidential campaigns. Office-holding is regarded by the author as of foremost importance in evaluating the political significance of the negro. The book deals with facts rather than with fundamental considerations as to the place of the negro in politics. The conclusion seems to be that if the negro is to achieve power, he must adopt the tactics of the Anti-Saloon League. (*American Political Science Review,* 1932:386).

The review is simple, direct, and taut. It is not expressive and evaluative. The reviewer gives the reader no indication of his judgement of the work except in his reference to the Anti-Saloon League, an early pressure group in American Politics (see Odegard, 1928). The suggestion here seems to be that blacks might need to become a pressure group to enhance their role in national politics.

The only other work written by a black to be reviewed in the political science journals was Robert Browne's *Race Relations in International Affairs.* The 574-word review appeared in the *Western Political Quarterly* and was authored by Professor Clark S. Knowlton of the New Mexico Highlands University (Knowlton, 1962).

The reviewer, after describing the work, turns critical and introspective. He writes: "There are certainly a number of incredulous and naive assumptions in this work" (p. 539). He adds: "The author in his zeal has certainly overdrawn his pictures" (p. 540). The latter reflects comments that are rather introspective. There are critical insights about the emergent African states from the book. The reviewer ignored and failed to comment on the author's concept of "neutraracialism." This keystone feature of the book was not brought to the attention of the political science community.

Two of the remaining works considered here (by Charles Hamilton and Fleming) were pamphlets and probably were not sent to the journals for review. Yet, in the bibliographic section of the *American Political Science Review,* enterprising scholars might have noted them anyway. For instance, the *Western Political Quarterly* did list the Taper and the Lloyd books in the Books Received section but did not review them. The *American Political Science Review*, however, did not list any of these works in the Book Received section.

As for the Tatum and St. James works, both were published by small presses—the St. James work has recently been republished in a second, revised edition—but they failed to be reviewed in the leading journals. This was not the case with such black journals as the *Quarterly Review of Higher Education among Negroes, Journal of Negro History, Phylon,* and the *Journal of Negro Education,* which did review these books (see Record, 1952).

The same fate, however, did not befall the works of white scholars on some aspects of black politics. Nine of the eleven works (82 percent) (Gosnell, Price, Odgen, Vose, Wilson, Westin, Berger, Garfinkel, and Ten Broek) appeared in one or more of the four journals under consideration. Seemingly, only the civil rights and protest books were not sent to, or received by, the major journals.

Overall then, only *one* of the works by a black political scientist appeared in these journals from 1903 (1885 was the beginning date for the *Political Science Quarterly* and 1906 was the beginning date for the *Review*) through 1965, and some nine of the works of white political scientists, making a total of ten books in sixty-two years. Needless to say, not much on black politics, or Negro politics as it was called, reached the academic community via its major journals. What did reach the academic community were monographs, and these were regional and spotty, if not scattered. At best these books presented a factional, if not highly limited, picture of this area, with several books promoting a distinct racial ideology that gave a negative portrayal of black politics. There is, then, little wonder that black politics was imbued with such a stigma, and almost no commitment and/or support from the general academic community.

But even if one overlooks the ten books in the journals and considers the larger body of works, no holistic portrait is available. Many of the books come from sociologists, quite a few from historians, several from research organizations like the Southern Regional Council, and some from just interested observers. Several of the works are obscure and difficult to find, while others are brief pamphlets and occasional papers. It appears that few researchers were interested in the topic. Hence, prior to 1965, to view or understand black politics one had to truly use the imagination. The literature in its broad scope left a great deal to be desired.

Before closing, however, a major work on black politics that was never published must be noted: the Ralph Bunche monographs prepared for the Gunnar Myrdal study. It was a major effort by a black political scientist to do a comprehensive, albeit hurried, and systematic study of black politics.[20] When it did emerge in published form, it was a truncated travesty of the original version.[21] Many scholars borrowed from the work, but it still remains buried.

Reflecting back, then, on the pioneering works in black politics in the formative years, 1903–1965, a small beginning was made, but the work was basically ignored by the academic community. Thus, when the field blossomed in the period 1965–1980, few scholars in the academic community were prepared. It is the literature in this critical period that helped to move the field forward. The literature in this period unquestionably stands in need of assessment, both in relationship to its predecessors and in relationship to later works.[22]

Appendix

The ninety-two books surveyed from the period under scrutiny comprise thirteen categories. The categories, and the books within each category, are arranged in rank ordering by year of publication.

Electoral Studies

American Negro Academy. 1905. *The Negro and the Elective Franchise*. Washington, D.C.: American Negro Academy.

Hamilton, James. 1910. *Negro Suffrage and Congressional Representation*. New York: Winthrop Press.

Olbrich, Emil. 1912. *The Development of Sentiment on Negro Suffrage to 1860*. Madison: University of Wisconsin Press.

Smith, W. R. 1914. *Negro Suffrage in the South*. New York: Columbia University Press.

Wardlaw, Ralph. 1932. *Negro Suffrage in Georgia, 1867–1930*. New York: Phelp-Stokes Fund.

Lewinson, Paul. 1932. *Race, Class, and Party: A History of Negro Suffrage*. New York: Oxford University Press.

Ford, James. 1937. *The Negro and the Democratic Front*. New York: International Publishers.

Mabry, William. 1938. *Studies in the Disfranchisement of the Negro in the South*. Durham: Duke University Press.

Logan, Rayford, ed. 1940. *The Attitude of the Southern White Press Toward Negro Suffrage*. Washington, D.C.: Foundation Publishers.

Jackson, Luther P. 1948. "Race and Suffrage in the South Since 1940." *New South*, (June/July): entire issue.

Moon, Henry Lee. 1948. *Balance of Power: The Negro Vote*. New York: Doubleday.

Lloyd, R. Grann. 1952. *White Supremacy in the United States*. Washington, D.C.: Public Affairs Press.

Thompson, Charles, ed. 1957. "The Negro Voter in the South." *Journal of Negro Education*, (Summer): entire issue.

Price, Margaret. 1947. *The Negro Voter in the South*. Atlanta: Southern Regional Council.

———. *The Negro and the Ballot*. Atlanta: Southern Regional Council.

Odgen, Frederick. 1958. *The Poll Tax in the South*. Alabama: University of Alabama Press.

Fleming, G. James. 1960. *An All-Negro Ticket in Baltimore*. New York: Holt.

Taper, Benard. 1962. *Gomillion Versus Lightfoot: The Tuskegee Gerrymander Case*. New York: McGraw-Hill.

Aiken, Charles, ed. 1962. *The Negro Voter*. San Francisco: Chandler.

Hamilton, Charles. 1962. *Minority Politics in Black Belt Alabama*. New York: McGraw-Hill.

Jarrette, Alfred Q. 1964. *Politics and the Negro*. Boston: VinJaro Educational Publishers.

Protest and Pressure Politics

Jack, Robert L. 1943. *History of the National Association for the Advancement of Colored People*. Boston: Mead Publishing Company.

Powell, Adam Clayton. 1945. *Marching Blacks*. New York: Dial Press.

Saddler, Gordon T. 1956. *The NAACP: The Struggle in the Fulfillment of American Idealism*. New York: Welch Publishing Company.

St. James, Warren D. 1958. *The National Association for the Advancement of Colored People*. New York: Exposition Press.

Garfinkel, Herbert. 1959. *When Negroes March*. Glencoe: Free Press.

Knovitz, Milton. 1961. *A Century of Civil Rights*. New York: Columbia University Press.

Clark, Jacquelyne. 1962. *These Rights They Seek*. Washington, D.C.: Public Affairs Press.

Peck, James. 1962. *Freedom Ride*. New York: Simon and Schuster.

Hughes, Langston. 1963. *Fight for Freedom: The Story of the National Association for the Advancement of Colored People*. New York: W. W. Norton.

Clark, Kenneth, ed. 1963. *The Negro Protest*. Boston: Beacon Press.

King, Martin Luther, Jr. 1964. *Why We Can't Wait*. New York: Harper & Row.

McCord, William. 1965. *Mississippi: The Long Hot Summer*. New York: W. W. Norton.

Belfrage, Sally. 1965. *Freedom Summer*. New York: Viking Press.

Sutherland, Elizabeth, ed. 1965. *Letters from Mississippi*. New York: McGraw-Hill.

Zinn, Howard. 1964. *SNCC: The New Abolitionists*. Boston: Beacon Press.

Young, Whitney, Jr. 1964. *To Be Equal*. New York: McGraw-Hill.

Burns, W. Hayward. 1963. *The Voices of Negro Protest in America*. New York: Oxford University Press.

Sindler, Allan. 1965. *Negro Protest and Local Politics in Durham, North Carolina*. New York: McGraw-Hill.

Holt, Len. 1965. *The Summer That Didn't End*. New York: Morrow.

Westin, Alan, ed. 1964. *Freedom Now: The Civil Rights Struggle in America*. New York: Basic Books.

Leadership Studies

Burgess, M. Elaine. 1962. *Negro Leadership in a Southern City*. Chapel Hill: University of North Carolina Press.

Larkins, John. 1959. *Patterns of Leadership Among Negroes in North Carolina*. North Carolina: Irving-Stone.

Reddick, L. D. 1959. *Crusader Without Violence*. New York: Harper & Row.

King, M. L., Jr. 1957. *Strike Toward Freedom*. New York: Harper & Row.

Kugelmass, J. Alvin, and Ralph J. Bunche. 1952. *Fighter for Freedom*. New York: Messner.

Clayton, Edward T. 1964. *The Negro Politician: His Successes and Failure*. Chicago: Johnson Publishing.

Thompson, Daniel T. 1963. *The Negro Leadership Class.* Englewood Cliffs, N.J.: Prentice-Hall.

Bennett, Lerone, Jr. 1964. *What Manner of Man.* Chicago: Johnson Publishing.

Broderick, Francis L. 1959. *W. E. B. Du Bois: Negro Leader in a Time of Crisis.* Stanford: Stanford University Press.

Rudwick, Elliott. 1960. *W. E. B. Du Bois: A Study in Minority Group Leadership.* Philadelphia: University of Pennsylvania Press.

State Politics

Brewer, J. Mason. 1935. *Negro Legislators of Texas.* Dallas: Mathis Publishing Company.

Morton, R. L. 1919. *The Negro in Virginia Politics.* Charlottesville: University of Virginia Press.

Jackson, Luther P. 1945. *Negro Officeholders in Virginia, 1865–1895.* Norfolk: Guide Quality Press.

Mabry, William A. 1940. *The Negro in North Carolina Politics Since Reconstruction.* Durham: Duke University Press.

Edmunds, Helen. 1951. *The Negro and Fusion Politics in North Carolina.* Chapel Hill: University of North Carolina Press.

Price, Hugh D. 1957. *The Negro and Southern Politics: A Chapter of Florida History.* New York: New York University Press.

Mungo, Scott. 1965. *The Negro in Tennessee Politics and Governmental Affairs.* Nashville: Privately Printed.

Party Politics

Nowlin, William. 1931. *The Negro in American National Politics.* Boston: Stratford.

Tatum, Elbert Lee. 1951. *The Changed Political Thought of the Negro, 1951–1960.* New York: Exposition Press.

Record, Wilson. 1951. *The Negro and the Communist Party.* Chapel Hill: University of North Carolina Press.

———. *Race and Radicalism: The NAACP and the Communist Party in Conflict.* New York: Cornell University Press.

Nolan, William A. 1951. *Communism Versus the Negro.* Chicago: Henry Regency Company.

Hirshon, Stanley P. 1962. *Farewell to the Bloody Shirts: National Republican and the Southern Negro.* Bloomington: Indiana University Press.

Judicial Studies

Nelson, Bernard. 1946. *The Fourteenth Amendment and the Negro Since 1920.* Washington, D.C.: Catholic University Press.

Vose, Clement. 1959. *Caucasians Only.* Berkeley: University of California Press.

Tussman, Joseph, ed. 1963. *The Supreme Court on Racial Discrimination.* New York: Oxford University Press.

Broek, Jacbus Ten. 1965. *Equal under the Law.* New York: Collier Books.

King, D. B., and Charles Quick, eds. 1965. *Legal Aspects of the Civil Rights Movement.* Detroit: Wayne State University Press.

Clark, Tom C., and Philip B. Perlman. 1948. *Prejudice and Property: An Historic Brief Against Racial Covenants*. Washington, D.C.: Public Affairs Press.

Hopkins, Vincent C. 1951. *Dred Scott's Case*. New York: Fordham University Press.

Broek, Jacbus Ten. 1951. *The Antislavery Origins of the Fourteenth Amendment*. Berkeley: University of California Press.

Berger, Monroe. 1957. *Equality by Statute: Legal Controls Over Group Discrimination*. New York: Doubleday.

Congressional Studies

Lynch, James R. 1913. *The Facts of Reconstruction*. New York: Neale Publishing Company.

Smith, Samuel D. 1949. *The Negro in Congress, 1870–1901*. Chapel Hill: University of North Carolina.

Mosely, J. H. 1960. *Sixty Years in Congress and Twenty-Eight Out*. New York: Vantage Press.

Hickey, Weil, and Ed Edwin. 1965. *Adam Clayton Powell and the Politics of Race*. New York: Fleet Publishing Company.

Haygood, David. 1960. *The Purge That Failed: Tammany v. Powell*. New York: McGraw-Hill.

Presidential Politics

Morrow, E. Frederic. 1963. *Black Man in the White House*. New York: Coward-McCown.

Quarles, Benjamin. 1962. *Lincoln and the Negro*. New York: Oxford University Press.

Golden, Harry. 1964. *Mr. Kennedy and the Negro*. Cleveland: World Publishing Company.

Bureaucratic (Regulatory) Studies

Kesselman, Louis. 1948. *The Social Politics of F.E.P.C.* Chapel Hill: University of North Carolina Press.

Carr, Robert. 1947. *Federal Protection of Civil Rights: Quest for a Sword*. Ithaca: Cornell University Press.

Ruchmanes, Louis. 1953. *Race, Jobs, and Politics*. New York: Columbia University Press.

Urban Politics

Gosnell, Harold. 1935. *Negro Politicians*. Chicago: University of Chicago Press.

Wilson, James Q. 1960. *Negro Politics*. Glencoe: Free Press.

Ideology

Du Bois, W. E. B. 1935. *Black Reconstruction in America*. Cleveland: World Publishing Company.

Meier, August. 1963. *Negro Thought in America, 1800–1915*. Ann Arbor: University of Michigan Press.

International Politics

Bunche, Ralph J. 1936. *A World View of Race*. Washington, D.C.: The Associates in Negro Folk Education.
Browne, Robert. 1961. *Race Relations in International Affairs*. Washington, D.C.: Public Affairs Press.

Federalism

Marshall, Burke. 1964. *Federalism and Civil Rights*. New York: Columbia University Press.

Notes

1. See Garnet, 1969. Garnet reissued Walker's 1829 appeal in 1848 with his declaration against slavery attached.
2. See Somit and Tananhaus, 1964:66 for the ranking of great men, and Somit and Tananhaus, 1967:49–54.
3. By 1965, the number of black political scientists stood at only sixty-two (see Prestage, 1969).
4. This listing of protest leaders does not include James Ford and W. E. B. Du Bois, because we did not want to count the same individual twice.
5. See Mendelson, 1961, for a summary of the 1961 U.S. Civil Rights Commission Report.
6. For a historical work on the policy desires of black political leadership, see Logan, 1944.
7. The point here is that there was no systematic treatment of blacks and the Constitution but instead a wide range of different constitutional matters.
8. For a historical state study see Logan, 1964.
9. For another historical work see De Santis, 1962.
10. For one study that does use it see Burk, 1984:77–88. For another popular study, which makes no use of the volume, see Greenstein, 1982.
11. Gosnell made records of the Negro political meetings he attended over the four years and published them in the *Review*, See Gosnell, 1934. Wilson gives the reader no such insight for his book. There is no list of the total number of people interviewed in each city, their affiliation, etc. One is left to guess about the data base.
12. When it came out, Gosnell's book won the John Ansfield prize and its $1,000 award for the best book of the year in race relations. See John T. Salter's review of Harold Gosnell's book (Salter, 1936).
13. For a somewhat critical review of Wilson's book, see Sayre, 1962. For a glowing review, see Garfinkel, 1961. Surprising, however, is the review by black political scientist Samuel Dubois Cook (1961). It both accepts and rejects some of Wilson's findings. In one statement, Cook offers that Wilson's findings bring "tears to one's eyes."
14. For another perspective on Meier, see Jones and Willingham, 1970.

15. For another ideological work on a black religious group, see E. O. Essien-Udom, 1964.
16. For more on Bunche, see Henry, 1983. "Ralph Bunche and the APSA" in *PS* (Fall, 1983), pp. 706-711.
17. For another analysis, by a black novelist, of how race may impact international relations see Wright, 1956. It is a discussion of race and nonalignment at the Bandung Conference.
18. Seemingly these works led black sociologist St. Clair Drake to develop an Afrocentric approach (see Drake, 1958).
19. For instance, the only new work, on the white primary events, was written by a black female historian. See Hine, 1979.
20. For a badly botched, deliberately misarranged, skewed, and improperly credited and edited version of the Bunche manuscript, see Bunche, 1973.
21. For an extended critique of this Grantham version, see Walton, forthcoming.
22. For an appraisal of the readers on the subject, see Walton, McLemore, Gray, 1973:134–44. For the readers on black political thought, see Walton, 1971.

References

American Political Science Review. 1932. Review of *The Negro in American National Politics* by William F. Nowlin. (April):386.

Bunche, Ralph. 1936. *A World View of Race*. Washington, D.C.: The Associates in Negro Folk Education.

Bunche, Ralph. 1973. *The Political Status of the Negro in the Age of FDR*. Edited and introduced by Dewey Grantham. Chicago: University of Chicago Press.

Burk, Robert F. 1984. *The Eisenhower Administration and Black Civil Rights*. Knoxville: University of Tennessee Press.

Cook, Samuel Dubois. 1961. Review of *Negro Politics* by James Q. Wilson. *Journal of Negro History*, (October):253–55.

De Santis, Vincent P. 1962. *Republicans Face the Southern Question: The New Departure Years, 1877–1897*. Bloomington: Indiana University Press.

Drake, St. Clair. 1958. *An Approach to the Evolution of African Societies in Africa Seen by American Negro Soldiers*. New York: The American Society of African Culture.

Du Bois, W. E. B. 1945. *Color and Democracy: Colonies and Peace*. New York: Harcourt, Brace, and World.

———. 1965. *The World and Africa*. New York: International Publishers.

Essien-Udom. 1964. *Black Nationalism*. New York: Dell.

Fortune, Timothy Thomas. 1884. *Black and White: Labor and Politics in the South*. New York.

———. 1886. *The Negro in Politics*. New York.

Garfinkel, Herbert. 1961. Review of *Negro Politics* by James Q. Wilson. *American Political Science Review*, (December):934–35.

Garnet, Henry Highland, ed. 1969. *Walker's Appeal in Four Articles*. New York: Arno Press.

———. 1969. *The Past and Present Condition and the Destiny of the Colored Race: A Discourse*. Miami: Mnemosyne Publishing Co.

Gibbs, Mifflin W. 1902. *Shadow and Light: An Autobiography*. Washington, D.C.

Gosnell, Harold. 1934. "Political Meetings in the Chicago 'Black Belt.' " *American Political Science Review*, (April):254–58.

Greenstein, Fred. 1982. *The Hidden Hand President: Eisenhower as a Leader*. New York: Basic Books.

Henry, Charles P. 1983. "Ralph Bunche and the APSA." *PS*, (Fall):706–11.

Hine, Darlene Clark. 1979. *Black Victory*. New York: KTO Press.

Holt, Len. 1965. *The Summer That Didn't End*. New York: William Morrow.

Jones, Mack, and Alex Willingham. 1970. "The White Custodians of the Black Experience." *Social Science Quarterly*1 (June):31-35.

Knowlton, Clark S. 1962. Review of *Race Relations in International Affairs* by Robert S. Browne. *Western Political Quarterly*, 15 (September):539–40.

Langston, John Mercer. 1883. *Freedom and Citizenship*. Washington, D.C.: Darby.

———. 1894. *From the Virginia Plantation to the National Capitol*. Conn.: American Publishing Company.

Logan, Frense. 1964. *The Negro in North Carolina, 1876–1894*. Chapel Hill: University of North Carolina Press.

Logan, Rayford W. 1945a. *The Negro and the Post-War World: A Primer*. Washington D.C.: Minorities Publishers.

———. 1945b. *The Senate and the Versailles Mandate System*. Washington, D.C.: Minorities Publishers.

———. 1952. *The Operation of the Mandate System in Africa: 1919–1927*. Washington, D.C.: Foundation Publishers.

Logan, Rayford W., ed. 1944. *What the Negro Wants*. Chapel Hill: University of North Carolina Press.

Lynch, John Roy. 1970. *Reminiscences of an Active Life: The Autobiography of John Roy Lynch*. Edited, with introduction, by John Hope Franklin. Chicago: University of Chicago Press.

McAdam, Doug. 1988. *Freedom Summer*. New York: Oxford University Press.

Mendelson, Wallace. 1961. *Discrimination*. Englewood Cliffs, N.J.: Prentice-Hall.

Odegard, Peter H. 1928. *Pressure Politics: The Story of the Anti-Saloon League*. New York: Columbia University Press.

Prestage, Jewel. 1969. "Report of the Conference on Political Science Curriculum at Predominately Black Institutions." *PS*, (Summer):322–36.

Record, Wilson. 1952. Review of *The Changed Political Thought of the Negro* by Elbert Lee Tatum. *Phylon*, (Second Quarter):174–76.

Richardson, Marilyn, ed. 1987. *Maria W. Stewart: America's First Black Woman Political Writer. Essays and Speeches*. Bloomington: Indiana University Press.

Salter, John T. 1936. Review of *Negro Politicians* by Harold Gosnell. *American Political Science Review*, (February):180.

Sayre, Wallace S. 1962. Review of *Negro Politics* by James Q. Wilson. *Political Science Quarterly*, (March):149–50.

Somit, Albert, and Joseph Tananhaus. 1964. *American Political Science: A Profile of a Discipline*. New York: Athenton Press.

———. 1967. *The Development of American Political Science*. Boston: Allyn and Bacon.

Southern Regional Council. 1960. *The Federal Executive and Civil Rights*. Atlanta: Southern Regional Council.

Walton, Hanes, Jr. 1971. "Black Political Thought: The Problem of Characterization." *Journal of Black Studies*, (Third Quarter):214–18.

———. 1972a. *Black Politics*. Philadelphia: Lippincott.

———. 1972b. "The South West African Mandate." *Faculty Research Bulletin*, (December):93–100.

———. 1982. *Black Political Parties: An Historical and Political Analysis*. New York: Free Press.

———. 1985. "The Recent Literature on Black Politics." *PS*, (Fall):769–79.

———. 1989. "The Current Literature on Black Politics." *National Political Science Review*, 1:152–68.

———. Forthcoming. "Black Southern Politics: The Influence of Bunche, Martin, and Key." Chapter 11 in Hanes Walton, Jr., ed., *Black Politics and Black Political Behavior: A Linkage Analysis.*

Walton, Hanes, Jr., Leslie Burl McLemore, and C. Vernon Gray. 1973. "Black Politics: The View from the Readers." *American Politics Quarterly (Third Quarter)*, pp. 43–50.

Wilson, James Q. 1960. *Negro Politics: The Search for Leadership*. Illinois: Free Press.

Wright, Richard. 1956. *The Color Curtain*. New York: World Publishing Co.

Independent Leveraging and Local Community Development

Mary Coleman

Jackson State University

Ronald Walters, 1988, **Black Presidential Politics in America: A Strategic Approach,** New York: Albany State University at New York Press, xi + 225 pp. ISBN 0-88706-546-5 (cloth)/ISBN 0-88706-547-3 (paper).

In this seminal work Ronald Walters examines the ways in which blacks participate in the process of presidential selection. He examines party primaries, party conventions, and, to a lesser extent, state and local politics as they present opportunities for a permanent minority to influence public policy. He establishes the fact that blacks have been a part of the winning coalition since the late 1800s, and markedly so in 1912 in the election between the Democrat Wilson, the Republican Taft and the Moose Lodge party candidate Theodore Roosevelt. In the 1912 election, the black (largely southern) vote was split between Taft and Roosevelt, with blacks in Northern cities casting ballots for Wilson.

The evolution of black electoral participation in the presidential selection process has been characterized by strategic voting and has resulted in a pivotal role for the black vote in 1960, 1968, and 1976. This has been so even though blacks constitute only 15 percent of the American electorate, though a much greater share of the Democratic party membership.

Walters poses two questions: Has the strategic role of the black vote secured black public-policy interests and goals as it has for other groups? Are blacks able to utilize political participation in the same manner as the composite of these groups—the white majority? To the first query he answers that blacks have been a part of the winning coalition, but they have not had their policy interests satisfied by subsequent presidential actions, as they are a permanent minority, unlike other groups. Further, he notes, the failure of blacks to have regular access to an effective ve-

hicle of legitimate decision making exacerbates the differential in status
and in perspective between blacks and whites to the point of serious
social cleavage.

Why and/or how have blacks failed to have their policy interests satisfied by subsequent presidential actions? The partial answer has several
interrelated components: the role of black leadership, from Booker T.
Washington to the Reverend Jesse Jackson; the role of black elected officials (political integration); the role and resources of black organizations
(dependent versus independent orientations); and the various ideologies
and strategies attendant thereto. All of these political resources—leadership, elected officials, and organizations—would be committed to mar-
shaling a disciplined black vote within, or external to, the existing two-
party system. Though disciplined, the strategic black vote would be
characterized by its malleability—as a political resource it would "oscil-
late and realign itself as the political situation demands" (p. 114).

This approach faces two challenges: the need to eliminate or neutralize black or white intermediaries, especially those holding elected office
or having a loyalty to one or both existing parties, and the need to create
a widely shared belief system regarding the efficacy of an autonomously
driven black or multiethnic structure at both the national and local levels. This structure would exercise competence in agenda building and in
astutely monitoring "the political situation." Walters has not demonstrated an explicit understanding of the relative payoff from this strategy.
However, such an explicitly stated understanding would be imperative
to a successful new beginning in this direction.

To what extent, if any, are these challenges and the understanding
implicit in such challenges surmountable? According to Walters, the key
"to the exercise of independent leverage, the meaning of which is that
the black vote will be controlled by the black community rather than the
major Democratic nominee," is organization (p. 112). Walters notes that
by 1971 the idea of a black political party had become an expression of
black independent politics. However, the National Black Independent
party movement contained strong nationalist currents—currents antithetical to the American system and its presidential process.

This poses the intriguing question of the necessity not for an either/or
approach to presidential electoral strategy, but rather, for developing an
autonomous community base and appropriate leadership structures
through which to become economically and therefore politically influen-
tial. In this way, the disruptive force emanating from political integration—especially the existing relationships between black elected officials
and the Democratic party and other leadership arenas—can be accommodated. The viability of the organization thus hinges, no less than it
does in the two-party system, on the commitment of participants to
maintain it. Its maintenance, however, must serve the interests of its
most strategically important elements. Walters notes that the electoral
arena is not a panacea, but neither is it, in my view, practically or theoretically useful to disentangle economic-resource strategies from electoral strategies for a permanent minority.

Now to the least successful element of Walter's work: his discussion of the Reverend Jesse Jackson's 1984 campaign as independent leveraging. Mr. Jackson's organizational base was the black community—its churches, its fraternal organizations, and its people and their resources. Does this, however, constitute an autonomous campaign? It does, indeed, illuminate the political isolation of a candidate and the permanent minority's interest agenda from other publics and their Democratic and Republican standard bearers. What are the criteria for an autonomous candidacy within the two-party system? Mr. Jackson mobilized a distinct constituency, and his style and the results of his activities have a distinct flavor. But does this constitute autonomy? In Mr. Jackson's campaign, elements of dependent and independent leveraging coexisted. Sentiment and logic coexisted. But ultimately, as Walters notes, assent to party loyalty gave way to low-level bargaining results. But had not Mr. Jackson and black voters assented when he, as leader and not merely as candidate, and they, as followers, entered the presidential process as participants? If Mr. Jackson's candidacies have been the best-case scenarios for independent leveraging, then as a rule the process of selection in presidential politics leads to low-level bargaining results for a permanent minority.

Walters's examination suggests a very limited utility for investing blacks' resources in dependent leveraging, of which, in my view, Mr. Jackson's candidacies in 1984 and 1988 were only significantly different variations. The historical consequences of racism as articulated by Mr. Jackson and as reflected in issue preferences, over time, have given expression to an unlikely basis for consensus building beyond the mere maintenance of the Democratic party. Blacks and whites in the Republican party have fewer percentage points separating them on basic ideological issues, such as military capability, welfare reform, and tax cuts, than blacks and whites in the Democratic party (p. 187). When presidential candidates cannot easily absorb the interests of blacks into the politics of voting reallocation (such as the Voting Rights Act (VRA) and its amendments) or the politics of symbolism, presidential politics is not as strategically meaningful as a permanent minority would need it to be, and, therefore, dependent leveraging strategies will likely prevail. Nonetheless, Walters reaffirms a black presidential candidacy within the Democratic party "as a powerful vehicle for constructing bargaining options" (p. 195). In this reaffirmation the writer seems to be in conflict with current political facts. The lack of certainty regarding binding commitments and the eventuality of honoring them remain insolvable dilemmas within the parameters of the ideological preferences and values of the white majority.

To the extent that such a candidacy can accomplish the organization and direction of black political resources (p. 195) such resources might usefully be institutionalized from within local black communities. The emphasis, however, must be economic and political at regional and national levels. In this way such an infrastructure, if systematic in its operations, and successful in articulating a functional ideology, may extend to a presidential effort. Its primary political function should not be to win a presidential election, but to slate candidates at local, state, regional, and national levels, who, if elected, have the capacity to assist a black policy agenda. A concomitant leadership structure, operative and legitimately perceived by the black public, must also prevail. Leadership can therefore influence who becomes an elected official. At present, recruitment structures in the black public do not generally facilitate a politics of reason and sentiment: they facilitate a politics of individual ambition without regard to agenda building. And it is therefore heavily dependent on national symbols of leadership and personality.

Overall, Walters's examination is an important contribution to the field of minority and black politics, and will be of interest to students of political behavior and organizational theory.

Bibliographic Essays
Race, Class, and Urban Politics

Race, Ethnicity, and
the Politics of Resources

Charles V. Hamilton

Columbia University

Robert D. Bullard, 1987, **Invisible Houston: The Black Experience in Boom and Bust,** College Station: Texas A & M Press *xiv* + 160 pp., ISBN 0-89096-357-6 (paper).

Gregory D. Squires, Larry Bennett, Kathleen McCourt, and Philip Nyden, 1987, **Chicago: Race, Class, and the Response to Urban Decline,** Philadelphia: Temple University Press, *xii* + 230 pp., ISBN 0-87722-487-0 (cloth).

Dianne M. Pinderhughes, 1987, **Race and Ethnicity in Chicago Politics: A Reexamination of Pluralist Theory,** Urbana: University of Illinois Press, *xix* + 318 pp., ISBN 0-252-01294-1 (cloth).

The most obvious and relevant fact about the political struggle of African Americans is that that struggle had its origin in a system of slavery, followed by several decades of legal segregation and discrimination. This initial condition set the stage for all else that ensued. As a "nation of immigrants," most ethnic groups came to this country seeking to acquire property; blacks came to this country *as* property. Although discriminated against and subjected to various requirements to obtain citizenship, European ethnics were nonetheless treated (albeit woefully in many cases) as human beings. Blacks were (except for the small number of free persons) chattel—bought, sold, and owned.

American society has not handled this historical fact well, sometimes referring to it as "an American dilemma," or using it as an analytical springboard to discuss the progressive, evolutionary nature of the polity. As expected, social scientists have engaged in protracted debates about the relative status and development of various groups in society. They have developed theoretical frameworks to explain the fate of those groups, especially over the last hundred years, since the late nineteenth century. Political scientists and sociologists have generally subscribed to a notion of "pluralism," which essentially outlines a process of eventual inclusion in the society on a reasonably equitable basis with other socio-economic groups of comparable status. The political system, with its fragmented parts, ultimately functions to the positive benefit of those who properly organize themselves and pursue a relentless process of political bargaining. This is the pluralist faith, challenged, to be sure, by more skeptical critics, but widely accepted. The theory does not over-look historical variations with different groups, but it does insist that the basic ethnic and racial differences between those groups will give way to factors more responsive to socioeconomic characteristics. As groups ob-tain higher economic status, their ethnic and racial identities become less politically important.

Many economists (and their social-sciences colleagues) have adopted their own evolutionary analysis based on economic growth. They are confident that society is not only best able to, but, in fact, will accom-modate and develop lower-status groups as the economy grows. "A ris-ing tide lifts all boats." The task, in such circumstances, is to pay attention to the important components of the economic system, espe-cially the market economy—keeping it as free as possible from public-sector regulation, and giving as much latitude as possible to private-sector forces to create capital, pursue economic development, and thereby provide the economic means for the labor market to grow and prosper. Thus, in this view, lower-status groups should, if properly pre-pared to take advantage of the economic growth, be able to develop along with the growing economy. And, of course, racial barriers of an earlier time would erode in the face of this inevitable economic growth.

The three books reviewed here join these perennial debates, and each in its own way challenges the widely held political and economic con-ventional wisdom.

Bullard's *Invisible Houston* gives a brief history of race and politics in that Texas city, but the main focus is on the 1970s and 1980s. In the 1970s, Houston, Texas, experienced considerable economic growth, thanks to the oil boom, less union constraints, and a politics that favored creating "a good business climate." But, the author indicates, "The New South has, unfortunately, meant business as usual for millions of blacks" (p. 6). Later, he concludes: "Discrimination has reached a level of sophistication that makes it easy to practice and difficult (if not impos-sible) to prove in a legal sense" (p. 58). Most of the empirical data are taken from census materials and recent studies showing the gap be-tween incomes of blacks and whites, housing disparities, law enforce-ment practices, and employment conditions. Essentially, his conclusion is that black Houstonians for the most part did not share in the boom years of that city's economic growth in the 1970s. An interesting and useful chapter focused on environmental issues. Here, he describes how the African-American communities—lacking sufficient political and eco-nomic clout—have been the disproportionate victims of waste-disposal facilities and discriminatory land-use decisions.

There were the makings of a small black entrepreneurial group in Houston early on, but this receded in the face of inability to get capital and compete with more economically resourceful white competitors. All this is interesting when one comes to the last chapter of Bullard's book, "The Quest for Equal Rights." African Americans in Houston were the source of some major Supreme Court decisions on education and voting rights, establishing the right to attend nonsegregated schools and overcoming party primary restrictions. Very much of the black talent and energy had to be directed to those efforts in a protracted, and reasonably successful, struggle in the "politics of rights."

What Bullard does with Houston, Squires, Bennett, McCourt, and Nyden do with their treatment of the much academically studied city of Chicago. Basically, they reject the notion that an emphasis on economic growth will be substantially sufficient to bring social justice. That city's political machine over the years catered to the business and financial interests—pursuing a "growth ideology"—to the detriment of lower-income groups and neighborhoods. "Chicago needs to stimulate economic activity but it must be activity responsive to social needs, not just market signals" (p. 183). The authors make clear what they perceive to be the more viable forms of the political struggle to help bring this about. They are impressed with the Saul Alinsky-style of neighborhood organizing as at least one viable approach to countering the strong built-in tendencies in the business and political (even after a Harold Washington victory in 1983) arenas for focusing on the more affluent. Indeed, sections of the city can, in fact, prosper, leaving others behind.

They describe some community-based efforts, some successful, others not. In each instance, they take care to identify "winners and losers," and they give some account of the political processes contributing to the results. The authors raise the correct questions as they adopt what they call a posture of "cautious optimism."

> Will Chicago continue to operate as a growth machine, or will it adopt a public balance sheet? That is, will the city and the wider community be exploited as a vehicle for private capital accumulation whereby all efforts are geared toward the creation of the proverbial "good business climate" in hopes that anticipated economic growth will automatically lead to the enrichment of all? (p. 182)
>
> What will happen should private capital feel threatened by public sector and community-based efforts to guide private investment and capital allocation decision-making? . . . Will more businesses simply choose to leave Chicago? Can capital go on strike? (p. 185)

Of course, they do not have the answers to these questions. No one does. But the book, as with Bullard's on Houston, is an honest effort to point up some blatant pitfalls and social inequities in pursuing certain kinds of urban-development policies. The too-smug economic-growth theory has to contend with these analyses.

Pinderhughes's account of Chicago's experience with race and ethnic politics takes us back in time—to the turn of the century—and compares blacks, Poles, and Italians. As a political scientist, she deals with the relevant literature on pluralism as she charts the political paths of these three groups. Her conclusion is that the rather facile equation of race and ethnicity in American politics is flawed. Her concern is with "political integration": how it has worked in Chicago with the three groups. Beginning historically, and later focusing on issues of criminal justice and education, she concluded: "Blacks are not just another ethnic group . . . because the limits to their participation in the polity and economy are of a nature and character beyond anything that immigrant groups have faced" (p. 258).

One useful contribution of this study is that it goes beyond the relatively simplistic analysis of racial goals—status/welfare, integrationist/nationalist—and describes a much more complicated situation whereby many African Americans seek to end "externally imposed collectivism" at the same time hoping to "pursue internally generated collectivism with impunity" (p. 129). In this sense, of course, they are little different from Poles, Italians, or most other ethnic groups that have attempted to balance the demands for political integration with the desires for group identity and cohesion. But when these seemingly contradictory, but clearly not, preferences emerge with African Americans, they are not easily understood or accepted by the larger society. They appear "divisive" and "separatist," in the negative connotation of that term. Pinderhughes's book is one of the best academic analyses of this phenomenon in terms of how it could emerge, as well as its political implications on the urban scene. The book combines theory and empiricism to achieve a level of sophistication not often obtained in works on this subject. And the ethnic comparative context makes the study that much more valuable—in fact, future studies ought to concentrate more on the comparative in this mode.

Squires and his colleagues tell us pretty convincingly what has been happening with Chicago's urban development policies. Pinderhughes provides an excellent historical context for understanding how these situations came about. Both bring honest and perceptive interpretations to a field so fraught with naive assumptions and the inability to come to terms with the discomforting character of America's heritage of slavery and the lingering legacy of past and continued segregation and discrimination.

Pinderhughes pays close attention, as one would expect of a political scientist, to the role and impact of Chicago's "political machine." For African Americans to utilize that vehicle in a way reasonably approximating the manner of European ethnics would imply according race and ethnicity similar status in society. Machines rely on bargaining situations, but the factor of race, Pinderhughes concludes, which was preeminent in the minds of many white Chicagoans, could never be a legitimate negotiable item for blacks. Thus, for Pinderhughes, the entire basis of understanding black politics in the framework of a pluralist analysis became problematic at best.

All three books offer enough empirical data to keep their readers attentive. No one should expect that these accounts will escape the theoretical-analytical fracas.

Ultimately, what we are seeing in the latter years of the twentieth century is an African-American political struggle that will continue to pursue civil rights issues, defined in terms of segregation and discrimination based on race, and an increasing emphasis on the "politics of resources." That is, whether it is through coordinated community-wide organizations described by Bullard in Houston, more concentrated neighborhood-based Alinsky-type participatory structures preferred by Squires et al., or the remaking of the citywide electoral politics with alliances with other groups started by Harold Washington (but prematurely ended with his death), the focus of urban politics will be clear. What will be sought will not be the symbolic rewards of token appointees or externally controlled leaders. These kinds of benefits—divisible, individualistic—could always be parceled out to new groups entering the society. The public sector could rely on a generally growing private-sector economy to take care of the needs of most immigrants—albeit at first minimally *and* within the context of a racially segregated market economy. The urban machine did not have to deliver very much to purchase loyalty. This is no longer the case. The lower-status constituencies in these urban centers today must pursue a very different politics—one that focuses on the delivery of substantial resources to masses of people—*in*divisible benefits. The market economy, understandably interested in private profits, will yield only so much, but neither must it expect to preempt the decision-making agenda. This is the "politics of resources" that will be played out in these urban areas in the near term. The old theories (pluralism, economic growth) and the simplistic dichotomies (integration/nationalism, for example) will not contribute much to an understanding of these complex problems. The authors of these three books have done their part in clearing away some of the distracting intellectual underbush.

Separate and Unequal Societies in Urban Politics

Susan Welch

University of Nebraska

Robert D. Bullard, 1987, **Invisible Houston: The Black Experience in Boom and Bust,** College Station: Texas A & M Press, *xiv* + 160 pp., ISBN 0-89096-312-6 (cloth)/0-89096-357-6 (paper).

Dianne M. Pinderhughes, 1987, **Race and Ethnicity in Chicago Politics: A Reexamination of Pluralist Theory**, Urbana: University of Illinois Press, *xix* + 318 pp., ISBN 0-252-01294-1 (cloth).

Gregory D. Squires, Larry Bennett, Kathleen McCourt, and Philip Nyden, 1987, **Chicago: Race, Class, and the Response to Urban Decline,** Philadelphia: Temple University Press, *xii* + 230 pp., ISBN 0-87722-487-0 (cloth).

Over twenty years ago, the Kerner Commission reported that "our nation was moving toward two societies, one black, one white, separate and unequal" (National Advisory Commission, 1968:1). These three studies by Robert Bullard, Dianne Pinderhughes, and the quartet of Gregory D. Squires, Larry Bennett, Kathleen McCourt, and Philip Nyden, illustrate that, despite great gains in education and occupational status by millions of blacks since then, two largely separate and unequal societies continue to exist in our urban areas. Whether they live in cities in the rust belt, such as Chicago, or in cities of the sometimes-booming sunbelt, such as Houston, the opportunities for blacks are still limited by their racial and economic status.

Despite this common theme in the message of the three books, they are very different in their focus, scope, methods, and rationale. Robert Bullard's *Invisible Houston* spotlights the status of blacks living in Houston, Texas, the South's largest and richest black community (a fact I learned from reading the book). A sociologist, Bullard sketches the situation facing Houston's blacks in areas such as housing and neighborhood development, employment, the environment, law enforcement, civil rights, and political power. The book contains not only the usual text and graphs, but many photographs that add much to the presentation of the material.

In examining these topics, Bullard traces the historical development of Houston's black community in terms of its size, spatial distribution, and the impact of racial discrimination on it. He also provides some comparative data from other cities. Drawing on census data and case-study material, he illustrates the demographic, social, and political status of black Houstonians.

On the whole, Bullard sacrifices depth of treatment of particular issues and conditions for breadth of coverage. The reader learns a little about a lot of aspects of the lives of Houston's blacks. This is a useful outline, but this reader wished for more detail and more evidence. For example, the topics of black empowerment, black leadership, and civil rights in Houston each received about five pages, some of which were pictures. While *Invisible Houston* was not a book specifically about black political power, this brief treatment was too sketchy to be useful. More questions were raised than answered. To cite an example that begs for a more in-depth treatment, the author states, at the end of a summary discussion of black leadership, that

> recent black opposition to the racist white rule of the South African government has brought numerous black organizations and their constituents closer together not only in their protests against apartheid, but in their assessment of the condition of the blacks in the United States. By taking this worldview, black Houstonians are beginning to define their situation in the broad context of other oppressed people of color (p. 119).

These sentences cry out for illustration and evidence. How were black organizations and their constituents brought together? What evidence do we have? What evidence is there of changing definitions of black Houstonians' situation? How has this affected black organizational strength and black political behavior? While this is only one example, there are many like this that leave the reader asking for more information, evidence, and examples.

In sum, while the book will probably not have a wide audience, it will be useful for those interested in Houston politics, and Texas politics more generally. For those unfamiliar with the status of blacks in the United States, it provides much valuable information. For all of us, it is a useful reminder that even in boom towns and boom times, there are many, particularly in the black community, who suffer from deprivation.

Pinderhughes's *Race and Ethnicity in Chicago Politics* and *Chicago: Race, Class, and the Response to Urban Decline* by Squires and his associates complement each other nicely in their treatment of the dynamics of Chicago politics. Though they are both generally critical of what Chicago's leaders have done to the city during most of the twentieth century, their approaches are quite different.

Pinderhughes's work is the more theoretically sophisticated. She examines the black experience in Chicago in light of theories of pluralism.

By contrasting the experience of Chicago's black urban immigrant population with Polish and Italian immigrant communities during the first part of this century, she shows that the mechanisms available to white ethnics to assimilate and to gain economic and political power were often denied to blacks. While Polish and Italian Americans experienced discrimination and poverty, the discrimination suffered by African Americans was much more pervasive and enduring. These conclusions are not new; indeed, the Kerner Commission report itself devoted a brief chapter (chapter 9) to debunking the myths that the experience of the white immigrant and black slave and ex-slave were parallel. And, of course, several analysts of black politics, such as Charles Hamilton (1981) and Mathew Holden (1973), have pointed to the weaknesses of pluralism in explaining blacks' political status. Nonetheless, Pinderhughes's work makes an important contribution to our understanding of the relative status of black and white immigrants to northern cities in the early twentieth century. And it provides yet another illustration of the weaknesses of pluralist theory in understanding the special situation of America's racial minorities.

The heart of the study is a careful examination of a wide variety of census and other documentary reports (e.g., Chicago School Directories and Police Reports at the turn of the century), now-forgotten scholarly analyses of sometimes fairly esoteric aspects of early-twentieth-century life in Chicago (e.g., Herbst's study of the role of blacks in Chicago's meat-packing and slaughtering industries, published in 1932, and Thrasher's study of 1,313 Chicago gangs, published in 1936, to cite two examples), and many political science and sociological studies of the black, Italian, and Polish communities of Chicago. Indeed, the scope and variety of materials consulted for this study are quite exemplary and give the book an impressive depth. These studies are used to draw a picture of the status of black, Polish, and Italian Chicagoans as political participants in Chicago's machine politics, as individuals seeking to establish neighborhoods and secure employment, as participants in organized (and not-so-organized) crime, and as citizens wanting quality education and some representation in educational policy-making. In each of these areas, she illustrates the discriminatory treatment of the black community. For example, ironically, even as participants in organized crime, black Chicagoans were victims of discrimination. As lower-level employees of underworld organizations, they were the most vulnerable to police action. Their money did not buy the same secure protection from police intervention as did the money of the white ethnics higher in the organized-crime hierarchy.

Though by far the greatest portion of this work focuses on Chicago in the 1910s through 1940s, Pinderhughes also examines Chicago politics through the Daley era and to the earliest period of the Washington administration. Her analysis of the breakup of the Daley machine over the past decade is illuminating, though necessarily much sketchier than the historical analyses that form the heart of the book.

This book will be of interest and value to political scientists interested in pluralism and ethnic politics, as well as to urban scholars more generally. Shortcomings of the book are few and relate more to style than substance. I personally would prefer a succinct rendering of her main arguments and evidence in a concluding chapter. In particular, I would be interested in Pinderhughes's interpretation of how the election of Harold Washington and his successes and failures in office confirm or contradict her conclusions about pluralism and blacks. Moreover, a slightly heavier-handed copy editor might have eliminated some redundancies and made portions of the book more readable. But these are minor quibbles about what is a fine book. I am sure most readers will look forward to her further analyses of the racial and ethnic politics of the Washington and post-Washington eras in Chicago.

The book by Squires and his associates does not have the theoretical underpinnings of the Pinderhughes book, but it is a solid, scholarly work that will also be valuable to urban scholars. The thesis of *Chicago: Race, Class and the Response to Urban Decline* is that the "growth at all costs" philosophy espoused by Chicago's leadership over the past several decades has been detrimental to most of Chicago's residents. This growth ideology has resulted in a healthy and attractive downtown at the expense of most of Chicago's neighborhoods, black and white. Moreover, Squires and his colleagues argue that the downtown-centered growth philosophy has exacerbated the problems of poverty, unemployment, racial friction, and crime in Chicago. The interests of corporate Chicago and its wealthy elite have predominated over the interests of Chicago's middle and, especially, working, classes.

The authors pursue this argument in a cogent way throughout the book. After an introductory chapter, they describe the rise and fall of Chicago's industrial base and describe current trends in the Chicago economy. They then turn to a description of the growth and decline of the Daley machine, ending with a brief glimpse at the Washington campaign and election. Chapter 4 outlines the racial demography of Chicago and the housing policies that have made Chicago one of the most, if not the most segregated city in the United States. In chapter 5, the authors examine conflict and cooperation among neighborhood and community groups and their attempts to combat the downtown-centered growth philosophy of Chicago's elites. Chapter 6 deals specifically with the private-public cooperation that has guided Chicago's redevelopment and transformed its downtown in the past thirty years, while the final chapter asks whether the Washington administration heralds the beginning of a new direction in Chicago politics whereby public and private actions will be directed toward more democratic and humane ends.

These two works on Chicago share many common perspectives, including the view that racial discrimination continues to be a festering sore damaging the lives of hundreds of thousands of individual citizens and the life of the community as a whole. Both place their hopes in the election of Harold Washington and some of the forces that brought him to office (both books were published before Washington's death). One interesting difference is between their views of Chicago's white ethnics.

Pinderhughes views these groups as having had real political power through the mechanism of Chicago's political machine. Italian and Polish Americans, along with Irish Americans and other twentieth-century immigrants, often benefited from the repression of Chicago's black citizens. They profited when black neighborhoods received less than their fair share of public goods, and they profited when the private marketplace worked to cheat black Chicagoans out of good jobs and decent housing at the same price that whites paid.

On the other hand, though they give significant attention to racial discrimination and friction between blacks and whites in Chicago, Squires and his colleagues' primary argument is that the growth ideology has been almost as disfunctional for Chicago's working-class white ethnic citizens and neighborhoods as it has been for its black citizens and neighborhoods. Thus, most white ethnics, as lower- and middle-income residents, are really victims too. They, along with blacks, have suffered when economic incentives are directed toward downtown rather than toward neighborhood rejuvenation and when problems relating to the health and welfare of Chicago citizens are swept under the rug.

These two perspectives are not irreconcilable, in that both sets of authors would probably agree that the political machine provided benefits to white ethnic neighborhoods that it did not provide to black ones, and that most white ethnic citizens (as contrasted with their political leaders) had little say in major decisions shaping Chicago. Nonetheless, the different emphases of the two books make a thought-provoking contrast.

My criticisms of the Squires, Bennett, McCourt, and Nyden book are also fairly minor. One is that in their discussion of the internal distribution of public services they give no attention to the empirical research that has been done by Kenneth Mladenka and others on the way benefits are distributed among Chicago's wards and neighborhoods in recent years. These findings indicate that some of these benefits are distributed in ways that are more complex than simple race-and-class prejudice would dictate. Even Pinderhughes's analysis of the Chicago school system fifty years ago seems to indicate that sometimes pragmatism tempered prejudice in the distribution of some resources, and research on more contemporary eras indicates that bureaucratic routines and historical accidents do play a role in the distribution of resources.

A second criticism is that I would have linked a fuller discussion of the alternative policies they favor. I am certainly sympathetic to their critical perspective toward the "growth machine" and its consequences. This perspective has a much broader applicability than just to Chicago. Few among us have not felt a sense of injustice when, in our own communities, civic leaders pare human service budgets, yet give handouts to developers through tax write-offs or eagerly vote to waive planning and zoning requirements to accommodate strip development or the building of new shopping malls. Nevertheless, I would have appreciated a fuller discussion of policy alternatives that Chicago's lead-

might pursue to rebuild neighborhoods and re-install a sense of community and participation to Chicago's citizens. Again, however, this criticism should not overshadow praise for this very thought-provoking
book.

References

Hamilton, Charles V. 1981. "New Elites and Pluralism." In Richard M. Pious,
ed., *Power to Govern. Proceedings of the Academy of Political Science* 34: 167–73.

Herbst, Alma. 1932. *The Negro in the Slaughtering and Meat-Packing Industry in
Chicago.* Boston: Houghton Mifflin.

Holden, Mathew. 1973. *The Politics of the Black Nation.* New York: Chandler.

National Advisory Commission on Civil Disorders. 1968. *Report.* New York:
New York Times Company, Bantam Edition.

Thrasher, Frederick. 1936. *The Gang: A Study of 1,313 Gangs in Chicago.* Chicago:
University of Chicago Press.

Social Science, Public Policy, and Persistent Poverty among Urban Blacks: A Review of the Literature

Roland Anglin

Rutgers University

Paul E. Peterson (ed), 1985, **The New Urban Reality,** Washington D.C.: Brookings Institute, *vii* + 301 pp., ISBN 0-8157-7017-0 (paper).

Changes in the American economy have prompted a rush of studies on the cumulative effect of these shifts on the urban political economy. Many questions posed by these studies are engaging. For example: Is the central city obsolete (Peterson 1985)? Who controls and guides spatial development in the postindustrial city (Stone and Sanders, 1987; Logan and Molotch, 1987)? Has the postindustrial economy spawned a new type of poverty more persistent than previous incarnations (Nathan, 1987)? What social groups are affected most by economic change (Kasarda, 1985; Hudson Institute, 1987)? And perhaps the most important question: What role does government have in all these questions (Kantor, 1988)?

In his edited volume, *The New Urban Reality,* Paul Peterson provides a meeting place for discussing some of these questions. The papers are diverse in subject and content. Nevertheless, they converge into a pointed assessment of America's older urban cities and what to do about the increasing correlation between race and poverty (Peterson, 1985: 12).

This review concentrates on three voices in *The New Urban Reality*. This is not to slight the other contributors in the volume—all of whom in some measure add to the debate. Yet the selections by Paul Peterson, William Wilson, and Gary Orfield stand out in terms of breadth, argument and the nature of their policy recommendations. Rather than examining each contributor lightly and without substance, it was decided that picking these three constitutes a representative barometer of current thoughts on the nexus of race, poverty, and the city.

The Eclipse of the Industrial City

Peterson sets the tone of the volume with a provocative thesis. For Peterson, basic changes in the American economy have caused older urban areas to lose their comparative advantage. Agglomeration economies that gave rise to the industrial city have been nullified by advances in communications technology and the ability to rapidly move goods by planes and trucks. Additionally, the industrial complex, formerly located in these cities, has now branched out to low-density sites in the United States and offshore. The result, Peterson says, is that industrial cities have become "institutional anachronisms" (Peterson, 1985:1).

The policy question, for Peterson, is what to do about these older cities lacking employment opportunities yet laden with high-need minorities? The latter point is especially trenchant for Peterson and other contributors to *The New Urban Reality*. There is great concern that economic change impacts greatly—if not unevenly on urban blacks (Peterson, 1985:14–15).

While Peterson shows obvious concern for the plight of poor blacks, he is opposed to past and perhaps future federal attempts at stalling or reversing urban change. Peterson believes that such efforts run counter to prevailing market trends. Thus, government should not interfere in the efficiency of various markets. Peterson would much rather see a national system of equalized welfare payments. The thought, here, is that older, northern states tend to award higher per capita welfare payments. This discourages the poor from seeking better job opportunities in states with low welfare benefits but more job opportunities. Essentially, Peterson locates many of the problems of poor urban blacks in the spatial mismatch between people and jobs (Kasarda, 1985; Ellwood, 1986).

Peterson strongly argues that the changed nature of the urban economy has stymied the city's traditional role as a staging area for upward mobility. Yet to vest a national welfare system with the onus of matching low-skilled black urban dwellers to jobs in growth areas is curious.

For Peterson's policy recommendation to have value, one must make the assumption that welfare is the main source of income for much of the underclass. Yes, welfare is a prime source of income for many female-headed households with children in urban ghettos. Yet, what about the men of the underclass? Are we to assume that black, unemployed men are so enticed by welfare funds (presumably obtained from the mothers of their children) that they would also move to new areas of growth?

Then again, why is welfare such an attractive alternative when there are great profits to be made in the drug economy and other illicit markets (Viscusi, 1986)? While these are some of the issues one might raise with Peterson, it is clear there are many unanswered questions about the correlation between welfare and individual action.[1] With so many questions, a public policy based on welfare reform or equalized welfare payments across jurisdictions might be inadequate.

William Wilson, in his contribution to *The New Urban Reality*, does not take issue with Peterson's focus nor his conclusions. Wilson, however, places the issue of the urban underclass in a larger analytic context. Wilson examines the extent to which economic plus social and demographic factors lead to the formation of the urban underclass.[2]

Wilson argues on several fronts in his contribution to *The New Urban Reality* and in his larger work, *The Truly Disadvantaged* (1987). Broadly, Wilson takes issue with those claiming liberal government policies have created a dependent class through the welfare system. Many policy intellectuals, such as Charles Murray, have gained wide currency contending that through welfare, government has caused a whole host of ills— including increased illegitimacy, rising school-dropout rates, and high crime (Murray, 1984; Gilder, 1980).

For Murray, and others less prone to broad sweeps of causation (Lemann, 1986), dependence on welfare has become ingrained in the culture and attitudes of this particular subgroup. Wilson is concerned with the lack of rigor used by some (including Murray) citing welfare as the cause of all ills. For Wilson, these commentators use welfare as a shibboleth without recognizing the complexity of social and economic forces shaping the behavior of the underclass (Wilson, 1987:18).

The Issue of Race

In a related theme, Wilson argues, as he did in his now widely known work *The Declining Significance of Race* (1980), that creation of the black underclass cannot be understood as an artifact of American racism (Wilson, 1980; 1985:142–45). That is to say, racism is not the defining factor in gaining access to power and privilege in American society. This is in sharp contradiction to those arguing that race is still the defining variable in determining black upward mobility (Pinkney, 1985).

Using census data, Professor Wilson contends that the rise of an underclass is not simply the product of one variable (Wilson, 1985:141). Rather, the "profound" changes in poor black communities result from three interrelated factors: access to social mobility, a relatively young underclass, and economic change (Wilson, 1985:142–57).

In considering social mobility, Wilson discusses the role of the civil rights movement in opening the doors for black Americans (Wilson, 1987: chapter 5). Why, though, should increasing social mobility for blacks correlate with the rise of the underclass? Wilson argues that the Civil Rights Movement, apart from the obvious changes it engendered in American society, helped initiate public policies that bifurcated the black community.

Professor Wilson's point is clear: the move toward affirmative action in several spheres (e.g., open housing and promoting increased numbers of blacks in the professions) helped many blacks to gain access to the middle class (Wilson, 1987:112–15). Wilson asks us to entertain the argument that many of these individuals could have gained access without the extra help (Wilson, 1987:115–18). These individuals possessed the intangibles, whatever they are, that allow access to the middle-class mainstream. Conversely, those in need of real help (i.e., those not possessing these intangibles) languished in ghetto warrens (Wilson, 1987:118).

By removing overt discrimination and substituting even minor policies of redress, society gave an added advantage to those already able to compete. Wilson adopts the prevailing wisdom that many of the programs or policies of the "Great Society" period did not succeed in reaching those in need of help.

If we accept Wilson, then increasing social mobility was not a utilitarian outcome. The base effect was to destabilize the fabric of urban black communities. Because of "historic" discrimination, blacks of different classes were forced to live in the same communities (Spear, 1967). While this was noxious because choice opportunities for capable black Americans were denied, at least the lower classes had role models of success. Now, Wilson argues, choice opportunities opened access to different housing markets. The black middle classes left, leaving an imbalance. At present, there are no "positive" models of success for young blacks. Thus, the result of this "isolation" is the congealment of a set of values not conducive to upward mobility.

It must be said, though, that Wilson is not saying that absent role models is the only negative result of the black middle class leaving the city. Wilson makes the point that, overall, the loss of the middle class decimated the viability of community institutions through a sort of domestic brain and capital drain (Wilson et al., 1988:147).

The lack of role models becomes even more poignant considering Wilson's demographic finding that much of the underclass is relatively young. Migratory patterns from the South to the North continued well into the twentieth century. Unlike European immigration, which was restricted at a certain point, America could not effectively apply such restriction to blacks. Thus, the age structure of urban underclass communities remained young. A younger population means less skill accretion and, consequently, lower incomes. Important for Wilson, though, is the disruptive behavior and attitudes held by some in this younger cohort. Behavioral norms such as illegitimacy and sociopathic criminal behavior, helped along by the density of public housing, proliferate because these actions go unchecked by competing value systems (Wilson, 1985:149–52).

Wilson, although giving much credence to the social-mobility thesis and the demographic concentration argument, still assigns the greatest explanatory weight to the changing economy. Wilson argues that when black migrants were coming to the city in great numbers, the industrial complex was changing. Low-skilled—but relatively high-paying—occupations were giving way to occupations requiring more education. In addition, these jobs were not located in proximity to the underclass. The result has been devastating for the black family. With unemployment for black males often running three times that of their white male counterparts, it was hard if not impossible to form stable, thriving family units (Wilson, 1985:152–57).

With urban black communities under siege by all three factors, Wilson is able to make a solid case that the resulting formation of an underclass was an inevitability.

Policy Recommendations

William Wilson's solution, while measured and grounded in extensive analysis, still operates at a very macro level. Wilson argues that, if the policy goal is to reduce family dislocation and other pathologies of the underclass, the emphasis must be on macroeconomic prescriptions. That is, there must be a national policy of growth and maintenance of tight labor markets. Such a full-employment economy has to be helped along by efficient labor-market policies such as training and subsidies for relocation (Wilson, 1985:159–60; Wilson, 1987: chapter 7).[3]

Wilson's analysis is convincing. In fact, if Wilson's study has a problem, it is not in the analysis but in his policy recommendations. If we accept that the underclass is a product of spatial concentration and isolation, then a policy of macroeconomic tinkering would only indirectly address that situation.[4] Thus, the tide of economic growth raises many ships, but Wilson has already argued that because of spatial isolation the underclass is bereft of skills that make them competitive in wider labor markets. How are members of the underclass going to acquire (1) the skills and (2) access to jobs in the unfolding economy?

Wilson may reply that it is the responsibility of government to provide effective job training so the underclass can be employable or, again, subsidize relocation. Such an answer is limited, because the United States has not had major success in job training (Baumer and Van Horn, 1985). The argument can be made that if we cannot effectively train them, maybe the solution is to subsidize relocation.

This assumes that localities with labor-deficient economies will welcome workers without regard to anything but their ability to work. In pure form this is an attractive solution. Yet one has to pose the fairly obvious question: Is the marginal benefit to localities (potential workers) enough to offset the marginal disutility? That disutility is the potential (or perceived) problems brought with any social grouping that has been isolated from the social mainstream (Danielson, 1976). With members of the underclass one has to ask: Why should communities experiencing growth accept individuals with different mores and work habits? What is the incentive? There really is no incentive if one accepts the thesis that localities maximize either high-income individuals or firms that contribute to the tax base (Danielson, 1976; Peterson, 1981).

The Configuration of Race, Class, and Space

Gary Orfield, in his contribution to *The New Urban Reality,* takes a quite different approach than Peterson and Wilson. Where Wilson acknowledges the ghetto as a dominant variable in perpetuating the underclass, it is not, for Wilson, the prime causal factor in the phenomenon of the underclass.

Orfield is quite clear: he locates the creation of the black urban poor in the historical construction of the ghetto (Orfield, 1985: 162–65). Orfield and Wilson differ in this vein. Wilson acknowledges racism in the historical creation of the ghetto. Yet Wilson would not agree that historical racism is a residual constraint on black upward mobility.

Orfield maintains that one cannot understand the behavior of latter-day urban dwellers without understanding that space, historically, has never been neutral. Rather space—as geographers term it—has been used as an aggressive agent for inequality (Orfield, 1985: 164–69; Spear, 1967).

Thus Orfield notes that even though the civil rights movement created economic opportunities for many black Americans, the ghetto survived. More to the point, while barriers were relaxed in the larger society, nothing was substantively done to destroy this dysfunctional entity. Consequently, the concentration of inferior schools, segregated housing, substandard government services was able to grow worse (Orfield, 1985:175–78).

For Orfield, it is not that choice has created such a great bifurcation in the black community. Black Americans, and now Hispanic Americans, are still denied choice opportunities in various markets. Instead of the rather optimistic vision of substantial numbers of blacks entering the middle class, Orfield would point out that "ghettoization" has become a metropolitan problem (Orfield, 1985:168). In other words, some blacks might possess the income to acquire better surroundings, but due to racism, blacks are often resegregated when they move into new areas (Logan and Schneider, 1984). With resegregation, urban minorities are still faced with the problems of limited choice and inferior services (Orfield, 1985:168–71).[5]

Orfield, relying on his argument that spatial structure has constrained choice opportunities for poor urban blacks, contends that traditional policies aimed at leveling the ghetto failed. Orfield states that if society wants to destroy the ghetto it has to commit itself to integration. Integration has to come through aggressive policies for fair housing and planned integration.

The conceptual foundation for integration is strong. In practice, the policy and the methods for implementation (both residential and through schools) have provoked a storm of controversy. Community battles against bussing and open housing have raged since both were court ordered some thirty years ago. This is not to say bussing and open housing measures have not met with success. There have been notable successes—especially in the South. But strong resistance has limited integration as a comprehensive policy measure.

Although Orfield cites some victories in managed integration, the fact still remains that most middle-class Americans—black or white—do not want low-income blacks in their neighborhoods. Unless new or improved methods can be found to convince Americans that integration is a worthy public-policy goal, such a policy will never alleviate the problems of the urban black poor.

Conclusions

The three analyses presented above comprise a sort of analytic standard. Separately, they set the prescriptive tone for welfare reform, increased attention to a national growth policy (with attention to human capital), and increased housing and employment choices for low-income blacks through spatial desegregation.

All three views have their individual strengths and weaknesses. A common weakness, however, is the slight attention paid to the structural capacity of various national and local institutions that have to wrestle with urban poverty. It is not enough to propose a national system of equalized welfare payments without probing how communities will afford to build moderate-to-low-income housing and increase municipal services to absorb high-need groups.

Then again, a national growth policy (as proposed by Wilson) with an effective job-training component and relocation is fine. However, with an economy currently growing strongly and near what some economists would term full employment, the question becomes: Do we need a national growth policy (Economic Report of the President, 1988)? Arguably, this is an impossible policy to construct; thus, why waste intellectual and political resources in advocating its construction?

The question should be: Can our system of federalism train and educate the hard-core urban unemployed to take jobs in the new and evolving economy (Hudson Institute, 1987)? The answer could well be one of limited administrative and political capacity at the local and national level. That is, the question is state-centered and not society-centered. If so, the most complete analysis of what causes the rise of the urban underclass may be an ineffectual exercise.

On balance, increasing housing choices and labor market opportunities (through desegregation) is quite proactive, given local problems of financing schools and providing public services to underclass communities. Nevertheless, continued attention must be given to attempts at community economic development and access to viable community institutions. Such a two-pronged effort has often proceeded as a mutually exclusive process. It is not.

Choice must be given to those who have the ability and drive to succeed in the mainstream. And spatial deconcentration makes the multiple problems of the underclass more manageable. Yet those who are left behind cannot be consigned to permanent poverty because of urban triage. All levels of government must *commit* to making poor urban communities viable (Mayor's Commission on Black New Yorkers, 1988; Kantor, 1988).

There are those commentators who would cite the failure of past attempts at a community-development strategy. There is little need to debate at this time whether urban renewal or the "Great Society" worked. It is fairly obvious that spot infusions of money and attention are wholly inadequate. Real community development is more than a city department or satellite agency in a neighborhood shoveling money into small scale projects. Community development encompasses a continuing effort at promoting effective schools and efficient neighborhood services, opening closed employment opportunities in the public and private sector, and, yes, creating the incentive for a viable economic base in the community (Mayor's Commission on Black New Yorkers, 1988).[6] These are not things subject to ideological challenge, but, rather, they constitute the essence and firmament of a strong democracy.

In closing, the discussions in *The New Urban Reality* form the backdrop for larger policy debates. As such, the entire book is an invaluable volume. Despite the overstated theme that urban cities are an anachronism, cities are surviving. They have acquired new functions and comparative advantages (Noyelle and Stanback, 1984). To imagine that older American cities are an anachronism is to argue a cataclysm that is not yet evident. Cities go through cycles. We are simply experiencing the unfolding of yet another cycle (Noyelle and Stanback, 1984).

Policy analysts concerned about the underclass, however, have to wrestle with the tough issues of how the urban black poor will be accorded the opportunities to achieve upward mobility (Mayor's Commission on Black New Yorkers, 1988). These are issues of institutional access—and not problems of individual rectitude. Too often the debate has concentrated unnecessarily on the latter.

Notes

1. There is scant evidence in the literature supporting a correlation between welfare and personal decisions such as residential mobility or family structure. See, for example, Ellwood and Summers (1986a).
2. This group experiences severe if not permanent unemployment, commits crimes out of proportion to their numbers in society, and suffers from high rates of illegitimacy.
3. Wilson proposes a range of ameliorative programs, many of them resembling social-welfare programs found in Europe. Some of these policies include a family allowance and improved child-welfare benefits.
4. Wilson is very clear: he is against "race-specific" policies fearing that such policies would not gain widespread political support.
5. Orfield maintains that limited choice in education and other public services has exacerbated the effects of a changing urban economy. Orfield asserts this situation is especially hard on male members of minority groups simply because the changing economy looks favorably on those with clerical skills—usually women (Orfield, 1985:177). Traditionally, these males lack such skills and certainly lack the "educational credentials to compete for the higher paid, traditionally male occupations in the white-collar work force" (Orfield, 1985:177).
6. A recent study commissioned by the mayor of New York (Mayor's Commission on Black New Yorkers, 1988) makes the point that the problems of poor

New Yorkers still rest with race. The commission's report documents that black New Yorkers are still unemployed at higher rates than average even with a booming city economy. According to the commission, the main problem is a lack of access to key institutions, such as a quality educational system. The commission also reported discrimination in private and public labor markets, which acts as a major hindrance to upward mobility for poor blacks. The main recommendations were increased attention to school reform and opening labor markets closed by racism. See Pomer (1986) and Hayward and Coverman (1987) for support of the argument that racism still plays a significant part in occupational mobility.

References

Baumer, Donald, and Carl Van Horn. 1985. *The Politics of Unemployment.* Washington, D.C.: Congressional Quarterly Press.
Danielson, Michael. 1976. *The Politics of Exclusion.* N.Y.: Columbia University Press.
Hudson Institute. 1987. *Workforce 2000: Work and Workers for the 21st Century.* Indianapolis: Hudson Institute.
Economic Report of the President. 1988. *The Annual Report of the Council of Economic Advisors.* Washington, D.C.: The U.S. Printing Office.
Ellwood, David and Lawrence Summers. 1986a. "Poverty in America: Is Welfare the Answer or the Problem?" In Sheldon Danziger and Daniel Weinberg, eds., *Fighting Poverty: What Works and What Doesn't.* Cambridge: Harvard University Press.
——— 1986b. "The Spatial Mismatch Hypothesis: Are There Teenage Jobs Missing in the Ghetto?" In Richard Freeman and Harry Holzer, eds., *The Black Youth Unemployment Crisis.* Chicago: The University of Chicago Press.
Gilder, George. 1980. *Wealth and Poverty.* N.Y.: Basic Books.
Kantor, Paul. 1988. *The Dependent City: The Changing Political Economy of Urban America.* Glenview: Scott, Foresman and Company.
Kasarda, John. 1985. "Urban Change and Minority Opportunities." In Paul Peterson, ed., *The New Urban Reality.* Washington, D.C.: Brookings Institution.
Lemann, Nicholas. 1986. "The Origins of the Underclass." *The Atlantic,* (June).
Murray, Charles. 1984. *Losing Ground: American Social Policy 1950–1980.* N.Y.: Basic Books.
Mayor's Commission on Black New Yorkers. 1988. *The Report of the Mayor's Commission on Black New Yorkers.* New York: Office of the Mayor.
Hayward, Mark, and Shelley Coverman. 1987. "Change in the Racial Composition of Occupations, 1960–1970." *Sociological Perspectives,* 30(2).
Logan, John, and Mark Schneider. 1984. "Racial Segregation and Racial Change in American Suburbs, 1970–1980." *American Journal of Sociology,* 89(4).
Logan, John, and Harvey Molotch. 1987. *Urban Fortunes: The Political Economy of Place.* Berkeley: University of California Press.
Nathan, Richard. 1987. "Will the Underclass Always Be With Us?" *Society,* (March/April).
Noyelle, Thierry, and Thomas Stanback. 1984. *The Economic Transformation of American Cities.* Totowa: Rowman and Allaheld.

Orfield, Gary. 1985. "Ghettoization and Its Alternatives." In Paul Peterson, ed., *The New Urban Reality*. Washington, D.C.: Brookings Institution.

Peterson, Paul. 1985. "Technology, Race, and Urban Policy." In Paul Peterson, ed., *The New Urban Reality*. Washington, D.C.: Brookings Institution.

Peterson, Paul. 1981. *City Limits*. Chicago: University of Chicago Press.

Pinkney, Alonso. 1985. *The Myth of Black Progress*. N.Y.: Cambridge University Press.

Pomer, Marshall. 1986. "Labor Market Structure, Intergenerational Mobility, and Discrimination: Black Male Advancement out of Low Paying Occupations, 1962–1973." *American Sociological Review*, 51.

Spear, Allan. 1967. *Black Chicago: The Making of a Negro Ghetto 1890–1920*. Chicago: University of Chicago Press.

Stone, Clarence, and Heywood Sanders. 1987. *The Politics of Urban Development*. Lawrence: The University of Kansas Press.

Viscusi, W. Kip. 1986. "Market Incentives for Criminal Behavior." In Richard Freeman and Harry Holzer, eds., *The Black Youth Unemployment Crisis*. Chicago: University of Chicago Press.

Wilson, William. 1980. *The Declining Significance of Race: Blacks and Changing American Institutions*. Chicago: University of Chicago Press.

———. 1985. "The Urban Underclass in Advanced Industrial Society." In Paul Peterson, ed., *The New Urban Reality*. Washington, D.C.: Brookings Institution.

——— 1987. *The Truly Disadvantaged: The Inner City, the Underclass and Public Policy*. Chicago: University of Chicago Press.

Wilson, William, Robert Aponte, Joleen Kirschenman, and Loic Wacquant. 1988. "The Ghetto Underclass and the Changing Structure of Urban Poverty." In Fred Harris and Roger Wilkins, eds., *Quiet Riots: Race and Poverty in the United States*. N.Y.: Pantheon Books.

Urban Politics

Zelma A. Mosley

University of Delaware

Stephen L. Elkin, 1987, **City and Regime in the American Republic,** Chicago: University of Chicago Press, 220 pp., ISBN 0-226-20465-0 (cloth)/0-226-20466-9 (paper).
Ted Robert Gurr and Desmond S. King, 1987, **The State and the City,** Chicago: University of Chicago Press, 242 pp., ISBN 0-226-31090-6 (cloth)/0-226-31091-4 (paper).

Students of urban politics are engrossed in an intense ideological debate about urban political economies. The books by Elkin, and Gurr and King continue the debate waged among neo-Marxists, neoconservatives, liberals, conservatives, elite theorists, pluralists, and others by addressing in distinct ways the dynamics of rational choice in city politics. On one hand, Elkin, in *City and Regime in the American Republic,* considers the political institutions that best serve the "commercial public interest." On the other hand, Gurr and King, in *The State and the City,* proceed in the tradition of urban political economic analysis, focusing on choices of national and local government officials. Both works raise questions about the treatment of race and ethnicity in the theoretical debate being waged in the study of urban political, economic, and social phenomena.

City and Regime in the American Republic is a state-market interpretation of urban politics. Elkin looks beyond the conventional political science concern for political equality and social problem solving in cities by addressing what cities should be. He proposes that city political institutions need to be rearranged to achieve both equality and efficiency in the urban political economy. The themes of efficiency and equality guide the work. The efficiency theme is pursued by asking whether city political institutions are organized to promote social intelligence in problem solving. Elkin pursues the equality theme by asking whether popular control in cities is characterized by bias such that some interests are systematically favored over others.

244

In the first half of the book, Elkin reviews evidence indicating that cities have failed in their attempt to provide political equality and social intelligence. He finds public officials are disposed to favor some actors and some kinds of policies over others, and some political actors are in a better position than others to achieve their purpose. He concludes popular control has failed.[1] More specifically, he discovers that popular control is unduly receptive to the economic preferences of the business sector. As a result, cities are characterized by systematic bias and fall short in problem solving. He makes the point that popular control of authority, if honored, does not call for a trade-off between efficiency and equality. These assertions are based on a weak assessment of the politics of city services and city jobs and a more complete analysis of land-use patterns.

According to Elkin, the structural factors that define the division of labor between state and market create urban political economies that revolve around three axes: (1) an alliance between public officials and the local business sector, focused on promoting economic growth in the city, (2) efforts by local politicians to organize and maintain electoral coalitions, and (3) efforts by bureaucrats to gain autonomy in shaping politics that guide their sphere of activity. He views racial politics in the city as revolving around these axes. This conclusion is based on the observation that "the black mobilization of the 1960s in northern cities and in some southern ones had the principal impact of altering both the players in the politics of the functional bureaucracies and the pool from which the public side of the politics of growth was drawn" (p. 53). Elkin contends the principal features of the axes remained intact. Perhaps racial conflict figures more prominently than Elkin concedes. Nevertheless, Elkin does not provide adequate supporting evidence for his assertions about racial conflict in cities.

Elkin's discussion of the various types of urban political economies presents shortcomings as well. Federalist political economies, created after the political mobilization of the mid and late 1960s, feature the use of federal money for coalition-building efforts. A natural alliance between local businessmen and public officials characterizes an entrepreneurial political economy. Lastly, a pluralist political economy features an ethnically and racially heterogeneous coalition. Elkin refers to the findings of Edward C. Banfield in *Big City Politics* and J. David Greenstone and Paul E. Peterson in *Race and Authority in Urban Politics* to justify the classification of Chicago as a version of the pluralist political economy. A reading of *Race and Ethnicity in Chicago Politics* by Dianne Pinderhughes would indicate race does not fit a pluralist conception of the urban political economy.

In the last part of the book, Elkin presents a theoretical discussion of the political way of life that values popular control and economic prosperity and of the political judgement necessary to guide the reform of institutions of popular control in ways that will serve those values. In pondering these concerns, Elkin raises the question of whether a regime can prosper while pursuing both popular control and a property-based market system. He argues that these two aspirations are not necessarily incompatible. Rather, he offers the thesis that institutional arrangements need to tie the self-interest of individuals to the common good of a commercial republic. This is striking, particularly since, in the case of blacks, institutional racism is so deeply embedded in American society that the distinction between the self-interest of the individual and the self-interest of the group is not clear. Elkin says that a balance must be struck among procedural morality, political equality, and social intelligence in city political institutions.

While *City and Regime* concentrates on the shortcomings of city political institutions in furthering regime purposes, Gurr and King, in *The State and the City*, focus on the limits imposed by the interests of the national state in advancing and legitimizing itself. Gurr and King present a general analysis of the role of the state and the evolution of the role of the state in reshaping cities over the last thirty years. They use a "state-centered" approach that emphasizes the significance of state action—both national and local—for cities. Gurr and King argue that national and local states have their own distinctive interests in cities and have autonomy in how they pursue those interests, and that the changing character of cities in advanced industrial societies is not merely the result of inevitable economic processes but, instead, is affected by the decisions of national and local public officials. The authors err by not figuring into their formulations a discussion of power and privilege disparities among state officials.

According to Gurr and King, the autonomy of local government has declined as a result of the internationalization of production. This means that control of urban economic change is ever more removed from the local economy, and consequently less subject to management by the local government. As the industrial base declines, the local state becomes increasingly dependent on the national government. Gurr and King contend that the arrangement of city political institutions, while vital in the Elkin analysis, become subordinate to national state interests. In Gurr and King's "state-centered" analysis, the dependence of cities upon the national government depends on their economic, political, and administrative importance in the national system of cities. Also, levels of disorder, social stress, and political mobilization come into play.

Gurr and King draw evidence from cities in the United States and Great Britain to support their contentions. They find that urban decline in the United States is associated with increased dependence on federal and state revenues. But the authors attribute unwarranted importance to federal bureaucrats in the allocation of federal aid. They disregard political reality by not taking into account the role of members of Congress—politicians—in the allocation of federal aid. Furthermore, empirical support for their conclusion is weak. Their major assumption concerning national state interest garners minimal support in the empirical analysis. After identifying several ways in which the national state may be involved in local economies, Gurr and King fail to include them in the regression analysis.

Despite the interest the national state has in postindustrial cities, Gurr and King argue, national governments have withdrawn, allowing the future of old industrial cities in the United States and Great Britain to be decided by the private sector. Gurr and King suggest that if pressures from the fiscal health of cities results in urban crises which affect the national state's interest, a new thrust of national-state intervention in cities, similar to that of the 1930s and 1960s, will occur. But they do not provide strong evidence to support the national-state-interest assumption.

In the concluding chapter, Gurr and King identify four types of cities that they believe depict the decline or growth of the city in the national market economy and the level of activity brought about by state power and policy. The fourfold typology reflects the authors' interest in the way state policies interact with economic forces to reshape the cities of advanced industrial societies; the four types of city are (1) old industrial cities that are economically stagnant, (2) new industrial cities that were made vigorous by the movement or the relocation of capital and the development of high-technology industries, (3) administrative cities that depend heavily on public-sector employment, and (4) welfare cities that have a growing poor population and are dependent on government transfer payments.

The first two chapters and chapter 6—the concluding chapter—of *The State and the City* are valuable for understanding the contemporary trend in research on urban political economies. The authors provide a useful summary of the ideological debate in the study of urban politics and insights for understanding urban development. Gurr and King do offer some insights about the unfolding market economy in inner cities. In that regard, *The State and the City* may be useful for understanding the contemporary black urban underclass.

Both of the works reviewed criticize theoretical perspectives from both the left and the right and offer alternative approaches to the study of urban politics. According to Elkin in *City and Regime*, it is important to connect a strong democratic sensibility to a Madisonian account of the American regime. Further development of the formulation should address how racial conflict confounds the link between popular control, political equality, and efficiency. In *The State and the City*, Gurr and King offer the examination of the interaction between public and private decisions as the appropriate perspective for understanding urban politics. More rigorous analysis is essential. Furthermore, both works fail to give adequate attention to the persistence of race and ethnicity in the political economy of the city. Clearly, this was not the intention of either of the authors. Nevertheless, if advances are to be made toward a comprehensive understanding of urban politics, the persistence of race and ethnicity must be taken into account.

Note

1. By "popular control" Elkin means the effort to connect the use of public authority to the opinions of the citizenry. Formulations by Charles E. Lindbolm in *The Intelligence of Democracy* suggest the promise of popular control is that it will make the benefits of collective life available to a wide range of citizens and will utilize the intelligence of a wide range of citizens.

Race, Class, and Politics: A Conceptual Critique of William J. Wilson's Model of American Racial History

Eric Moskowitz

College of Wooster

William J. Wilson's The Declining Significance of Race *became one of the most controversial analyses of U.S. race relations in recent memory. Most of this controversy surrounded Wilson's interpretation of the simultaneous growth of a successful black middle class and an entrapped black urban underclass in contemporary America. Unfortunately, despite all the controversy over his contemporary analysis, little attention has been paid to Wilson's ambitious attempt to create a comprehensive model of U.S. race relations that seeks to explain the variations in the levels and forms of racial antagonism across a series of historical epochs.*

The core of Wilson's model maintains that, in a complex industrial economy, racial oppression will exist at higher levels when the white and black working classes are in economic competition with one another and when the white working class has the political power to enforce a racial solution to their economic problem. However, when one carefully sifts through Wilson's model and his application of it to U.S. racial history, a number of problems arise. Two of his central concepts, economic competition and political power, are too ambiguously defined to be of any use for other analysts. Moreover, the model is unable to explain significant differences in both the level and form of racial oppression in different historical eras. Many of the problems of Wilson's model are ultimately attributable to his overdependence on a very narrowly defined materialist interpretation of race relations.

William Julius Wilson's *The Declining Significance of Race* was highly controversial when it was first published. Most of the controversy concerned Wilson's assertion that race was no longer a significant variable for explaining the economic position of blacks in contemporary America. But in the heat of that dispute, another significant component of the book was overlooked. The first half of the book attempts to explain the variation in race relations in the United States across historical periods. This historical analysis is the focus of this review. Race is one of the most significant factors in the historical evolution of the American political economy. Wilson has made an ambitious attempt to create a model that will explain that racial history. This model deserves further attention.

Competing Class Models of Racial Antagonism

Wilson takes two class-based models of racism (orthodox Marxist theory and split labor market theory) and compares their utility for explaining racial antagonism in differing eras of U.S. history. Ultimately, Wilson will argue that neither theory can explain all periods adequately. While never explicitly offering an alternative model, a careful reader will find the outline of such a model in Wilson's historical examination. Wilson describes the orthodox Marxist explanation of racism as a two-class model (Wilson, 1980: 4–5. Unless otherwise noted, further references are to Wilson, 1980). The capitalist class's goal is to maximize profits. Toward that goal capitalists isolate blacks in both economy and society. This racial oppression produces a marginal black working class and a relatively privileged white working class. This serves capitalist interests because it (1) destroys working-class unity, (2) sets up a black reserve army of labor useful for pressuring white laborers, and (3) provides white workers with a false sense of socioeconomic success.

In contrast, Wilson depicts the split labor market (SLM) approach as a three-class model consisting of capitalists, high-priced labor, and low-priced labor (pp. 5–8). This model postulates that, when the labor market is split into pools of high- and low-priced labor and that cleavage is also coterminous with racial distinctions, then racial antagonisms will develop. The high-priced labor group will use racial oppression either to exclude the lower-priced group or to set up a racial stratification system in the interest of avoiding competition from this lower-priced labor in the marketplace. Thus, in the SLM model the catalyst for racial antagonism is a white labor aristocracy seeking to avoid the competition of cheaper black labor. Capitalists, who have an interest in cheaper labor, acquiesce to this racial stratification to preserve white labor's cooperation in the production process.

Wilson then evaluates the ability of these two models to explain the variety of racial regimes in U.S. history. He specifies seven different racial systems: the Antebellum South, the Antebellum North, the Reconstruction South, the Post Reconstruction South, the Late Nineteenth Century North (1870–1900), the Industrial North (1900–1950), and the Modern Industrial System (from 1950). Wilson also categorizes the race relations of each racial regime as either paternalistic racial domination, competitive racial domination, or fluid race relations.

Citing van den Berghe, Wilson states that "paternalistic racial patterns reveal close symbiotic relationships marked by dominance and subservi-

ence, great social distance and little physical distance, and clearly symbolized rituals of racial etiquette" (p. 13). Wilson categorizes both the
Antebellum South and the Reconstruction South as paternalistic racial
regimes. Competitive race relations are an alternative form of racial exploitation that include social and economic racial stratification, residential segregation, loss of political rights, and public violence. According to
Wilson, the Antebellum North, the Post-Reconstruction South, and the
Industrial North fall into this category. Wilson finds that the Late Nineteenth Century North and the contemporary Modern Industrial eras are
not marked by comprehensive racial exploitation. Significant aspects of
black life chances are not constrained by racial domination in these eras
of fluid race relations.

Wilson's Model of Race Relations

Wilson uses his historical evaluation of the Marxist and SLM explanations as an opportunity to develop implicitly his own model of race relations. Wilson's predisposition to a materialist interpretation of race
relations can be seen in both his focus on two-class-based models and
his explicit rejection of a significant independent role for racial-belief systems (pp. 9–12, 148–49). Nonetheless, he does not simply rely on these
class-based models. Wilson also seeks to incorporate an independent political factor into his own explanation of race relations:

> Although I stress the economic basis of structured racial inequality in the
> preindustrial and industrial periods of race relations, I also attempt to show
> how the polity more or less interacted with the economy either to reinforce
> patterns of racial stratification or to mediate various forms of racial con-
> flict. . . . Thus, my central argument is that different systems of production
> and/or different arrangements of the polity have imposed different con-
> straints on the way in which racial groups have interacted in the United
> States. (P. 3)

As seen in this passage, Wilson's explanation of patterns in race relations will involve a combination of the two economically oriented theories (through a sensitivity to 'systems of production') with an awareness
of the political dimension.

Wilson will use three basic factors to construct his own interpretation
of race relations in U.S. history. The economic factors are derived from
his comparison of Marxist and SLM theories. As portrayed by Wilson,
both theories assume that the interests and motivations of classes will be
determined by their roles in the economic system. Both also assume that
a class will act in its own economic self-interest. The theories differ, according to Wilson, in the specification of which class has the motivation
and ability to use racial exploitation of blacks for their own class ends.

The first concept that Wilson extracts from his theoretical comparison
deals with the constitution of the economic system in a given era. The
type of economic system will shape group interests, relations, and

power. Wilson argues that the level of *complexity of the economic system* importantly affects race relations. For Wilson, all other things being equal, a more diversified industrial economy produces more possibilities for group mobility. Potential for mobility, in turn, produces high levels of economic competition among racial groups. Since all things are rarely equal among racial groups (migration patterns, geographic separation, occupation skill levels, etc.), Wilson also uses a separate *economic competition* factor to denote whether economic competition among racial groups actually exists. Wilson then adds a political factor that takes into account the relative *political power* of white economic elites, white workers, and blacks. The interaction of these three variables produces the form of racial relations for each era.

A brief description of Wilson's analysis of several racial eras may provide a sense of both the power and limitations of his model. According to Wilson, in the Antebellum South a simple agrarian economy greatly minimized the direct economic competition between racial groups. Moreover, since the planters dominated southern society, economy, and polity, the white working class was powerless to impose either occupational stratification or exclusion upon blacks to reduce whatever economic competition did exist. The result was a planter-controlled paternalistic exploitation of black slaves.

A number of the relevant variables are different in Wilson's analysis of the Antebellum North. Most significant is the diversity of the economy, which leads to economic competition between black and white workers. But this economic competition is only a necessary, not sufficient, cause for a competitive style of racial relations. It must be present with white working-class power to produce a pattern of competitive segregation. Wilson makes the case that competitive racial antagonism depends upon the white working class having both the motive (economic competition) and the ability (political power) to enforce this racial stratification system. As the U.S. economy becomes increasingly complex, these two factors become the center of Wilson's late-nineteenth and twentieth century analyses. Thus, when Wilson analyzes the Post-Reconstruction era in the South and the twentieth century industrial period in the North, both fit quite neatly into the same pattern as the Antebellum North. They are marked by both economic competition between racial groups and significant white working-class power. The result in all three historical periods is the competitive form of racial antagonism, with both exclusion and stratification present.

Two other historical periods are not categorized by Wilson as having competitive racial exploitation. As one might expect, they will also differ on one of his two crucial variables. The white working class in the North from 1870–1900 had significant political power, but, because working-class economic competition was negligible, they had no interest in creating a system of racial stratification. This becomes an era of fluid race relations. Conversely, Wilson describes the Reconstruction era in the South as one in which there is growing economic competition but white working-class power is not sufficient to enforce a competitive racial regime. Instead a planter-merchant alliance dominates and enforces a regime of paternalistic exploitation.

Economic Competition in Wilson's Model

At first glance this historical analysis of Wilson's is quite impressive. A substantial amount of American racial history seems to be explained on the basis of primarily two factors—economic competition and white working-class power. Nonetheless, there are a number of problems with Wilson's historical analysis. His analysis of economic competition is marred by conceptual ambiguity, causal inconsistency and mechanistic materialism, and the failure to adequately distinguish independent from dependent variables.

Conceptual Ambiguity

Wilson's central variable of economic competition is not well defined. In his historical analysis, Wilson presents very little data to substantiate his categorization of the level of competition in particular eras. This is particularly bothersome for his claim that the northern economy from 1870–1900 was noncompetitive. By Wilson's own account in the eras just prior to and just subsequent to this period, economic competition was present in the North. Through all three periods, Wilson specifies the northern economy as diversified, thus changes in the economic structure are evidently not significant here. Instead, Wilson relies on differential rates of ethnic occupational mobility and on the low percentage of blacks in the North to explain low levels of economic competition. Wilson claims that "there was little racial competition during the late nineteenth century because the German and Irish immigrants had significantly improved their economic status in the trades and municipal employment. They therefore had little occupational contacts with blacks, who were concentrated on the lower rungs of the occupational ladder" (p. 63). Wilson goes on to state that direct economic competition was further reduced by the small number of blacks living in the North at this time.

Wilson's explanation is problematic. He presents no data to support his claims of the occupational structure of the North. By failing to provide such crucial data, Wilson not only leaves his argument without an empirical foundation, but, more important for later analysis, he avoids crucial conceptual discussions about the parameters of a competitive occupational structure. For instance, how similar must racial occupational distributions be to qualify as competitive?

Causal Inconsistency and Mechanistic Materialism

Additional problems with Wilson's use of economic competition can be highlighted by comparing his analyses of the North in the late nineteenth century with other northern eras. As just noted, Wilson describes the late nineteenth century northern labor market as having white immigrants safely entrenched in a niche above that of black workers. Compare that to his description of the northern labor market of 1900–1950:

> Most of the black workers who migrated to the northern industrial centers went directly into low paying, unskilled or semi-skilled work. . . . What was distinctive about these jobs, however, is that both native and americanized foreign born white workers tended to reject them in favor of more desirable employment. (P. 73)

According to Wilson, in the late nineteenth century this labor segmentation led to a lack of economic competition and hence an era of racial harmony; but in the twentieth century this labor segmentation is associated with a competitive form of racial antagonism. Wilson attempts to explain this apparent causal inconsistency by noting the increase in black migration to the North in the 1900–1950 era and the potential threat this posed to white workers. (pp. 65–70) But this explanation, too, is problematic. If one looks at the proportion of blacks in the northern population during the 1870–1900 period and the early part of the industrial era, 1900–1915, there is very little difference (Katznelson, 1976:32). These facts call into question Wilson's explanation of racial antagonism grounded almost solely in material factors like occupational structure and migration patterns. Instead, one might want to explore the possibility that the racial harmony of the 1870–1900 era is significantly associated with the Civil War's impact on northern racial beliefs and behavior.

Failure to Distinguish Independent and Dependent Variables

Another problem with Wilson's use of economic competition as an independent variable is also suggested by his analysis of the late nineteenth century North. The differential occupational hierarchy that Wilson believes ultimately leads to racial harmony in this period could just as readily be seen as a racial stratification system, the very essence of the competitive form of racial antagonism. In fact, Wilson later describes the labor market of this period in just such a manner:

> Throughout the latter half of the nineteenth century, northern industrialists had tended to ignore black workers, primarily because the immigration of European ethnics provided them with an adequate and continuous cheap labor supply. It was therefore much easier, and not unprofitable, for industrialists to adhere to explicit racial norms of unequal treatment for blacks and to satisfy white workers' demands that Negroes be excluded from industry. (P. 67)

This is a rather serious conceptual weakness. There seems to be a significant entanglement of one of Wilson's vital causal factors (economic competition) with his dependent variable (the form of racial relations). It would seem that competition in the labor market is being used as both part of the explanation and part of that which is to be explained. This confusion is related not only to the way in which Wilson has defined economic competition but to his broad definition of racial antagonism as well. He states that racial antagonism "includes all aspects of intergroup conflict, from beliefs and ideologies (e.g., racism), to overt behavior (e.g., discrimination), to institutions (e.g., segregationist laws)" (p. 6). One can assume, then, that racial conflict or competition within the labor market is thus captured in this dependent variable, while, as we have seen, it is simultaneously used as an important explanatory variable.

Wilson's analysis of this era slips into this conceptual morass partially because he chooses to focus on noneconomic aspects of racial relations. His evidence for racial harmony is made up of the passage of state civil rights laws, black voting rights, black access to public facilities, and the lack of residential segregation. None of these encompass employment opportunities. Thus, he is able to find racial harmony in the North from 1870–1900. Given the primacy Wilson attaches to the economic sector for affecting black life chances (p. *ix*), one might wonder why Wilson has labeled this a period of racial amity.

Political Power in Wilson's Model

As noted earlier, the inclusion of a political dimension distinguishes Wilson's work from the more purely economic models that he builds upon. Adding a political variable may ameliorate his model's tendency toward economic determinism and may help explain variations in race relations not possible to explain simply by depending upon economic competition. Nonetheless, his political analysis is weakened by a failure to adequately specify the basis for political power and an inability to explain the various forms that racial antagonism takes.

The Basis of Political Power

Wilson's treatment of the basis of political power is brief and cryptic. Since the distribution of political power varies across historical eras, its causes are of some significance for understanding both contemporary and future racial patterns. Wilson's analysis of white working-class power is critical because of its relationship with competitive racial antagonism in his model. The most detailed analysis of white working-class power occurs in his attempt to distinguish the more powerful northern workers from their impotent southern brethren during the Antebellum period.

> In comparison with their southern counterparts, northern white workers were more concentrated and better organized, and hence more able to protect their economic interests during the Antebellum period. The differences

in resources possessed by northern and southern workers were basically related to the different systems of production in the North and in the South. . . . [I]n a diversified economy, workers in the North were more centrally involved in the production process and therefore the power gap between the workers and the capitalist class was not nearly as great. (P. 47)

For Wilson, much of political power is simply a derivative of economics, more specifically, the system of production. Wilson talks of economic power being transferred or transformed to political power (pp. 60–61). Wilson does not develop in much detail the linkages between the economy and the polity. As can be seen from the citation above, Wilson argues that in a more diversified industrial economy white workers are in a more vital position in the economy. They can use that to bargain with the capitalists. Moreover, the scale of the workplace increasingly concentrates workers, further facilitating class communication and ultimately class organization. In discussing the Post-Reconstruction South, Wilson also notes the importance of transportation and communication technologies, which allow greater mobilization of the rural and urban white working class (pp. 55–56).

By adopting this economic vision of political power, Wilson loses much of the value of adding a political dimension. In this form it doesn't provide a significant break from economic determinism. In addition, Wilson does not explore with any precision the possible interactions among his economic and political variables. The result of his brief analysis is to leave many important political questions unanswered. Why was the level of antagonism directed at blacks lower in the North than in the South from 1900 to 1950? Of special interest here is Wilson's discussion of the ability of black workers to break into the northern industrial labor market. Furthermore, why do the forms of racial antagonism differ in the North and South in this period?

Wilson's model does not handle the issue of level of antagonism very well. While both regions heavily repressed blacks in the first half of the twentieth century, clearly the level of violence, as well as the economic, social, and political deprivation were substantially higher in the South. The dilemma for Wilson's model is that the driving force in both racial regimes is the white working class, and that the power of the white working class is derived from the centrality of their position in the regional economy. But industrialization and economic diversity were greater in the first half of the twentieth century in the North than they were in either the Antebellum North or the Post-Reconstruction South. Thus, the white working class should have been more powerful in this northern era, yet, as Wilson describes the North from 1900–1950, whites are less successful in imposing competitive styles of racial antagonism. At various points in his analysis of the twentieth century North, Wilson notes white working-class inability to impose a Jim Crow system, to disenfranchise blacks, or to keep black presence in industry from growing (pp. 79, 84).

Of most importance for the Wilson model is the situation in the economic sphere. Wilson observes:

Nonetheless, we can only assume that the steady growth of blacks in industry during and following World War I, despite discriminatory practices in many firms, indicated that white workers had not developed sufficient resources in their struggles with management to impose segregation barriers in order to avoid being undercut by black labor in certain jobs. (P. 84)

Several points need to be addressed. First, Wilson may overestimate the "steady growth of blacks in industry" following World War I and consequently underestimate white working class power. At best, black industrial employment growth was intermittent (Pinderhughes, 1987: 16–24.) Second, there is the paradox of the weaker white working class in the North. Economic diversity and industrialization have come further along in the North of 1915 than either the Antebellum North or the South of the early twentieth century, yet blacks were unable to make employment advances in those latter two racial regimes. Given the previous economic framework for analyzing political power, the case for a weaker white working class in the industrial North is not appealing on its face. Does it make sense in terms of Wilson's own model to consider the white working class of the South more powerful than that of the North in the World War I era? By Wilson's own description, isn't the North the more diversified and industrialized economy? And doesn't the North's white working class have a much longer history of political participation and organization, according to Wilson?

Lastly, Wilson provides little evidence for his conclusions about white working-class power. Instead, Wilson slips into tautology as support. How does he know that the power of the twentieth century northern working class is low? It is "indicated" since there had been a steady growth of blacks in northern industry. What allowed blacks to break into the industrial labor market? Low levels of white working-class power. This entire argument is simply not very convincing.

Inability to Explain Forms of Racism

Wilson's argument takes on more subtlety when he addresses the related topic of the varied forms of repression. Wilson explains the Industrial North's lack of statutory Jim Crow and disenfranchisement in terms of the level of white unity. He argues that, unlike the South, which had a "united white segregation movement . . . in the North, on the other hand, a united white movement against blacks never crystallized" (p. 83). But what determines white racial unity? In his discussion of this phenomenon, Wilson refers to a capitalist need to use black strikebreakers to control white labor in the North. Apparently, this white capitalist interest in black labor was enough to diminish working-class ability to impose formal segregation and disenfranchisement. But it is not clear why white capitalists in the rapidly industrializing South would not have the same interest in manipulating white workers with black labor. Some support for this counterhypothesis can be found in Wilson's chart on the use of black strikebreakers. Six of the twenty-two specified cases are from the South or the border states. Nine of the sixteen northern cases are in Chicago. This is hardly definitive evidence for a systematic difference in labor strategies between northern and southern capital (p. 72).

Wilson's discussion of the northern urban ethnic machine raises other important issues for understanding white working-class power. While noting that white ethnics did not disenfranchise northern blacks, he argues that their use of gerrymandering and other political subterfuges were quite effective in limiting black political influence despite black retention of the vote in the North. Wilson argues that the urban, ethnic-based machine provided political and social power for its white working-class clients. White workers were able to use ethnic solidarity and patronage to build political cohesion and power in these working-class communities (pp. 79–81). Blacks were only permitted to participate in city-wide buffer institutions and were not able to develop neighborhood-based party organization. Wilson ultimately concludes that

> White ethnic control of the city machines was so complete throughout the first half of the twentieth century that blacks were never able to compete for municipal political rewards such as patronage jobs and government contracts and services. Accordingly, the racial conflicts that permeated the economic and social orders never really penetrated the political sector. (P. 85)

It is undoubtedly useful to bring into play factors like ethnic cohesion, party organization, and political institutionalization to help explain working-class political power. Ultimately Wilson's effort founders, however, because it isn't well integrated into his previous arguments. While before it appeared that a group's political power was directly linked to its economic position, this discussion of the machine accepts the possibility of political power being independent of the economic system. But Wilson provides no clues about the interaction between the economic and political sectors in the Industrial North. How is it that northern workers were losing the battle to exclude black workers at the same time that their control of urban machines was so complete? Why couldn't or didn't they use that political control to influence labor practices? Such exclusionary practices were institutionalized in the South, where both the political and economic power of the white working class would appear to be more limited. Other more general questions need to be addressed as well: Under what circumstances can groups build significant political power despite weaknesses in their economic position? What are the limiting factors for such noneconomic-based political power?

Consideration of such questions might have led Wilson to reevaluate the impact of the urban machine. Some have argued that the white ethnic machine tended to focus workers on particularistic neighborhood and ethnic issues, with the result that class-oriented, macroeconomic concerns were organized out of politics (Katznelson, 1981; Erie, 1978). Answering such questions might have also pushed Wilson to look once again, more systematically, at the question of culture and ideology. For instance, if the northern white machine was so powerful and northern white hostility toward blacks was so great, why did the machine settle for gerrymandering and buffer institutions instead of southern style disenfranchisement?

Ironically, part of that answer may lie in the work of Katznelson, on whom Wilson greatly relies in his section on the urban machine. Wilson uses Katznelson's concept of the buffer institution to explain black political weaknesses in this era. Katznelson seeks to show how some forms of representation may act to control rather than empower mass political participants. Political buffering is one such social-control mechanism. But Wilson overlooks Katznelson's explanation of the significance of the study of the forms of representation. Katznelson argues that these less-than-fully-empowering forms of representation are necessary for liberal capitalism. This form of social control in the guise of representation is liberal capitalism's modus vivendi between the politics of mass participation and the economics of inequality (Katznelson, 1976: p. *xxi*). These constrained forms of participation are necessary to meet liberalism's political and cultural requisites of mass participation while still protecting capitalism's requisite of economic inequality. While Wilson has amply explored the impact of economic inequality, he fails to recognize the impact of political culture, tradition, and institutions. The ideological structures of the North made it very unlikely that statutory Jim Crow and disenfranchisement could be imposed. The North was a liberal society with all its constraints, the South was not (Hartz, 1955).

Some Tentative Conclusions on Race and Class Interaction

Wilson's analysis of the varied patterns of race relations is a valuable and ambitious undertaking. His use of historical analysis allows him to explore the underlying structure of race relations in the United States over time. His work is further sharpened by the use of that historical material to evaluate two competing models of race relations. Unfortunately, there are several aspects of the study that keep it from being fully successful. The failure to define several critical concepts precisely enough inevitably leads to unnecessary confusion. There is also a tendency to explain too much with materialistic analysis. His attempts at political analysis, all too often, are directly derived from his economic variables and underplay relevant noneconomic factors. When Wilson does raise more-autonomous political phenomena as with the urban machine, his discussion does not seem well integrated into his overall analysis. He needs to specify far more clearly how these economic variables interact with the political variables. The economy may act as a significant constraint on political behavior and institutions, but so may the polity limit the economy. This system of mutual constraints needs to be a central focus of our understanding of race relations.

Some of the weaknesses in Wilson's explanation, nonetheless, may provide us with guideposts for future research on race and class interactions. One way may be to build outward from Wilson's core concept of economic incentives as the explanation for variations in race relations toward approaches that are less purely materialist in orientation and that treat race as a more autonomous factor in the explanation. Thus, we can start by first looking at the role of economic incentive structures in race relations, then move on to the role of other nonracial incentive structures, and then conclude by considering race as a primary factor in itself.

One of the major substantive problems with Wilson's interpretation of the role of economic incentives in the creation of racial antagonism is his implicit assumption that in a complex, competitive economy the motivation for racial domination lies in the working class. While one would not want to underemphasize the racism that has existed in the U.S. labor movement, the situation is far more complex than Wilson allows. Wilson underplays both management's economic incentives to maintain racial antagonism and the labor movement's incorporation of the black working class under certain circumstances.

For instance, the black experience in the coal mining industry in the late nineteenth century and the early twentieth century does not fit the Wilson model. Blacks made up a significant portion of bituminous coal miners in the North and South in this period. Blacks were active in coal mining in states like Pennsylvania, Ohio, Illinois, West Virginia, and Alabama. This would seem to be a competitive economic situation both in the North and the South. Yet Gutman shows that blacks were both significantly included in the membership of the United Mine Workers (UMW) and modestly represented in the UMW leadership at both the local and national levels (Gutman, 1977). Moreover, the UMW leadership fought the institutionalization of Jim Crow in the South in this period. Conversely, Gutman offers evidence of mine owners exploiting black miners by using them as temporary strikebreakers and on a permanent basis by paying them less than white miners.

Gutman offers two basic factors to explain racial conditions in the American coal mines. The first fits within an economic-incentives framework. He simply argues that unionization of black miners was in the material interest of white miners, both to lessen the threat of management use of black strikebreakers and to avoid having black miners' working conditions drag down white working standards (Gutman, 1977:157–58, 168). But he quickly adds that the exclusion of blacks might have also solved this material interest. Gutman argues that this exclusionist path was not chosen by the white union, at least partly because it would have violated ideological norms of the UMW. He maintains that a union like the UMW, based on the principle of industrial organization, would have had a difficult time justifying exclusion of any kind. Moreover, the union leadership of this time was part of a general reform movement premised on evangelical principles of human solidarity (Gutman, 1977:158).

This brief discussion of the mine industry indicates that the relationship between working-class-based racism and economic competition is not simple. The material origins of racial domination may often rest within the capitalist class. Moreover, under certain circumstances (including the possession by blacks of the requisite industrial skills), it may be in the material interests of white workers to cooperate with black workers. The economic strategy that whites choose is affected by the ideological norms of the white working-class organizations involved in the economic conflict with the white capitalist class. Thus, economic interest is more complex than Wilson allows and, furthermore, economic interests will now always solely determine the outcome of race relations.

Race relations can also be shaped by such noneconomic factors as status, prestige, and tradition. Frederickson focuses on these factors for his explanation of several historical periods in U.S. race relations. For instance, in Frederickson's account of the Post-Reconstruction South, he notes that black employment opportunities in this era were severely restricted. But he does not attribute this to the motivating factor of direct racial economic competition. Quite the contrary, he maintains that direct economic competition was quite minimal in this era in the South. With the demise of slavery, large landowners, fearful of an argricultural labor shortage, soon created new methods for binding blacks to the land. Sharecropping, farm credit, and convict leasing all effectively limited black employment opportunities outside the rural economy. In the non-agricultural economy, factory work was white work, while domestic work was for blacks. Blacks were perceived as incapable of performing well with machinery. Employers also sought to maintain the racist social structure by placing poor whites in the new factories a notch above blacks (Frederickson, 1981:209). The only nonagricultural sector with considerable racial overlap was in low-skilled, extractive work like that in the coal and timber industries (Frederickson, 1981:215).

Frederickson labels this a period of neither economic cooperation nor competition, but rather segmentation. Blacks and whites were in different segments of the economy. He goes on to state that

> The compartmentalization of economic function along racial lines was the result not so much of competitive pressures by lower-class whites as of retarded economic development and cultural continuity. Economic opportunity was severely limited for almost everyone in this society, and the parceling out of low-paying jobs among whites and blacks tended to follow antebellum precedent, where this was possible, or the needs of local employers where it was not. The general notion that the dirtiest and most unpleasant work should be done by blacks was accepted by almost all whites. (Frederickson, 1981:215)

One can see the role of both social status ("unpleasant work") and tradition ("antebellum precedent" and "accepted by almost all whites") in shaping the racial allocation of occupations. The racial practices of this era are apparently not simply explained by rational, calculating economic motivations, but rather are also based on a southern social structure.

Political variables make up another set of important noneconomic factors affecting racial relations. Politics encompasses both the interests of

various segments of society in gaining control of the government and
the ideological understandings of that governmental process by members of society. State actors have political interests to protect, and they
may often be willing to manipulate race relations toward those ends. C.
Vann Woodward's analysis of the evolution of Jim Crow racial oppression in the South relies primarily on just such political interests. According to Woodward, conservative Southern Democrats adopted a program
of paternalistic racial subordination in the 1870s as they sought electoral
support from the black community (1974:47–59). They sought to use this
support to defeat both their white Republican and Independent/Green-
back political opponents.

   In the late nineteenth century they changed this strategy for essentially political reasons as well. A wave of Populist opposition to the
conservative Democrats' business-oriented programs began to spread
throughout the South. Early Populists made an attempt to incorporate
blacks into their movement (Woodward, 1974:60–65). "Alarmed by the
success that the Populists were enjoying with their appeal to the Negro
voter, the conservatives themselves raised the cry of 'Negro domination'
and white supremacy and enlisted the Negrophobe elements" (Woodward, 1974:79). Under this political onslaught, southern Populists began
to blame blacks for their movement's problems (Woodward, 1974:81).
The result was that both the Southern Democrats and the Populists
agreed to the disenfranchisement of black voters and the imposition of
Jim Crow laws. Northern Republicans did not intervene to protect black
southerners, because by the late 1870s they were looking for a reconcil-
iation with the white South (Woodward, 1974:70). Republicans also recognized that they did not need the black vote to maintain control of
the national government (Marable, 1984:7). Thus, we see that political
factors can be a significant force in the shift from a paternalistic racial
regime to a competitive one, and the impetus for competitive racism
can be located in the white upper class (the conservative Democrats in
this case).

   Society's ideological understanding of legitimate governmental processes is another aspect of politics that may also influence race relations.
We need not go into great detail on this point. Our previous discussion
of Katznelson on the racial limits imposed by the social acceptance of
liberalism already suggests the importance of political culture on race
relations.

   The issue of culture raises one last point. If one looks at the history of
the United States from its inception to today, it would seem hard to deny
that race has been a significant factor in American society. Whatever its
genesis, analysts need to consider the possibility that at some level race
is now an independent variable, not simply reducible to other factors
(Omi and Winant, 1986). Issues and political groups have for so long
been defined, at least partially, in racial terms that these racial understandings have become an autonomous force. Racial definitions and understandings can have an independent impact on social, economic, and
political outcomes in the United States.

This conclusion has not offered an alternative comprehensive model of race relations. Instead, it has sought to place the Wilson model in a broader context: to suggest that economic relationships might be more complex, that noneconomic factors can be significant, and that race should also be considered as an independent force in social relationships. The next step is to explore more systematically how these various factors interact with one another across history to produce varying forms of race relations.

References

Erie, Steven. 1978. "Politics, the Public Sector and Irish Social Mobility." *Western Political Quarterly*, 31: 274–89.

Frederickson, George. 1981. *White Supremacy.* Oxford: Oxford University Press.

Gutman, Herbert. 1977. "The Negro and the United Mine Workers of America." *Work, Culture and Society in Industrializing America.* New York: Vintage Books.

Hartz, Louis, 1955. *The Liberal Tradition in America.* New York: Harcourt, Brace.

Katznelson, Ira. 1976. *Black Men, White Cities.* Chicago: University of Chicago Press.

———. 1981. *City Trenches.* Chicago: University of Chicago Press.

Marable, Manning. 1984. *Race, Reform and Rebellion.* Jackson: University Press of Mississippi.

Omi, Michael, and Howard Winant. 1986. *Racial Formation in the United States.* New York: Routledge and Kegan Paul.

Pinderhughes, Dianne. 1987. *Race and Ethnicity in Chicago Politics.* Urbana: University of Illinois Press.

Wilson, William J. 1980. *The Declining Significance of Race.* Chicago: University of Chicago Press.

Woodward, C. Vann. 1974. *The Strange Career of Jim Crow.* 3rd rev. ed. New York: Oxford University Press.

Book Reviews

Cynthia Harrison, *On Account of Sex: The Politics of Women's Issues 1945–1968* (Berkeley: University of California Press, 1988), *xv* + 337 pp.; ISBN 0-520-06121-7 (cloth).

This book's most compelling features are a congressional chronology of the proposed Equal Rights Amendment to the Constitution and inception and passage of the Equal Pay Act, an outline of events preceding formation of President Kennedy's commission on the Status of Women (PCSW), and a description of the interplay of political institutions and representation of some women's interests. However, the book provides neither the "broad and incisive analysis" nor the "impressive, new understanding of three decades" that its jacket blurb proclaims.

Several times (pp. *xiii*, 12, 162), the author asserts that black women put race first. Hence, hers is a study of the politics of "primarily educated, middle class white women" (p. *xiii*). Use of fewer than six selections from the archives of the National Council of Negro Women (NCNW) tends to create an image of regressive positions on women's issues. Although references to black women in a book of this genre are refreshing, regrettably their outcome is stale.

The purpose served by stating that 'race' is a primary emergency to African-American women does not excuse a dogged tendency to ignore their interests. Contemporary scholars need to recognize considerations entering into black women's interest representation, for example, to white women, to give context to the priorities assigned.

As participants on two panels indicated during the November 1987 conference at the University of Massachusetts-Amherst, "African-American women and the Vote: 1837 to 1965," "defining for themselves" has not been simple. Nonetheless, as Martha Norman put it, these aggrieved women moved to change the sociopolitical boundaries of their lives. Bettye Collier-Thomas, director of the NCNW's archives, called for more detailed studies than we now have of the black women's club movement as an organizational base. Both Collier-Thomas's and Norman's remarks dealt with research priorities relevant to the period that Harrison studies.

Despite a focus on development of "the old suffrage coalition" (p. 7), Harrison does not share the priorities. She dismisses the civil rights movement of the 1940s and 1950s as one basis for analysis of women's issue politics, 1945–68: "The fight for civil rights for blacks and the struggle on behalf of women remained separate" (p. 13, p. 16).

Convened by Rosa Parks and Coretta Scott King, and held in October 1988, a national conference, "Women in the Civil Rights Movement: Trailblazers and Torchbearers, 1941–1965," devoted a full day to the theme "Carry the Torch: In the Intersection of Race, Class, and Gender." Joyce

Ladner remembered gender-free models provided by older activist women; Gloria Wade Gayles, the physical vulnerability of movement women. Sara Evans found that from such experiences came the possibility for questioning what society defined gender to be. A question came from the floor: How could the modern feminist movement have taken so many things from black women's kitchens and created something so alien to black women's experiences?

Harrison's treatment of white reformers' attention to black issues displays limited range and sensitivity. She shows that the PCSW considered black women to present special interests (p. 161), and emphasizes the relatively more "hospitable" approach of the Women's Bureau (WB) of the U.S. Labor Department (DOL) than of the National Woman's Party (NWP) to these women "as a special group requiring its assistance in the fight for economic opportunities" (p. 12). After this paternalism, Harrison never considers what assistance white women required from African-American women, and attends little to the assistance they received.

References to contributions by Pauli Murray and Aileen Hernandez are almost unavoidable. But a reader looks in vain for extended commentary about Dorothy Irene Height—one of Washington's most powerful women, in 1957 elected NCNW president—and Dollie Lowther Robinson—described as "a long time union employee now at the [WB]" (p. 111)—among others.

Sometimes, though, even Harrison's briefest references reveal the error in her emphasis on the fundamental separation of the two movements. For example, Robinson is described in twenty-nine words as having pressured Kennedy to assign importance to eliminating the effects of gender and racial prejudice both. Murray's initial introduction stops with "black attorney long associated with the civil rights movement" (p. 126, 180). Assigned to a footnote is Murray's interest in birth-control laws despite the PCSW's hands-off attitude (p. 279). Former Equal Employment Opportunity Commissioner Aileen Hernandez, described only as "a black woman from California" (p.188), is mentioned, without comment, as having become a vice president of the newly formed National Organization for Women (NOW).

Also revealing are Harrison's omissions. A single letter dated 16 February 1964 is cited to show the influence of the NWP's reluctance to coalesce with the civil rights movement on some members' perceptions that Murray was using the women's movement to further the civil rights cause (p. 129). Not mentioned is Murray's later law-review article showing that U.S. slave codes were modeled after the common law's doctrine of coverture, which merged a married woman's legal identity with her husband's. That Hernandez became NOW's second national president, or that for twenty years Height was a staff member of the national board of the Young Women's Christian Association are also not mentioned.

Harrison mentions the NAACP's growth during World War II (p. 13), but not NOW's founders' desire in 1966 to create an NAACP for women, and so she barely touches on the source of this desire (p. 26). Minimizing African-American women's influence on white women, Harrison almost entirely avoids examining their stimulation of and participation in women's-issue arenas. Rather than help provide a reevaluation of black women's role in issue representation, for which Collier-Thomas called in Amherst, Harrison demonstrates its need.

This denial of diversity cannot legitimately be described as "incisive" that is, according to Webster's dictionary, "writing that seems to penetrate directly to the heart of the matter, resulting in a clear and unambiguous statement"), or as "broad." As such denial is not new, it does not deserve the accolade "impressive, new understanding of three decades."

There are other objections. The analysis of absolute numbers of presidential appointments of women falters for want of comparative figures for men and the failure to consider that total appointments increased yearly. The use of proportions reverses the course that Harrison describes (see Schramm, 1981). Further, mentors such as DOL secretary Frances Perkins and Health, Education, and Welfare secretary Overta Culp Hobby associate with women's appointments across time (Schramm, 1981:56–58; cf. Harrison, p. 63).

The de rigueur quotation of WB director Mary Anderson's characterization of Perkins as minimizing women's problems to avoid being herself stereotyped (p. 63, 82) ignores the reality of Perkins's life as a social feminist activist. She willingly entered appeals for women, for example, those homeless, or dismissed under the 1932 Economy Act's ill-advised section 213. She also was no token (but see p. 63) and is considered the most illustrious labor secretary ever to serve.

Because the concept of feminism is not susceptible to precise definition (Schramm, 1979:1–13), Harrison's discussion of coherent (and incoherent) definitions of feminism (pp. 140, 148, 192, 200) falters. Further, in the United States the concept always has been both normative and descriptive (Schramm, 1979:3); this is not the new situation Harrison claims (p. 220).

She describes NOW as "the first avowedly feminist organization to emerge since suffrage" (p. 112). But NOW's statement of purpose did not include the word 'feminist'; this became a major organizational issue in 1974. The National Black Feminist Organization, founded in 1973, has a stronger claim than NOW on the 'first organization' title. NOW experienced incoherence (but see p. 200), for example, during congressional hearings on Title IX when its Sports and Education Task Forces gave opposed testimonies about their desire for integration of women in sports. NOW is discussed better elsewhere.

The book is filled with incautious choices of language and misassumptions. Discussion of women's influence in office is plagued by unreasonable expectations: for example, presidential appointees are customarily beholden to the president's program (cf. p. 53). Discussion of the PCSW agenda compares poorly to Debra W. Stewart's fine work on local commissions as agenda setters. Attack on the NWP is relentless (see, e.g., pp. 10, 15, 22, 118–19, 122, 160), and points in the ERA's favor go unaddressed. It is said that, because of occupational segregation, "few women would benefit from equal pay legislation" (p. 89)—overlooking teachers, saleswomen, social workers, bookkeepers, factory workers, etc.

Harrison joins Paula Giddings, J. Stanley Lemons, Lois Scharf, Joseph Lash, this reviewer, and others in helping to show the twentieth century women's movement's continuity. Nonetheless, she might have been more responsible to the era 1945–68 than she has been.

Sarah Slavin
Buffalo State College

References

Schramm, Sarah Slavin. 1979. *Plow Women Rather Than Reapers: An Intellectual History of Feminism in the United States.* Metuchen, N.J.: Scarecrow Press.

———— . 1981. "Women and Representation: Self-Government and Role Change." *Western Political Quarterly*, 34 (1):46–59.

Robert A. Goldwin and Art Kaufman eds., *Slavery and Its Consequences: The Constitution, Equality, and Race* (Washington, D.C.: American Enterprise Institute, 1988) *ix* + 181 pp.; ISBN 0-8447-3650-3 (paper).

The U.S. Constitution of 1787 is an interest-specific document. It was written, ratified, and amended as a social contract between rich, white, property-owning males, who had affirmed John Locke's theory of private property through their practices of genocide against the native population, the enslavement of Africans, the indenturing of European dregs, and the paternalization of white women. In large measure, the Constitution, as social contract, sought to mediate the fundamental economic and class interests of its framers.

The framers fashioned citizenship and human rights to represent the explicit domain of property owners. Race, more than any other question, would be the fulcrum through which the Constitution would be given its most expressive utility.

Goldwin and Kaufman's *Slavery and Its Consequences: The Constitution, Equality, and Race* is a collection of essays that attempt to assess the framers' intentions regarding slavery and the resulting problems and consequences of the role of race and slavery in the Constitution. These essays are largely historical and interpretive in nature.

Fehrenbacher and Wiecek strike a similar theme in their essays by observing that slavery, as an institution, was "compatible with the American constitutional order." Slavery was not only central to the deliberations in the Constitutional Convention, but it

shaped the language in the Constitution, especially with regards to the Fugi- tive-Slave Clauses.

Herbert Storing's 1976 essay "Slavery and the Moral Foundations of the American Republic" takes up an analysis of the *Dred Scott v. Sandford* case (1857) in order to decry the moral failures of the constitutional framers. Storing conducts an analysis that is now accepted as the 'classic problemat'—the duality between the framers' ideas and beliefs about democracy and equality, and the belief that black people could not be citizens of the United States—free or not. As Storing put it, the framers, in "their accommodation to slavery, limited and confined it and carefully withheld any indication of moral approval." In fact, Storing believed that he had "rescued the Founders from the common charge that they shamefully excluded Negroes from the principles of the Declaration of Independence, that they regarded their enslavement as just, and that in their Constitution they protected property in man like any other property." Herein lies the chief problem with this volume from the American Enterprise Institute. It serves to obfuscate the problem of slavery by attempting to rescue the constitutional framers from their specific class and race interests.

The essays by Allen, Holland, Sedler, and Loury are companion pieces in today's right-wing propaganda. These essays treat matters of freedom and equality as abstractions devoid of human manipulation. They attempt to find constructs that leave the framers unculpable for slavery and the history of racial domination in the United States. These essays are designed to convince us that something called "racial preference" is now plaguing the land, and that freedom and equality cannot be applied on group bases.

Goldwin and Kaufman include

Abraham Lincoln's "Address at Cooper Institute" as the appendix to their volume. Lincoln's address is a statement in support of the view that the framers "designed the provisions to start the institution of slavery on the road to extinction." Today's "trickle-down" theory has been at work a long time.

As interpretative pieces the essays in Goldwin and Kaufman's volume are useful in understanding the decidedly right-wing thinking on the question of slavery, the Constitution, equality, and race. There is a distinct propaganda function in these essays, as well as a definite intent to reconstruct history and its incidents.

Perhaps an epilogue by the editors would have been useful to connect the points of continuity in the essays. We do not learn anything new from this volume. The essays suffer from the failure to lay bare the truth about the continuing consequences of slavery—the domination of African Americans under explicit racial and class arrangements.

Rickey Hill
South Carolina State
College

Wilbur Rich, *Coleman Young and Detroit Politics: From Social Activist to Power Broker* (Detroit: Wayne State University Press, 1989) 299 pp.; ISBN 0-8143-2093-7 (cloth).

Of the several political biographies of black mayors to arise in recent years, this is by far the most *significant*, not only because it covers a highly controversial and unique political figure, Coleman Young, but also because of the way it is conceptualized and methodologically structured, and because of the scholarly skills brought to bear on the subject matter—black urban and mayoral politics in Detroit, Michigan.

What makes this a classic study, a breakthrough book, and a one-of-a-kind work is that Professor Wilbur Rich addresses immediately (1) the matter of black political culture and socialization (in the first three chapters) and (2) how it has produced not only a score of black clientage leaders, but also a black nationalist like the Reverend Albert Cleage and a man for all seasons like Coleman Young; that is, how it has produced multiple types of black political leaders from the same contextual environment. This makes for intriguing and revealing insights. Then, Rich addresses how a left-wing social labor movement led by Walter Reuther supplanted Henry Ford's clientage politics in the black community with black labor activists, but shut the black labor leaders out of *all* of the union's administrative and leadership power positions, leaving the leaders only in the black community. He also shows that, once entrenched in power, Reuther transformed himself and the union into a right-wing organization that ultimately undercut black civil and political rights, in addition to freezing black labor activists into minor or pointless organizational roles. Reuther became a red-baiter (p. 67). It is here that Rich does what no other biographer of black mayors has done—shown how the civil rights movement in the South forced blacks out of their political deadlock and away from their politically stifling coalition with a new right-wing union movement bent on keeping blacks in their place.

Enter the white liberals. Here, Professor Rich shows how white liberals became new players in Detroit politics and helped the black shift from union paternalism. But the liberals failed both themselves and the fledgling black efforts toward independence when the first black mayoral candidate, Richard Austin, lost his bid because of their limited support.

Rich's book here offers so much in thematic value, ideas, insights, and details that the work has surpassed all would-be contenders.

But the stage is set for Coleman Young. Through his analysis of Young's four elections and political culture and socialization, Professor Rich reveals to the reader that there is no one more devoted to Detroit than Coleman Young. But, in doing this, Rich gives the reader a journey in black politics that is unequalled in knowledge and thought. He shows the reader what a black mayor can expect from (1) a rust-belt area with aggressive affirmative action policies, (2) inner-city whites who are left behind, (3) the captains of industry, (4) black political opposition, (5) the state government, and (6) a negative Republican administration. This would be enough in and of itself, yet Rich gives the reader more.

Professor Rich gives the reader three independent case studies: (1) on economic development, (2) on collective bargaining and affirmative action, and (3) on the fiscal crisis, that is, the near bankruptcy of the city in 1981. In each case, he details how Mayor Young rose to the occasion. These case studies are engrossing in both description and explanation. Moreover, the analysis is rooted in the best literature in the field.

Yet for all this penetrating analysis and insight and the positive assessment of Mayor Young's policies and programs, Professor Rich doesn't let the mayor off the hook. He shows that Young is, for all his populist rhetoric, a fiscal conservative, and that he has done little to elevate and improve the lot of poor blacks in the city, blacks who, Rich finds, are the mayor's strongest supporters. The mayor may have saved the city, but he has not yet saved its poor "inhabitants." He is passing that on to someone else. Perhaps the greatest achievement of this book, and the factor that will make it an all-time classic, is that Professor Rich shows that, even under adverse and oppressive conditions, the black community has processes and mechanisms in place to generate the type of political leadership that the community needs, despite similar mechanisms that whites put in place to keep this from happening. Here, one thinks inevitably of M. L. King, Jr. This is indeed a seminal work in black political recruitment practices in northern urban areas; in fact, it has no peer in the literature. Rich shows the reader the journey that Mayor Young travels from a left-wing activist to a fiscal conservative. Besides being a mayoral study, the books is a study of black political transformation.

Hopefully, Professor Rich will come back to this topic, when Mayor Young has finished his course in American politics, to complete this brilliantly developed study on black political leadership in the declining rust-belt section of urban America. In fact, Rich has an obligation to do so.

Hanes Walton, Jr.
Savannah State College

Thomas E. Cavanagh, ed., *Strategies for Mobilizing Black Voters: Four Case Studies* (Washington, D.C.: Joint Center for Political Studies, 1987) *xix* + 148 pp.; ISBN: 0-94141048X (paper).

While Cavanagh's book is advertised as a "how to" guide, it is much more than a guide. The book is a much-needed organization and update of research on black voting behavior in the United States. Moreover, although the foci of the book are electoral case studies of mayoral races in Chicago (by Daryl D. Woods), Philadelphia (by Sandra Featherman), Birmingham (by Margaret K. Latimer and Robert S. Montjoy), and North Carolina's Second Congressional District (by Thomas F. Eamon), Cavanagh's efforts as an editor are valuable in their own right. Cavanagh's chapters contribute to the value of the book because they go beyond the individual case studies. His chapters deal with issues generally not treated in voting studies—substantive issues like the organization of black communities—that help to explain variations from the behavior of the white majority.

Daryl Woods's chapter explaining Harold Washington's election as mayor of Chicago tells the story of a city and urban black population with a long history of community-based organizations. In many respects, this story is a version of a long-standing theme in Chicago politics, because it is about coalition formation and community mobilization in reaction to a powerful governing elite. Those familiar with the political history of Chicago will appreciate this case study for the organizational genius it describes. This is, at least in part, the story of a coalition that energized community power bases that have existed and evolved over the last generation. This is a well-told story, rich in detail.

Woods subtly tells the story of the use, in pursuit of a common goal, of the variety of resources that blacks controlled. This is the story of an urban black population that has come of age politically; it is the story of communities with savvy, experienced leaders, important media resources, and seasoned, sophisticated political "outsiders."

Sandra Featherman's study of W. Wilson Goode's primary battle against Frank Rizzo for the Democratic nomination as mayor of Philadelphia provides great detail on the registration efforts that preceded Goode's electoral victory. This is a useful counterpoint to the Chicago picture, because Philadelphia had fewer strong black community organi-

zations to provide experienced black political leaders. In Philadelphia, these roles were filled by black professionals—people whose educations and employment histories made them like traditional white civic activists. And, unlike Washington, Wilson Goode had a neutral local Democratic organization and considerable assistance from government officials in registration efforts.

It is almost reassuring that Margaret Latimer and Robert Montjoy begin their exposition of Richard Arrington's election as mayor of Birmingham in the context of the civil rights movement. While everyone may agree that the Civil Rights Act of 1964 and the Voting Rights Act of 1965 have been important in the development of black political power, the force of those acts seems less obvious and less important outside of the South. Moreover, it appears that the impetus for the formation of the local community organizations that were tapped in the Arrington campaign was the city's desire to qualify for (CDBG) funds. Thus, it appears that federal activities contributed significantly to the growth in black political power in Birmingham. Less well known, but of equal importance, are changes that occurred in the structure of Birmingham's city council in the early 1960s.

The situation in Birmingham is unique, even from other areas in Alabama, in part because of the unique setup of the Jefferson County (greater Birmingham) Office of the Board of Registrars—it is more professional and independent than other registrars' offices in the state. There are other unique aspects to the Birmingham case. For example, unlike either Chicago or Philadelphia, political communication in Birmingham is primarily by word of mouth. Such an approach is less costly than media-based campaigns but requires tremendous human resources to succeed.

The political-education efforts in Birmingham had to combat fear, a problem either not faced or not mentioned in the northern urban examples.

This is the only one of the case studies presented in which black efforts in subsequent campaigns are recorded and assessed. More important, the Birmingham story is impressive because of the tremendous change that it documents—a reversal in registration rates for black versus white voters—and because of the success of the get-out-the-vote campaigns built on the voter-registration drives.

Thomas Eamon's study of Henry Michaux's unsuccessful bid for North Carolina's Second Congressional seat is a useful and telling counterpoint to the other examples in the book. This case reminds us that electoral success is not guaranteed, and reinforces the dictum repeated through the other cases that success requires prolonged, coordinated voter-registration efforts.

The history of racial tension in North Carolina's Second Congressional District is more like that of Birmingham than of the northern examples. Unlike the Birmingham case, Michaux's race resulted in a racial split, with extraordinary turnouts in rural white polling places. Michaux went into the campaign after a reapportionment challenge that resulted in redrawn districts months before the election.

Unlike the stories of other candidates in *Strategies*, Michaux was a critical part of the voter-registration drive in North Carolina. This may be due to personal preference, or to a community less prepared to undertake a major voter-registration drive. By any criterion, the 29 percent increase reported in black voter registration is spectacular. But white registrants still outnumbered black registrants by more than 2 to 1. This kind of differential in voter balance makes success unlikely for a black candidate in a race-conscious district.

Another lesson, less-well spelled out than it might be, is to be drawn from Michaux's 44 percent Democratic primary victory in a race against two whites that became a defeat in the Democratic runoff. This kind of win-loss pattern is more common in multicandidate primaries.

All of the case studies pay homage to the old political dictum: Know the local community, its mores, and structures. The book will be useful to anyone interested in understanding, explaining, or changing the patterns of minority-voter participation. It will be valuable in any educational setting.

Marilyn K. Dantico
Arizona State
University

Marcus D. Pohlmann, *Political Power in the Postindustrial City: An Introduction to Urban Politics* (New York: Associated Faculty Press, 1986) *x* + 421 pp.; ISBN 0-8046-9389-7 (paper).

Political Power in the Postindustrial City is an important scholarly contribution to the study of urban and minority-group politics. It is also a welcome change from recent works that have blamed the "urban underclass" for many of the problems confronting urban America. Too many social scientists and neoconservatives have blamed disadvantaged blacks and Hispanics who are at the bottom of the socioeconomic totem pole for creating the urban dilemma. They cite welfare dependency, lack of employable skills, out-of-wedlock births, drug use, criminal behavior, and school failure, inter alia, as being the reasons why urban pathology exists today.

Therefore, it is indeed refreshing to see an analysis that does not blame the victims of urban malaise. Marcus Pohlmann suggests that "the twentieth century's postindustrial economy has given rise to a permanent underclass which has been colonized and whose interests are rapidly becoming almost completely subordinate to the interests of ever more mobile capital." The political and public-policy consequences of this phenomenon are seen through the two basic functions that capitalist economics require of their governments. According to Pohlmann, the first function is "accumulation." The role of government here is to "guarantee an adequate supply of venture capital and productive labor so that the capital-owning class will invest in ways that will lead to stable economic growth, e.g., by offering corporation tax abatements and subsidies as well as roads, sewers which provide the necessary infrastructure." In this instance, the role of government is to "compensate those who become economically dislocated in the process, so that the necessary level of social harmony can be maintained, e.g., by providing maintenance services and social welfare programs." The dilemma for cities occurs when the ownership of capital becomes monopolized and the capitalist class begins to pressure government into underwriting more of the costs of capital accumulation and production, while the benefits remain in private hands. This, in turn, forces the government to spend more and more on social expenditures in order to retain its legitimacy with the nonowners. This results in what James O'Connor refers to as the "fiscal crisis" of the state.

Pohlmann illustrates how these contradictory functions of government have unfolded in twelve northern cities. Referred to as "the Troubled Twelve," the cities are Baltimore, Boston, Chicago, Cleveland, Detroit, Milwaukee, Newark, New York City, Philadelphia, Pittsburgh, St. Louis, and Washington, D.C. In each of these cities, Pohlmann presents data that show how population decline has reduced the importance of these cities in state and federal elections, thus making it difficult for them to secure state and federal funds. In addition, he shows that manufacturing plants have departed, which increases the unemployment, and, last, that the overall quality of life in these cities has declined. Consequently, the governments of the Troubled Twelve are confronted with the increasing needs and demands for services, while simultaneously the flight of individuals and manufacturers has reduced their tax revenues. This, according to Pohlmann, is what creates the urban dilemma.

To make his case more poignant, Pohlmann gives two excellent case analyses of how political power was usurped from the inner-city poor in favor of corporate capital by examining the fiscal crises that confronted the cities of Cleveland and New York in the 1970s. In exchange for help from higher levels of government and the financial community, these city governments accepted the imposition of "Finance Control Boards." Pohlmann documents how these boards, containing more local corporate elites than local elected officials, were given final authority over city budgetary decisions. This substantially reduced the control that the poor might have had over basic policy decisions affecting their lives. Not surprisingly, legitimation expenditures (social-welfare benefits) were drastically reduced.

Other strengths of the book include the author's perception of how the circumstances existing in the "Troubled Twelve" may be viewed from differing ideological perspectives. Conservative, liberal, neoliberal, socialist, and fascist views are considered in light of present pol- icy proposals for ameliorating urban problems.

Regardless of his or her ideological position, the reader will find that this book is well documented, and its extensive bibliography and index enhance its usefulness in a classroom setting.

Michael O. Adams
Texas Southern
University

Susan Welch and Timothy Bledsoe,
Urban Reform and Its Consequences:
A Study in Representation (Chicago and London: University of Chicago Press, 1988) *xx* + 154 pp.; ISBN 0-226-89300-6 (paper).

Reform of urban political structures, while overtly aimed at achieving "good government," has often masked shifts in group representation. In the early days, Progressive reformers clearly and openly sought to limit the influence of working-class and immigrant neighborhoods through nonpartisanship and at-large elections. In modern times, at-large elections have been used to stifle black and Hispanic political representation.

The great political success of anti-party reformers has been widely recognized, but we know much less about whether the goals they sought have been achieved. Did their structures indeed create cities governed by the elite in the interests of business-defined efficiency? In *Urban Reform and Its Consequences*, Susan Welch and Timothy Bledsoe present a careful and effective analysis of the impact of the reform movement on city politics. Welch and Bledsoe utilize a survey of city council members in cities whose population ranges from fifty thousand to one million.

City councils have been severely neglected in the study of representation. When we study city political leaders, we often look at mayors. When we seek to explore legislative representation, we can consult the huge literature on Congress. It is, therefore, refreshing to find a study of representation that begins with the thousands of local politicians who win election to seats on city councils. Those who breathe the air of city politics know that city councils matter, and that council members are expected to represent the people in government.

Welch and Bledsoe ask whether the two leading urban reforms (nonpartisanship and at-large election of city councils) indeed create the results often hypothesized. Are politicians elected under these rules more likely to have a conservative bias, to be from higher-income groups, and to pay more attention to citywide concerns than to district concerns? Are city councils elected under these rules less likely to provide arenas of conflict for important community issues? If there are such effects, what are the individual roles of nonpartisanship and at-large elections in bringing them about?

The authors prepared a very concise questionnaire (attached as an appendix) that elicited material on these matters from the respondents. In total, they received responses from 975 council members, a rate of 61 percent. Through the use of bivariate and multivariate analyses, they assess the effects of reform and the roles of nonpartisanship and at-large structures. Their study avoids some of the pitfalls of previous research. For example, many cities in previous studies had both nonpartisan and at-large systems. That overlap made it difficult to separately assess the effect of each reform. The sample chosen by Welch and Bledsoe includes a wide variety of systems in various permutations.

The effects of political structure vary. The weakest effect is found on policy preferences of council members. Political structure seems to have no important impact on whether conservatives or liberals are elected to office. At the other extreme, levels of conflict vary greatly depending on nonpartisanship. In partisan councils, there is a strong and dominating party conflict, while in nonpartisan councils there is very little.

Most of the important, if modest, effects lie in the middle and are due largely to at-large versus district elections. At-large elections turn out to be significant in bringing higher-income and higher-status people into office. At-large elections lead members toward a citywide view, and away from representing a neighborhood constituency. Conversely, district elections are shown to be crucial elements in bringing diversity and responsiveness to city councils. The representation of working-class and neighborhood concerns, rather than those of business, seems to depend somewhat on the existence of district elections. Overall, at-large elections influence representation to a significantly greater degree than nonpartisanship.

This study has many strengths. Welch and Bledsoe ask the right questions about a subject that has often been marked more by assertions than evidence. They fill methodological gaps in the literature. Welch and Bledsoe are also careful not to overstate their results; they label effects "modest" when appropriate. While they purposely omit the six largest cities, the applicability of their results can be seen in the case of Los Angeles. In that city, a coalition of blacks and progressive whites won power in a system that is strongly nonpartisan but that has a council elected by district.

The implications drawn by the authors are particularly interesting. The book is not primarily about race and political structure, but it explicitly connects the struggle for racial equality to the movement for grass-roots representation. The authors note that the case for the impact of structure on minority representation has already been made; in fact, court decisions have taken the impact of district elections into account. But district elections have not only been essential to minority incorporation; they have also made city councils more responsive to interests other than those of business or the upper classes.

Second, the authors suggest that the modest effect of reform structures probably underestimates the impact of the reform movement. They argue that modern city politics, regardless of current structure, has been shaped by such antiparty forces as campaign money and mass media. Therefore, structural differences alone may have become smaller over time. But they insist that this makes the case for partisanship even more important. In fact, they argue that district elections in a partisan system still provide the best means of urban representation.

The authors are perhaps too ready to accept the notion that partisan conflict can be a sure road to representation. Their assumption that party conflict economically links together a package of issues relevant to the voters raises questions. At the city level, partisanship has been an inconsistent vehicle for progressive change. Strong parties have certainly been an impediment to black incorporation. The book makes a more persuasive argument for the value of district elections than for the virtues of partisan conflict.

Urban Reform and Its Consequences should be required reading for those concerned with the quality of urban government. It is an excellent, pathbreaking analysis. In addition to the importance of its overall conclusions, the study suggests the potential for

representation in city councils. It
ought to spark significant additional
research and further link the movements for minority representation
and progressive change.

Raphael J. Sonenshein
California State
University, Fullerton

Book Notes

Katherine Tate, Ronald E. Brown, Shirley J. Hatchett, and James S. Jackson,
The 1984 National Black Election Study Sourcebook (Ann Arbor, Mich.: Institute for Social Research, University of Michigan, 1988).

The 1984 National Black Election Study (NBES) of the Institute for Social Research provides the first opportunity for in-depth investigations of the political
attitudes, perceptions, and reported electoral behavior of a large representative
national sample of adult black Americans. Designed to permit direct access to
the study's basic findings, the volume's tabular format allows analysts freedom
to shape their own conclusions.

Albert K. Karnig and Paula D. McClain, eds., *Urban Minority Administrators:*
Politics, Policy, and Style (Westport, Conn.: Greenwood Press, 1988).

This work examines the impact of the increasing number of high-level minority administrative appointees through the views of minority administrators, together with analyses by three scholars in the field. The administrative group,
which includes two women, consists of two city managers, two police chiefs, a
deputy mayor, and the director of a quasi-governmental health organization.
The editors provide a framework for analyzing the role of minority administrators and their impact on policy issues in urban settings. They conclude the volume with an examination of differences and similarities in the experiences of
the contributing authors and attempt to place common issues in a broader context.

Hanes Walton, Jr., *When the Marching Stopped: The Politics of Civil Rights*
Regulatory Agencies (Albany, N.Y.: State University of New York Press, 1988).

This is a comprehensive and detailed analysis of the implementation of Title
VI (discrimination in programs receiving federal funds) and Title VII (employment discrimination) of the Civil Rights Act of 1964 across virtually all of the
statutory and executive agencies of the federal government from 1964 to 1982.
Extremely well documented, the book covers a number of important aspects of
the implementation process, for instance, the political bargaining surrounding
the creation of the Title VI offices within each department and the impact of
budget allocations for Title VI activities across agencies on the enforcement process. A unique approach to implementation research.